THE RESHAPING OF BRITAIN

The Reshaping of Britain

Church and State since the 1960s

A Personal Reflection

Clifford Hill

Wilberforce Publications
London

Published in Great Britain in 2018 by
Wilberforce Publications Limited
70 Wimpole Street, London W1G 8AX

Wilberforce Publications Limited is a wholly owned subsidary of Christian Concern

ISBN 978 0 9956832 9 7

Printed in Great Britain by Imprint Digital, Exeter
and worldwide by CreateSpace

Contents

ACKNOWLEDGEMENTS

This has not been an easy book to write. It has been spread over a period of nearly two years in the midst of a busy ministry. But it has drawn on my notes and records of the past 50 years. I am truly grateful to a number of my friends and colleagues who have shared in the journey recorded in this book.

It seems almost invidious to mention any names as there are so many to whom I owe a great debt of gratitude and whom I have been privileged to call my friends at different points in my journey – members of both Houses of Parliament, church leaders of all denominations including the new churches and the Caribbean and African churches. I have been hugely privileged to have a small share in the lives of many people in different walks of life from academia and politics to church and state, many of whom have already completed their journey in this life.

In particular I want to thank my two oldest surviving friends and colleagues, David Noakes and Michael Fenton Jones who have walked with me for most of the period covered in this book. I am also grateful to Gill and Crispin Brentford and Gordon Landreth who were hugely influential and supportive in the early days of the period of ministry recorded here.

I am very grateful to the trustees and staff of Issachar Ministries for their patience with me during the writing of this book and the love and support with which they have surrounded me.

Most of all my inexpressible gratitude to Monica, my wife of more than 60 years who has walked every step of the way with me. Although I have done the writing she has contributed enormously to every page — this is really a joint record of our journey together.

Finally, I want to say how grateful I am to Andrea Williams and John Scriven who have also been my friends for many years. They have made it possible to present this book to a wider readership than we could have covered through Issachar Ministries.

It is my hope that this book may be a useful reminder to those who have shared in the journey, but it may also be helpful to those who have more recently taken an interest in church and state: in providing a record of how we have reached this point in our national history, and that it may be influential in forming the path for the years to come.

INTRODUCTION

Learning from the past and providing hope for the future
Throughout the period of radical social change from the mid-1970s through the next thirty years, Monica and I were separately in a unique position of being close to the centre of power in most of the denominational churches in Britain, including the Church of England. From 1983 we also had close links with members in both Houses of Parliament. It has been a strange experience, because we have observed at first-hand the battle for the soul of the nation that has taken place within the churches and in secular society in the greatest period of social change in the history of Britain.

Monica was one of the prime movers in launching the British Church Growth Association in 1979, working closely with leaders of all the mainline denominations, and she led the Association for the next 25 years. I worked with, or had personal friendships with, church leaders and leaders of independent ministries. I also had close relationships with leaders in the black-majority churches, both African and Caribbean, which built upon links that stretched back to the beginning of our pastoral ministry in London. For much of the latter part of this period I was either a member or the Convenor of the 'Lords and Commons Family and Child Protection Group'. For a number of years, I also led the LCFCPG research team that, over a period of 30 years, produced eight reports on the family for MPs which enabled me to keep abreast of events in both Houses of Parliament as well as in the church.

It was my time in the 1970s with the Lambeth Group chaired by Archbishop Donald Coggan, and subsequently with the Evangelical Alliance, that provided my introduction to church leaders of all the mainline denominations. Friendships made in those days outlasted my official appointments and the fact that I was not sailing under any denominational flag was an advantage, as I was seen as a trusted independent counsellor. I travelled the length and breadth of the country with a ministry team and our own worship band in the 1980s and 90s, giving a biblical perspective on contemporary issues. We spoke at numerous meetings and spent time with church leaders in Scotland, Ireland (North and South) as well as in Wales and England, enabling us to gain a first-hand knowledge of what was happening in churches and local communities across the UK.

Prehistory

We go back a long way – I go back even farther! We were married in 1957. I had already been ordained five years, working in a tough inner-city church in Harlesden, north west London where I unwittingly became a pioneer working among Caribbean migrants. I didn't know I was doing anything out of the ordinary until the press began to take an interest in what was happening in my church where many Caribbeans mixed happily with the white congregation. These were days of mounting ethnic tension, but my church provided a warm welcome and practical help for the newcomers. The church house became known locally as the 'Jamaican labour exchange' as I was heavily involved in finding jobs and helping with accommodation for the homeless. It was a seven-bedroom house and we were always full. As I was unmarried, my parents had sold their house in salubrious Ruislip and moved in to keep house for me and they were wonderfully self-sacrificing in supporting me. On more than one occasion the police called me out in the early hours of the morning to prevent a street riot when the Caribbeans were having a party to which their white neighbours objected. My first book was published at the time of the Notting Hill riots which were rightly forecast in the book.[1]

Soon after we were married we moved to Tottenham, north London, to a much larger church and a strong middle-class, all-white congregation, many of whom came from outside the borough. We soon began attracting local people, both black and white and quite large numbers of young people who filled the galleries on Sunday evenings. The church seated 1000 and we were often full, although not everyone appreciated the changes that were taking place. A local magistrate and her husband found a black family sitting in their usual seat – they walked out and never came again. Life was not always easy, especially when the church was picketed by the 'National Front' and our house was attacked because of things I had said in a BBC radio programme which were picked up by the national press.

INTRODUCTION

After 10 years in Tottenham we felt strongly called to go to a small mission church in the East End of London where we could experiment with new concepts of outreach and community renewal that we called 'community-based evangelism'. We were particularly interested in community and we wanted to use 'community development' methods in communicating the gospel while at the same time meeting the needs of people in the area. We had done some of this in Tottenham but we were hindered by the very strong traditions of the church and its leaders, which prevented us from doing the kind of work to which we felt called. This book begins with the record of what happened to us in the East End.

The Prophetic Ministry

One of the great blessings of growing older is that you can see the long trail of events that have led up to what is happening today. The advantage of this for anyone in the prophetic ministry is that you can see the relevance of what you said 30 years ago and how the warnings you gave of what would happen are now everyday news. I don't claim to be a prophet; I am too well aware of my personal shortcomings. In any case, I don't believe there are any prophets today in the mould of the prophets of Israel whose writings are recorded in the Bible. They were in a unique position, ministering to a nation in a covenant relationship with God. They were used by God to reveal his nature and purposes – a task that was completed in the Person and Work of Jesus the Messiah.

I *do* say that I exercise a 'prophetic ministry': but I am by no means unique in this. Those involved in prophetic ministry are watchmen (or women) for the Lord – watching and praying and discerning the significance of what is happening in the world today. In my younger days, I used to say that a watchman is someone with a Bible in one hand and a newspaper in the other. I suppose today's equivalent would be someone with two mobile phones – one with readings from the Bible and the other logged onto the Internet news. In this way all believers could be watchmen and intercessors, asking God to show us the significance of what is happening in our lifetime so that we can be his witnesses to our generation.

I have made a lifetime habit, not only of watching current events, but noticing trends, which enables me to foresee the direction of social change, or things that are of spiritual significance. I am never really sure whether my academic training as a sociologist has led me to a particular understanding of contemporary events, or whether there is an element of revelation. For me they often blend together, but what is also needed, and is specifically the work of the Holy Spirit, is both discernment and distinguishing between spirits.

Discernment is not a spiritual gift, it comes with maturity and familiarity with the biblical word of God. Distinguishing between spirits is one of the manifestations of the Spirit of God, which Paul describes in 1 Corinthians 12.10, that enables a believer to know the *source* of something that is being communicated, particularly whether it is coming from the human imagination, from an alien spirit, or from the Holy Spirit.

Studying the Times

The 'watchman' is not simply an observer of what is happening, but there has to be *understanding* of the significance of events and what needs to be done in response. This is where the strong element of revelation comes in. Millions of people can see what is happening, but they have no understanding. They have knowledge, but without wisdom they don't know how to use it. This is why Paul links 'wisdom and knowledge' in the list of spiritual gifts in 1 Corinthians 12. The sociologist can perceive the significance of a train of events and can predict their likely outcome; but to understand the *spiritual* as well as the *social* significance of events requires the perception given by the Holy Spirit. That is the difference between the social observer or commentator, and those who exercise a prophetic ministry.

This was the ministry of the elders of the Tribe of Issachar who went to King David's coronation ceremony and offered their services. All the other tribes sent warriors, men armed for battle, to provide David with a powerful army to defend the nation. The men of Issachar were those who *understood the times and knew what Israel should do* (1 Chron 12.32). They must have formed a small but powerful group of intercessors and advisers around the new king as he took up his responsibilities for uniting the tribes of the nation and building a national identity and loyalty, not only to each other, but to be obedient to God in order to enjoy his blessings that brought peace and prosperity.

In a similar way, God gave both a prophetic and an intercessory-based ministry to the New Testament Church. This is seen in the church at Antioch where they were at prayer when the Holy Spirit spoke to them. As a result, those with prophetic insights were given foreknowledge of Paul's missionary calling and he was commissioned to begin his ministry. In a similar way the church today should be exercising both a prophetic and intercessory ministry.

It was God's intention that the church should be both priest and prophet to the nations. The priest speaks to God on behalf of the nation, and the prophet speaks to the nation on behalf of God.

In the Bible, Moses is the man who most clearly represents this dual ministry. Numerous times Moses had to get before God to plead on behalf of the nation, because he knew perfectly well that the nation thoroughly deserved judgement and did not deserve mercy or blessings. But he also presented the word of God to the nation and reported what he heard when he stood in the counsel of the Lord, bringing both warnings and words of encouragement.

Liberalism
In this book there will be numerous times in which we will refer to liberal theology. We should make it clear at this stage that our use of the term does not preclude genuine biblical study that aims to unpack the truth revealed in the Bible. The scholarly study of the Bible is a great benefit to Christians when it is treated as the word of God. Our concern is that liberal scholars have distorted biblical truth by pursuing their study from an erroneous standpoint of unbelief and their work has become destructive of faith rather than increasing the faith of students. Our use of the term 'liberalism' in this book is synonymous with 'unbelief'.

Community of Believers
Clearly, we are living in extraordinary days when all the nations and great institutions are being shaken. God is not only looking for individuals to act as watchmen, but for a community of believers who will be his witnesses to the nations, and declare his truth in a generation of fake news, lies and deception. Ideally, the church should be this community of believers. But in so many ways the churches have become institutions

after the pattern of the world, and this is especially so in Britain as will be seen through the pages of this book. But God's good purposes are never defeated by human unfaithfulness and today God is calling out a community of believers from among the faithful remnant scattered across the nation. The Apostle Peter described the church thus:

> But you are a chosen people, a royal priesthood, a holy nation, a people belonging to God, that you may declare the praises of him who called you out of darkness into his wonderful light
>
> (1 Pet 2.9, NIV).

The New Testament references to 'church', 'ecclesia', do not mean our man-made institutions or denominations. 'Ecclesia' should be translated, 'gathering', or more specifically 'a gathering of those who are called out from the world' to be the body of Christ. Sadly, the 'ecclesia' of the New Testament has become the global organisations of today following centuries of institutionalisation.

The Prophet Isaiah foresaw this when he was writing about the new community of believers after the exile in Babylon that ended in 539 BC. They would not only rebuild the ancient ruins of Jerusalem (Is 61.4) but they would be the forerunners of the new covenant prophesied by Jeremiah (31.31). This new covenant community would be called *"priests of the Lord... ministers of our God"* (see Is 61.6). God's promise was:

> "... In my faithfulness I will reward them and make an everlasting
> covenant with them.
> Their descendants will be known among the nations
> and their offspring among the peoples.
> All who see them will acknowledge
> that they are a people the LORD has blessed."
>
> (Is 61.8b-9, NIV)

Peter foresaw the significance of what was happening in the post-Pentecost community in Jerusalem, as large numbers of people responded to the preaching of the gospel about the Risen Jesus the Messiah. He said,

> "Indeed, all the prophets from Samuel on, as many as have spoken, have foretold these days. And you are heirs of the prophets and of the covenant God made with your fathers" (Acts 3.24-25).

Moses' Wish

This statement that the new community of believers that formed the New Testament Church (who were all Jews at that time) were the heirs of the prophets was a reflection of the words of Moses when the Spirit of God rested upon the elders of Israel and they prophesied. After rebuking Joshua, who wanted to stop Eldad and Medad, Moses said, *"Are you jealous for my sake? I wish that all the Lord's people were prophets and that the Lord would put his Spirit on them!"* (Num 11.29).

If ever there were a time for Moses' wish to become a reality it is surely today as we face the immense challenges developing in the 21st century. That is what this book is about – learning from the past and providing hope for the future.

Note
[1] Clifford Hill, *'BLACK-AND-WHITE IN HARMONY: The Drama of West Indians in the Big City from a London Minister's Notebook'*, Hodder and Stoughton, London, 1958.

Chapter One

ARCHBISHOP DONALD COGGAN

The Most Revd and Rt Hon Dr Donald Coggan
Archbishop of Canterbury November 1974 to January 1980
It was just another day at the office, nothing extraordinary. There was no indication that this was going to be the day that changed my life for ever. In my diary, there was a staff meeting followed by a time of prayer, and after lunch a visitor was booked to see me – a John Poulton. I didn't know him or where he was coming from; but I knew he had the title 'Canon', so I assumed he was an ordained minister in the Church of England.

We were used to visitors. They came from different parts of the country and from different professions — social workers, clergy and even the occasional journalist, wanting to see what was happening in the East End of London. Not that we were famous, but somehow word that something exciting was happening in the London Borough of Newham was filtering out on the grapevine long before the days of social media.

This was 1976, the 'Newham Community Renewal Programme' had been going just six years. But its work had escalated rapidly in an area of considerable urban deprivation where we were experimenting with new concepts in community development that had gripped the imagination of local churches. Some 40 were now linked together across the Borough, sharing resources, working together in local projects, and enjoying the benefits of a united vision for outreach – in fact attempting to reshape the inner city.

I liked John Poulton immediately and I walked with him around our office building on the first floor of our Harold Road Community Centre in West Ham. It was a former Methodist church that Monica had transformed, and physically rebuilt parts of it under a government employment scheme for long-term unemployed youth (some said 'unemployable'!). But even with this group of lads we had seen lives changed, as we were seeing in most of our centres.

As we walked through the offices I introduced John to members of the team and explained something of what was happening and how we were fulfilling our objectives of developing new concepts in urban mission – what we called 'community-based evangelism'. I explained that we worked in teams specialising in different social groups: working with children and young people, senior citizens, and different ethnic groups, particularly Caribbeans and Asians.

I told him about our other centres such as Trinity in East Ham, a former large old Presbyterian church which we had bought when it was closed as redundant. Monica had led a small team back in 1972 who had not only been successful in establishing community work but had also established Christian ministry in different forms as well as giving immigrant churches a base for their worship. It was the early days of the Charismatic Movement and we often had up to 800 people coming from far and wide to 'Prayer Praise and Healing' meetings on a Saturday night.

John collected various pamphlets and published reports on our work and we said goodbye. After he had gone I realised that he had told me almost nothing about himself, although I knew that he was working in London. It was several weeks later that I heard from him again and this time he identified himself as the Archbishop of Canterbury's Secretary for Evangelism. He asked if I would come to London to meet with him, although once again he did not say the purpose of the meeting. I assumed he simply wanted to know more about our work, although in my spirit I sensed that this could lead to a wider ministry. In my prayer times such possibilities had already been dropping into my mind.

London Meeting

I arrived early for the meeting, having driven up through the early morning rush hour, and being unfamiliar with commuter traffic in the

City of London I had left the East End early. I still have vivid memories of sitting in the car outside Lambeth Palace before that meeting and opening my Bible at random when my eyes lighted upon the first few verses of Isaiah 42, *"Here is my servant whom I uphold, my chosen one in whom I delight; I will put my Spirit on him and he will bring justice to the nations."* Of course, I knew perfectly well that this was the first of the great Servant Songs in Isaiah, referring to the coming of Messiah and to the Messianic mission of the idealised nation of Israel who were to be, *"a covenant for the people and a light for the Gentiles, to open eyes that are blind, to free captives from prison and to release from the dungeon those who sit in darkness"* (Is 42.6-7).

Nevertheless, I wondered if there was some way in which God was alerting me to the possibility of my being involved in some kind of ministry that would open eyes that were blind and release those who were living in darkness. We were certainly seeing lives transformed in the East End of London and our community development programme was growing in significance. I wondered if God was preparing me for something of wider significance. I was overwhelmed with a tremendous sense of unworthiness and yet of the mercy and graciousness of God who, despite our human sinfulness, is nevertheless gracious enough to forgive us and purify us for use in his service. I think I was experiencing something like Isaiah felt when he was called to ministry *"For I am a man of unclean lips, and I live among a people of unclean lips"* (Is 6.5).

Despite my spiritual intuition, the meeting with John Poulton proved surprising, as well as being a deeply moving experience. He said that the work that Monica and I had been leading in East London had been observed by others and the Archbishop had asked him to convey to us an invitation to do on a national scale something along the lines of the work we were doing in Newham. We talked for a while about the Archbishop's 'Call to the Nation' and the response from around the country. This indicated that the time was right for a creative initiative that would reach people in all walks of life through a community-based outreach of the gospel. The invitation to lead such an outreach under the auspices of the Archbishop was certainly attractive, but I said that I would need time to think and pray, and talk it through with Monica, and we had three children still at school; any move would affect them also.

The 'Call to The Nation'

Soon after his enthronement as the 101st Archbishop of Canterbury in January 1975, Dr Donald Coggan broadcast to the nation. His 'Call to the Nation' expressed concern over the growing threat from moral libertarianism and his own deeply held conviction that salvation is only to be found in the Lord Jesus Christ. He foresaw the nation drifting towards disaster and he believed that the only hope lay in turning back to God and reasserting the centrality of the biblical word of God in the life of the nation.

The response was incredible. Vast numbers of people from all walks of life responded positively to the Archbishop, applauding the lead he had given and pledging support. Within days the postbag at Lambeth Palace reached 27,000 – and this was only the postal mail. The positive response in the media, in newspaper articles and correspondence columns and through the broadcasting media was immense. The response was so great and unexpected that it took the Archbishop and church leaders of all denominations completely by surprise. No one had realised the deep hunger for righteousness that still flowed through the spiritual arteries of the nation. Significantly, the response came, not only from the elderly, and those with conservative tendencies, but also from young people who were looking for radical solutions to the problems of society.

It was clear from this response, that Dr Coggan had rightly caught the mood of the nation and that his words were also rightly set in the timing of the Lord. It was notable that during the 1970s young people were turning to God in large numbers. The largest student organisations in most British universities were Christian, notably evangelical. Christian Union meetings often drew large numbers of students who were eager for biblical teaching that was relevant to the great issues facing them in the modern world. I spoke to one such meeting in Birmingham University with more than 1000 students attending. A new kind of radicalism was developing among intellectual young people who were seeking solutions to the problems thrown up by the worldwide proliferation of weapons of mass destruction that could destroy the entire human civilisation. Organisations such as CND (The Campaign for Nuclear Disarmament) attracted millions of supporters, and protest marches and demonstrations were a regular feature of the decade.

Bishops' Opposition

Dr Coggan's call to the nation had been largely unpremeditated and was a response to the spontaneous urging of the Holy Spirit within him. As such he failed to consult with colleagues in the House of Bishops before taking this step. The result was predictable. More than half of the bishops in the Church of England by this time were theological liberals as were many clergy and Free Church ministers. The Bishops reacted in anger forming a cabal to present the Archbishop with the threat that if ever he stepped out of line again and made such an appeal to the public without consulting them, they would denounce him publicly. They further threatened that if he followed up his 'Call to the Nation' with a full-scale evangelical campaign they would not only oppose him but they would prevent any evangelical bishop getting into Lambeth Palace for a long time to come.

The seeds of compromise were thus sown and the pressures upon the Archbishop to back away from his clear uncompromising evangelical call to the nation appeared irresistible in the context of the urgent need to maintain unity within the Church of England and to avoid a public scandal. The demands for compromise and unity at all costs had probably never been greater since the days of the Oxford Movement in the 1840s or perhaps even the Glorious Revolution in 1688.

The Lambeth Group

Donald Coggan, however, did not immediately bow to the inevitable although, even at that time, he must have known that the writing was on the wall for any uncompromisingly evangelical outreach of the gospel into the nation. He knew the extent of theological liberalism among Anglican clergy. It was more than 12 years since John Robinson had published his *Honest to God*[1] that had popularised liberal theology, bringing to the attention of the public what had been taught to Anglican clergy and Nonconformist ministers for a generation. He nevertheless took steps to form what became known as 'The Lambeth Group' which had its first meeting in June 1976. The Group brought together denominational representatives to discuss the setting up of a national evangelistic outreach. It was hand-picked, all evangelicals; plus one or two charismatics such as David Pawson. Its task was to plan a major evangelical campaign; but the pressures upon the Archbishop within the Church of England made this increasingly difficult.

It was at this stage that Donald Coggan sent for me. I was a Nonconformist and not under the authority of the bishops. He seriously considered defying the pressure from liberal bishops and organising a national outreach from Lambeth Palace which I would direct in consultation with John Poulton and the Lambeth Group. Many hours were spent in discussion and prayer with Donald and John, weighing up the consequences of such an initiative to the future of the Church of England. Eventually Dr Coggan decided to compromise by making the Lambeth Group more inclusive and ecumenical by inviting denominational and diocesan representatives to join him in the Group. Some of those who came were not evangelicals and some were even hostile to any form of evangelism and were prepared to oppose a national evangelical initiative. This much larger group was formed in January 1978 – a 'Council of Reference' with 39 members, which paved the way for what became known as the 'Nationwide Initiative in Evangelism', or NIE. But Donald Coggan, John Poulton and I all knew that this effectively pronounced the death of a national gospel outreach.

Dr Kenneth Greet of the Methodist Church was one of those who joined the Lambeth Group and sharply opposed any form of overt evangelism. Pressure from the House of Bishops ensured the appointment of Dr David Brown, Bishop of Guildford, to the Council of Reference. He was chairman of the Church of England Board of Mission and Unity, which probably says it all – only the Church of England could put together two polar opposites 'mission' and 'unity' and expect either objective to be achievable!

In his earlier years, David Brown had been an evangelical so he knew all the language of evangelicalism, but in the Council of Reference he was outspoken as a liberal in agreement with Kenneth Greet. The two of them were determined to ensure that the NIE did not become some kind of national evangelistic crusade. They were particularly opposed to any suggestion of an invitation to the American evangelist Billy Graham who had led the highly successful Harringay meetings of 1954.

At the Lambeth Palace meetings, the two men were usually in close attendance beside the Archbishop. David Brown usually sat at his right hand, while on the other side sat two Methodists, Dr Harry Morton and Dr Kenneth Greet. Harry Morton was the influential General Secretary of the British Council of Churches, while Kenneth Greet was the General Secretary of the Methodist Church. They were both liberal theologians and gave strong support to the Bishop of Guildford in his endeavour firmly to oppose an evangelical crusade.

David Brown had a particular dislike for charismatic evangelicals so he was dismissive of David Pawson's contribution, but equally he was dismissive of Gordon Landreth, General Secretary of the Evangelical Alliance (EA). Gordon was formerly in the diplomatic service so he was always polite and thoughtful, but his opinions carried little weight with the heavyweight liberals. He gave the NIE his personal support but his influence was limited by the fact that he did not carry the backing of his own evangelical constituency (the EA Council).[2] The meetings of the Council of Reference continued until 1981 when the latter was replaced by an NIE Council until March 1983 when the NIE was disbanded.

Vision for Evangelism

Donald Coggan's vision for evangelism was very different from the 1954 Harringay Crusade led by Billy Graham. Coggan and Poulton both believed firmly in stimulating evangelism at the grassroots by encouraging all believers in their local churches to be active in sharing their faith with their neighbours. This concept of evangelism had first been introduced in the Church of England in a report in 1945. The ground-breaking report was entitled 'Towards the Conversion of England'. It was a plan drawn up by a group set up during the Second World War by Archbishop William Temple and dedicated to his memory. It recognised both the challenge and the unique opportunity for evangelism in the nation recovering from war. It stated:

In England, the church has to present the Christian gospel to multitudes in every section of society who believe in nothing; who have lost a whole dimension (the spiritual dimension) of life; and for whom life has no ultimate meaning. The paramount spiritual need of the non-worshipping members of the community (as evidenced by this survey) is the recovery of their consciousness of God. Only so can they regain a doctrine of man morally responsible to God, and a philosophy of life that sees the material world as the sacrament of the realities of the eternal. But the church is ill-equipped for its unparalleled task and opportunity.

The laity complain of a lack of creative leadership among all ranks of the clergy. The spiritual resources of the worshipping community are at a low ebb. Above all, the church has become confused and uncertain in the proclamation of its message, and its life has ceased to reflect clearly the truth of the gospel. It is for the church, in this day of God, by a rededication of itself to its Lord, to receive from him that baptism of Holy Spirit and of fire which will empower it to send the call and give the awaited lead.[3]

Donald Coggan had responded to this challenge and he had rightly read the state of the nation and had perceived the timing of the Lord. The post war period of reconstruction and readjustment with its booming economy and full employment was over. The 'swinging 60s' had brought new challenges to the values of the nation, but the 1970s was a period of unrest and instability when unemployment exceeded three million and there were constant strikes as industrial strife spread. It was exactly the right time for the church to take a creative lead in the nation with a new declaration of biblical truth and a fresh presentation of the gospel to meet the needs of the people.

The Broadcast
In his October 1975 'Call to the Nation' Dr Coggan had said:

"I'm not offering a detailed plan or any kind of blueprint as a way out of her troubles for Britain. There are no easy answers to our problems. I do not pretend to know all the answers. But this is the point I want to make – unless there is a concerted effort to lift our whole national debate up into the moral sphere, not being afraid to ask individuals as well as the community what is right and what is wrong, we shall never find the answers. I am concerned for the spirit which is abroad in the country, because our national problems will not be solved unless we improve it.

I also want to encourage the enormous number of good people in Britain. They want a better country. They are saddened by the low level to which we have fallen. But they have no spokesmen. It is the extremists who tend to receive the publicity, and often they win the round. What I am attempting is to strengthen this group of responsible people.

And here's a third aim. I want to see opening up all over Britain groups of men and women, of all denominations and of none, who will sit down and face these two questions:

'What sort of society do we want?' and

'What sort of people do we need to be in order to achieve it?'

"At first sight, these questions seem extremely simple. But set them side-by-side and they imply something which, to our great loss, we have largely forgotten in our nation today – which is that the sort of people we are makes the society we get. Put another way, it means that we cannot leave out the moral factor and succeed in the long run. It is in the light of this that I want to initiate this debate today. It is in the light of this overriding consideration that I want the groups to do their thinking, working at specific problems in their own localities."[4]

Pastoral Letter

The following Sunday a pastoral letter from the Archbishops of Canterbury and York was read in all Anglican churches, backing up the call to the nation and urging all Christians to get involved prayerfully and practically in changing the nation. The letter urged the Archbishops' conviction that every person counts. It said:

The time has therefore come when we feel it is our duty to call all Christian people:

1. To pray steadily and persistently and intelligently for our nation.
2. To think seriously about our society in the light of what we believe, asking such questions as 'what sort of society do we want' and 'what sort of people do we need to be in order to achieve it?'
3. To cooperate with Christians of every allegiance and with any others who are willing to be associated with us, so as to influence society in a positive and helpful way.
4. To live out the faith we profess that God reigns and that God cares.[5]

Positive Response

John Poulton wrote a little book *Dear Archbishop*[6], summarising the public response. Of foremost importance, he noticed that the Archbishops' statement that each man and woman matters had really caught the public's imagination. He said "This statement touched an exposed nerve. The Archbishop almost need have said nothing else." As one mother wrote, for all her family,

Thank you for voicing the thoughts and desires of millions of good ordinary people inside and outside the church, and for giving us hope that there is something we as individuals can do. It is so easy to feel terribly inadequate in the face of the present situation, to feel that our little bit is so insignificant it is not worth doing.[7]

Another correspondent wrote, "We are ordinary people, human and frail, but there is nothing we cannot do if we work with the power God gives us." And yet another said "The problem of the relevance of each ordinary man or woman to society, and to affect events, lies at the root of the hopelessness many feel." Another person wrote a sentiment that reflected the spontaneous response of a very large number of the general population:

I cannot help feeling that the tragedy of life today is that people feel they no longer matter, everyone is lost in the bigness of everything. Shops go from super to hyper, local authorities group together to take in larger and larger areas, and schools are quite disgustingly huge. If only we could be made to realise that our individual behaviour *does* matter, however small we might feel.

John Poulton, in his book, commented,

In many of the archbishop's letters there were expressions of appalled concern for what people felt to be the decadence of Britain today. This was the background against which Dr Coggan was heard appealing for a return to biblical standards and morality.[8]

The reaction in the newspapers and journals in the aftermath of Donald Coggan's speech widely acknowledged the sentiments expressed in these letters. There was a spiritual hunger in the nation and a deep concern for what was recognised as a rejection of the Christian heritage of the nation. This was an indication that the Archbishop was perfectly right in his timing – the nation was ready for a national initiative to communicate the gospel and a fresh presentation of biblical standards of personal and corporate morality, of justice and love, of faithfulness and integrity, of grace and truth.

Opposition

Serious opposition came, not from members of the public but from bishops in the Church of England. Dr Mervyn Stockwood, the Bishop of Southwark, led the attack with an article published in the Communist daily newspaper *Morning Star*, in which he declared that the Archbishop should not have focused on individual behaviour but that his 'Call' should have been an attack upon the *system* in Western society that shapes the lives of all individuals.

This was followed inevitably by a backlash in the right-wing press, criticising the bishop's disloyalty to the Archbishop, which prompted Donald Coggan to comment in the February 1976 General Synod. He said "A certain amount of controversy has been engendered, and that is all to the good, for one of the prime reasons for the 'Call' was to open up a debate on matters of serious concern."[9]

In his criticism, Mervyn Stockwood had stated that under a truly socialist system pornography and other evils of London's West End would be cleared up overnight! This was gleefully taken up by the tabloids and contributed to the nationwide discussion of social morality that had been engendered by the Archbishop's broadcast to the nation. But much of the discussion became centred upon political and social values rather than upon the spiritual issues that were the focus of the Archbishop's 'Call'.

The most serious and negative effect of Stockwood's intervention was that it showed the level of disunity within the Church of England and the major spiritual battle that was developing between the liberal bishops and those who wanted to see an evangelical presentation of the gospel in the nation. It signalled the beginning of the end of Donald Coggan's hopes of a fresh presentation of the gospel in Britain.

John Poulton

There were certainly similarities between what the Archbishop was calling for and what we were doing in East London, so I could not help responding positively to the suggestion that our work might have national significance. I returned home to share with Monica the astounding news that our work in the East End might have national significance. Of course, we were excited, but any enthusiasm for a wider role in our work was tempered by the fact that we had three children in different stages of their education and there were many practical things to consider.

Discussions with John Poulton now assumed the character of serious negotiations, although we also spent many hours discussing concepts of evangelism and community involvement. John affirmed that any new initiative in evangelism should not be along the lines of a nationwide 'Harringay Crusade' à la Billy Graham. He was deeply committed to local community development. I liked his phrase 'Whatever is not happening locally is not happening!'

This made a deep impression upon me because it struck exactly the same note that we had been following for a number of years in our community development programme in the East End of London. It accorded closely with my own understanding of 'community-based evangelism'. I had already talked about this with him during his visit to Newham and we spent some time together discussing the possibility of extending this as a strategy of mission right across the country.

This conversation with John Poulton sealed the beginnings of a friendship that was to develop as we worked closely together in the early stages of setting up a nationwide initiative in evangelism. I was given a desk in John Poulton's room in Lambeth Palace, although I was still leading the Renewal Programme in Newham. But my frequent trips to central London and innumerable meetings with denominational leaders, as well as the meetings of the Lambeth Group, and private, heart searching discussions with John Poulton, and occasional discussions with Donald Coggan, introduced me to an unfamiliar world.

I was only used to working in inner-city working-class areas among people lacking social influence and with only limited ambitions. This was my calling that had drawn me into ministry. In Lambeth, these were powerful people, leaders of great institutions, in strong contrast to the people I spent my life among – the people I loved and where I felt secure and needed. Was I really prepared to walk away from all that had been my world for the past twenty years?

Ecclesiastical Politics

I was introduced to the world of ecclesiastical politics and the rarefied atmosphere of high-level inter-church relationships of which I had previously been unaware. I rapidly learnt something of the inside workings of the Church of England and I saw at first hand the effects of the pressures upon the Archbishop of what (three archbishops later), during my years of friendship with Dr Rowan Williams, I came to dub 'the Lambeth Mafia'. The pressures upon the Archbishop came not only from senior figures in the hierarchy but also from the team of officials (the C of E's equivalent to the civil service) who were in charge of his diary and in many ways exercised a controlling influence in his life.

Donald Coggan's vision for a national outreach which would touch every section of the nation with the gospel through a community-based initiative caused him to want, not only all parish churches but, churches of *all denominations* to be involved. This, of course, assumed a level of unity that simply was not present either in the Anglican Church or among the Nonconformist denominations. The invitation to each of the Protestant denominations to participate meant inviting them to send a representative to the organising group that was rapidly outgrowing the original Lambeth Group.

It was at this stage when there were pressures for a fully ecumenical organisation that it became clear that I could not simply lead the movement as the Archbishop's nominee with the backing of the original Lambeth Group, as was originally discussed. I had been quite prepared to find my own financial support in the early days of the Lambeth Group when we were discussing the concept. I was no stranger to finding my own finance, and to do this with the backing of a small support group based at Lambeth Palace was the ideal that John Poulton and I originally embraced with the endorsement of Dr Coggan.

Sadly, this was not to be. The whole concept was rapidly becoming institutionalised, with denominational representatives nominated and a committee structure emerging, and a demand for clear lines of authority, reporting back to each of the denominations and diocesan boards for endorsement of decisions. It was all becoming highly structured and I was becoming less and less happy with the situation. It was developing like an offshoot of the British Council of Churches and less and less like a simple mission aiming at encouraging local community development and involvement in evangelism which was the original vision to which Monica and I had responded.

Bureaucratisation

It was now more than a year since John Poulton had first approached us. In that time, the whole Initiative had become bureaucratised with the appointment of the much-enlarged Council of Reference, and I was beginning to have serious doubts about its viability. I was asked to meet with a small group of denominational representatives who were to interview me and make recommendations to an appointments committee. I was determined to sharpen the focus and make it perfectly clear where I stood, in terms of my commitment both to radical social change and to evangelism. I wrote a long 'concept paper' running to about 20 pages. It outlined our work in the East End and showed how these concepts could be extended nationwide.

I circulated this to the members of the group before the meeting. Although I constantly referred to the work that I led in East London in terms of its creative social impact, I also described the moral and spiritual needs we were meeting in the East End, which I believed were replicated throughout the nation. I affirmed my commitment to evangelism, stating clearly my conviction that there is salvation only in the Lord Jesus Christ. I sounded warnings about over structuring the work and I said that we had to leave room for the leading of the Holy Spirit.

The meeting took place in Westminster Central Hall in Dr Kenneth Greet's office, who was then General Secretary of the Methodist Connection. My paper certainly had the effect of polarising the situation, as I had anticipated. Even so, I was shocked to hear Kenneth Greet at one point declare, **"There is far too much loose talk about leaving things to the Holy Spirit. What we need is sound organisation!"** I remember looking up at the large portrait of John Wesley on the wall behind his desk and I wondered what he would have thought hearing the leader of the church he founded saying such a thing. He was warmly supported by Canon Kenneth Craston and Harry Morton and from that moment I knew that a great spiritual battle was raging over the project to take the gospel to the nation and that I was likely to be the first casualty of war.

My fears proved well-founded, but the outcome was not immediately apparent. The bureaucratic structure already set in motion moved slowly and cumbersomely towards the issue of leadership which dragged on for several more months before it was finally resolved and I was told that my services were no longer required. A small executive committee had been established to make the final decision. It was chaired by John Poulton and had three Anglican representatives and four representatives of other denominations.

Hierarchy Pressure

After a long interview with me, all four of the denominational representatives voted for me, but all three Anglicans were under instructions from Bishop David Brown of Guildford to vote against me. I was deeply hurt later when I discovered that John Poulton had bowed to the pressures of the hierarchy and cast his vote with the three Anglican representatives. This made it a tie, and he then used his casting vote as chairman to swing the decision against my appointment. This was after all the days we had spent together planning and hoping and praying. It seemed unbelievable!

I subsequently received a letter from Jeffery Harris, the Methodist member on the group, expressing his profound sorrow at what had happened and saying that he firmly believed that I was the one who should lead the Initiative. David Pawson, whose church in Guildford supported our work in the East End, and several others from the original Lambeth Group who knew what had happened, also expressed various degrees of regret and astonishment.

The thing that I could not understand was: why had my good friend John Poulton behaved in such a way? Was this another example of the unjust pressures within the Church of England? For John, it was some years before he was able to discuss the matter freely with me. Bruised and battered, I crept back to the East End of London where most people suffered from the injustices of life and supported one another on the most difficult days when their hopes and dreams were shattered.

Brokenness

I had now joined the people I ministered to in a way that I had never imagined possible. Brokenness was not something I had ever personally experienced. How would God use this for the Kingdom? I had certainly not sought a national ministry. I was perfectly content working in the East End of London with the people I loved and where I would have been happy to spend the rest of my days. Why had God allowed this to happen?

But I was not the only one to be broken. I was particularly sad to see the personal impact upon Donald Coggan of the opposition of the liberal bishops and the way they used their power to silence him. He was passionately committed to the message he had broadcast to the nation and he was immensely encouraged and excited about the overwhelmingly positive response from the public. He knew it was the right time for the church to lead an evangelistic outreach, but he was blocked in any attempt at evangelism. He simply could not understand why all the clergy in the Church of England could not share his commitment to initiating and participating in a movement to promote moral and spiritual change in the nation.

On 23 July 1978, just a few days after John Poulton had blocked my appointment, Donald Coggan addressed the Lambeth Conference. There were 400 bishops and senior clerics of the worldwide Anglican Communion gathered in Canterbury. In his address Dr Coggan said:

> Some of you have given up believing that God still speaks to the church. God forgive us. We would not admit it; it would shock our congregations if we did. But we have stopped listening to God and our spiritual life has died on us, though we keep up the appearances and go through the motions.

He added,

> But many in the congregations know that God does speak, and that he makes his mind known to his followers.[10]

This last statement showed that he recognised a greater level of faith in the pew than in the pulpit. This had been confirmed to him by the

27,000 letters he had received from ordinary people, some of whom had a greater faith in God than their vicars.

Just six weeks later, John Poulton left the Archbishop's service and plunged into depression leading to a nervous breakdown. It is my understanding that Donald Coggan held John responsible for the debacle surrounding my non-appointment. It was John's decision to appoint a small group of ultra-liberal church leaders to interview me. He probably thought that with my academic background and my years of service in the inner-city, and the prominent role I had played in social justice issues related to immigration and the rise of the African and Caribbean churches in Britain, I would have been acceptable to the liberal church leaders as I was in the East End of London.

John's great commitment was to unity and he truly believed that it was essential to get the liberal church leaders involved in the Initiative for it to be a success, and his hope was that I would be able to persuade them that this would be a fully ecumenical project. He underestimated the destructive powers of darkness driving liberalism and its hatred of anything to do with evangelicalism and biblical truth. I am not minimising my own responsibility for what happened because I could easily have made no mention of my charismatic/evangelical convictions and simply emphasised my commitment to social justice and that side of our work in East London. But I did not feel that would have been honest.

My non-appointment and the termination of John Poulton's role triggered Donald Coggan's decision to leave Canterbury, although he held on to his office to the end of 1979, finally departing in January 1980. He continued to chair the meetings of the Council of Reference, which replaced the Lambeth Group, but he had no further interest in it. As Donald English, the Initiative Committee Chairman pointed out, "Dr Coggan's heart was no longer in the Initiative after the Lambeth Group was superseded. Although he chaired the Council of Reference, he quite deliberately distanced himself from its activities." [11]

In Chapter Three we will deal more fully with the 'Initiative' that replaced the Lambeth Group.

Notes

[1] John A.T. Robinson, *Honest to God*, SCM paperback, March 1963 (ninth impression September 1963) London 1963.

[2] The EA Council were firmly opposed to any form of ecumenism or compromise with liberalism, and therefore were not supportive of working with liberal churches.

[3] *Towards the Conversion of England*, The Press and Publications Board of the Church Assembly, London, 1945, p. 16.

[4] Archbishop Donald Coggan's Broadcast to the Nation from Lambeth Palace, London, 15th October 1975.

[5] John Poulton, *Dear Archbishop*, Hodder and Stoughton, London, 1976 pp. 20–22; 25–26.

[6] *Ibid.*, John Poulton.

[7] John Poulton, *op. cit.,* p. 29.

[8] John Poulton, *op. cit.*, p. 51.

[9] John Poulton, *op. cit.,* p. 79.

[10] Lambeth Palace, Archbishop Coggan's speeches.

[11] Roger Whitehead and Amy Sneddon, *An Unwanted Child?* The Story of the NIE, British Council of Churches, London, 1990, pp. 49–50.

Chapter Two

COMMUNITY-BASED EVANGELISM

Inner-City Mission

In order to understand why Archbishop Donald Coggan had sent John Poulton to Newham in the East End of London to invite Monica and me to lead a national evangelistic outreach, it would be useful at this point to give a brief description of the kind of work in which we were involved in Newham.

I was the Minister of the Congregational/Methodist Church in Wakefield Street, East Ham, in the East London Borough of Newham. Monica and I had previously had a ten-year pastoral ministry in Tottenham, north London, where we were reported to have the largest mixed-race congregation in Britain, which included many migrants from the Caribbean and Africa. I wrote a number of books, newspaper and journal articles about the migrants, and at one time I did a weekly broadcast on the BBC Caribbean Service a 'Letter from London' describing life in London among the immigrants — a sort of Alistair Cooke in reverse! I had also participated in numerous radio and TV programmes in the 1960s, and I served on the Home Office sponsored Commonwealth Immigrants Committee. In 1961 I went to Barbados, Trinidad and Jamaica on behalf of the British Council of Churches to establish links between the churches there and the churches in the UK where immigrants were settling.

Moving to East London had not been an easy decision. I was the Senior

Minister of a large congregation in Tottenham and I was well-known for my community involvement in a wide area of North London. The church building seated 1000 and we were often full and sometimes had to use the church hall as an overflow. I rarely preached to less than 500 people on a Sunday.

I was actively involved in local activities as well as on the national scene, and I was mayor's chaplain three times to different mayors who attended our church. Although our own church was flourishing there were many other churches in inner-city areas of North London where congregations were dwindling and churches were closing. It particularly disturbed us when a church in Dalston closed despite having vigorous youth work led by some energetic evangelical young leaders. The church was no longer considered financially viable and so it was closed, the buildings were sold by the denominational authorities who said that the money was needed for churches in other areas in outer London 'where the people were'! — as though those who remained were of no significance.

It was these short-sighted policies that disturbed us because we knew that when church buildings were sold for commercial development in inner-city areas they would never be replaced and the Christian presence would be diminished with no comeback. The policy of putting more resources into suburban areas represented a failure of mission in the inner-city. Although our own church in Tottenham was flourishing, there were strong traditions that limited our ability to experiment with new concepts of mission. We felt a strong call to go to an area where we could serve a small, struggling congregation and where we could develop these new community-based concepts as well as reshaping the future of the nation's inner cities.

This was not understood by our denominational authorities who wanted us to progress by serving one of the larger and more prestigious churches in high status areas. My name was mentioned as the next minister of the City Temple in Holborn in the City of London and several other distinguished churches. But we weren't interested in social status, our desire was to introduce new strategies of outreach where the church was weakest in inner-city areas. Inner cities have always been the entry-point for immigrants to the UK who were often political or economic refugees — such as the Huguenots, the Jews and those from the Caribbean, as the doors from the old Empire and the Commonwealth opened up. As with local residents, it was seen as a stepping stone to more affluent and acceptable areas. Even the church had been operating a 'redemption and lift'[1] policy which had to be reversed. Our objective was to bring the gospel to those living in areas of social deprivation as well as immigrants. The denominational authorities didn't see this as a priority, so they refused to support us in the way we requested. In fact, they endeavoured to obstruct rather than help.

Moving to the East End

Eventually we were invited to a small church in East Ham that had been destroyed by bombing but rebuilt on the same site in the period of post-World War II reconstruction of the 1950s. Its congregation had dwindled to about 20 members and they had sold the church house so there was no accommodation for a minister and they had no ability to pay a salary.

The nearby East Ham Methodist Central Hall buildings had also suffered in the war and their roof was eventually condemned as unsafe, but this had happened after the period of bomb damage compensation so they had no help. An arrangement had been made whereby the Methodist congregation moved to Wakefield Street Congregational Church and the two congregations were combined. We were invited by the Congregational members to share the pastoral work with a Methodist minister. This provided us with an ideal situation where we could experiment with new concepts of mission without carrying all the responsibilities of pastoral ministry. But, in order to do this, we not only had to provide our own support but we also had to buy a house in East Ham. We had always lived in church houses and been supported by the pastorate so this was a challenge.

I was fortunate enough to secure a Senior Lectureship in London University teaching Sociology for the BSc Soc, and specialising in Urban Studies and the Sociology of Religion. Academically I was well qualified in both sociology and theology but I had never taught either subject, and I had no teaching qualifications. Lecturing was particularly demanding during the first two years as I had no previous experience. I had no previous lecture notes to draw upon. It demanded not only a change of subject from theology to sociology but a change of presentation from the language of the pulpit to that of the lecture room. I spent eight years in higher education which I actually enjoyed, after the first two years, as I had time for research and writing. My senior post only required 12 hours' student contact a week so it was not difficult to find time to give to my church work as well, particularly as there was a lot of relevance between my lecturing, my research and my ministry work. I am fortunate that I do not need more than four or five hours sleep when I am under pressure.

When we left Tottenham, we had two school-age children and a baby. Tottenham was a tough inner-city area, but the East End of London was even more demanding. We commuted from the neighbouring borough of Ilford but moved as soon as possible to be one of the people. The night we moved into a house in East Ham an 18-year-old boy was stabbed to death on the pavement outside our house. We trembled before the Lord, wondering what sort of community we were bringing our children into. How would they fare in local schools which were renowned at that time for poor standards? We suffered far more for our children than we did for ourselves throughout our time in East Ham. This is not the place to speak of those traumas except to note that each of our children enjoyed amazing protection and achieved a university education which opened fruitful paths for them later in life. More importantly, each of them became strong Christians and married Christians. Today, at the time of writing, we have a daughter-in-law and a grandson who are both entering the Anglican ministry. We really praise God that three generations of our family are all committed Christians.

Founding the Renewal Programme
In 1970, we began our first attempts at developing new outreaches in mission which we called 'community-based evangelism'. The following year we founded the 'Newham Community Renewal Programme' which brought together the leaders of several local churches, sharing experience and discussing concepts. We obtained a grant for the salary of our first 'community worker' which was quickly followed by a second. The work grew rapidly and by our third year of operations we had a full-time staff of 12 and, although this had not been in our original plans, we had taken over a redundant Presbyterian Church with large buildings.

Two years later the Renewal Programme had expanded to 22 staff and many volunteers. It linked 40 churches of different denominations in an imaginative programme of sharing resources and outreach with teams of specialised community workers, drawn from young people we had trained and others who were in an ongoing training scheme. We had teams working in the Asian community, in the Caribbean community, and others working with senior citizens, and with children and young people, and we were also by then carrying responsibility for four redundant church buildings. It was the largest Christian mission outreach programme in the country and we were seeing particular success in reaching young people of all ethnic backgrounds and involving the churches in the area in 'doing things together which they could not do on their own'.

The way in which the large Presbyterian Church in East Ham (our first) became available to us was quite remarkable. The Presbyterian authorities had determined to close the church as being uneconomic to run as the congregation was less than 30 in number. Although our staff were all fully involved in other projects we could not allow this resource to be lost. Monica then gave up her part time teaching job and agreed to give more time to oversee this new project, so we asked if we could rent the premises so that they could be used for the local community.[2] This was permitted for a year, but with a further challenge in that we could not use it for Sunday worship! What an indictment on the church —they were not going to permit us to do something that they had not found viable. But during that period the project managed to cover all its costs and the community flourished. By the end of the first year we had 1000 people coming onto the premises each week. But then we faced the challenge of buying it, which is another story[3] of God's amazing provision!

Owning premises had opened up even more possibilities and we then held regular Saturday night meetings for 'Prayer Praise and Healing' which drew people from far and wide, often nearly filling this old Presbyterian Church which seated 800. People came from a wide area in and around the Borough. It was the early days of the Charismatic Movement and there was considerable interest and excitement when reports of meetings circulated quite widely. The work was becoming known in other inner-city areas around the country and we hosted a meeting in the East End for leaders doing similar work in Liverpool, Sheffield and Manchester. Together we discussed what was happening in each of our areas and discovered many common concerns and ways in which we could learn from one another.

New Concept of Mission

This began an inter-city conversation on urban mission where we shared news and concepts. This wider interaction produced invitations from different parts of the country to speak about the work in East London. Several of the affluent churches in Surrey and Sussex began to support our work financially and there was an interchange of community visits. We then began getting requests for students to do placements with us from both theological and social work educational institutions. We initiated a scheme for taking young people straight from university who wanted experience in inner-city Christian work that would give them not only experience but also training. This expanded the team and vastly increased our mission work.

We became used to enquiries from other churches and organisations interested in inner-city mission, but even so it was a surprise to receive a phone call from John Poulton, as part of his search for the right person who could lead a new nationwide initiative in evangelism following the Archbishop's 'Call to the Nation', although at the time we did not know who he was. We received John[4] as any other visitor, and showed him our work. He had said that he was particularly interested in discussing our concepts of 'community-based evangelism'.

There had been a remarkable response to the vision we had shared with church leaders throughout the Borough of Newham back in 1970. Virtually all the churches participated – Anglican, Baptist, Congregational, Methodist and Pentecostal. This was particularly remarkable because some of the churches had liberal ministers, while some of the evangelicals were only interested in evangelism and had no previous commitment to what they despised as 'social work'. But once they recognised that our intention was to build bridges into the community by meeting community needs which would give opportunities for communicating the gospel, they were happy to become involved.

By coming together in a united programme of activity that included both evangelistic and social concern, each of the churches were able to preserve their own identity and emphases. We combined to maximise appeals for grant aid from charity trusts and Government funds. Urban Aid grants were not easy to obtain for small organisations or individual churches in the 1970s, but through the Renewal Programme grants were obtained that could support united projects as well as smaller projects carried out by individual churches. The pooling of resources for holiday clubs for children in different neighbourhoods of the borough was something that appealed to most churches and greatly assisted their work.

Community Development

The Renewal Programme grew rapidly in strength as well as helping the different ethnic communities in social and spiritual objectives. When Idi Amin expelled the Asian population from Uganda we took a lead in helping them to settle in Newham and in teaching English as a Second Language. We also began taking responsibility for other redundant churches in East London and reopening them as Christian Community Centres. Their activities included Sunday worship and weeknight evangelistic meetings as well as a wide range of practical social activities to meet needs in the community. These were all part of the comprehensive outreach policy that then developed over a number of years.

Our many years of experience in Harlesden and in Tottenham of working among Caribbean and African people enabled us quickly to build relationships with these communities in the East End. Most of the problems we encountered were similar to those in North London. But relationships between the police and the immigrant communities in East London were poor. The 1970s was an era of 'Stop and Search' that led to many injustices and I was sometimes called out during the night to deal with difficult instances of wrongful arrest.

I was well known at the police stations in the Borough and I was often called upon to mediate where difficulties had arisen that were affecting community relationships that could have led to widespread social unrest. Monica and I both became fully involved in the life of the Borough and I served on several Council Committees which gave me access to those who held power in Local Government. A central part of our ethos in community work was that all our staff and volunteers should be fully indigenised in the locality. Monica and I set the tone in this. She was 'Monica' and I was 'Cliff' to everyone – even the kids in the street. But when I went into the Town Hall or the Police Station, I was 'Dr Hill'. I was a voice for the voiceless; and I used my professional middle-class status on behalf of the status-less.

Our work in the East End, although it included social action, did not have this as its primary focus. Our mission was to be fully rounded: committed to both meeting practical needs in the community and to sharing our faith with our neighbours. We were committed to both social activities and evangelistic work. Saturday night renewal meetings, already mentioned, for 'Prayer Praise and Healing' were at the core of our united outreach, drawing people from all sections of the community. Many people beyond the reach of ordinary church activities came to youth groups and 'gospel discos' which produced some remarkable results of changed lives. Luncheon clubs for the elderly, after-school clubs for latchkey children[5] followed, and a variety of programmes for the various ethnic groups in the neighbourhood, including language classes for the Asian community — especially Asian women.

The work of the Renewal Programme was unusual in a number of ways: it was both fully evangelical and fully committed to a radical programme of creative social change. We were not simply engaged in social provision which we considered 'social first-aid' – meeting immediate needs. We wanted to deal with the institutional causes of injustice, inequality and lack of provision for those who had special needs. It was this imaginative programme of outreach that had both social and spiritual objectives that caught the imagination of church leaders in Newham. This was why the work was supported by churches of all denominations and different theological persuasions, from Anglo-Catholic to Pentecostal. This was truly remarkable at that time. Its ethos was essentially developing community at a local level and encouraging ownership of local projects by local people.

Our concept of 'community-based-evangelism' included discerning the latent gifts and abilities of each individual who came to our centres. If possible, we involved them in some activity or group and gave them some responsibility. It was quite amazing how this policy led to changed lives and to people being open to the gospel. Young people in particular responded positively to being put in a position of trust, which for them was probably a completely new experience. In this way people learnt personal development. They acquired practical skills as well as community skills and developed personal relationships and friendships. This was a practical expression of community development principles within a distinctively Christian ethos. The work crossed both age and ethnic barriers with young people carrying out practical jobs for the elderly, which was an important part of community development, as well as developing a 'serving' mindset among young people. Inter-cultural meetings between different ethnic groups fulfilled a much-needed purpose at a practical level such as cooking and sharing different national foods.

Church Growth

Monica soon became nationally recognised as an authority on 'Church Growth', through her work in the East End of London. Since 1972 and our first redundant Presbyterian church, other churches destined for closure were offered to us. She took over several redundant church buildings, restoring them and planting them as Christian community centres offering a wide range of community activities, evangelism and worship. In each of the centres she established at least one Christian worshipping community, usually by offering accommodation to a local group from one of the ethnic communities. It was a work that she loved doing and we were both committed to developing local 'communities of believers' based upon the New Testament teaching of the 'priesthood of all believers'. We saw the fruit of the methods we were using both in our programme of training young leaders and in the work among local people of all ages.

In each of these centres we had to be creative in sharing the gospel and in Christian activities and teaching as well as covering all our costs until we succeeded in purchasing the buildings which were in a poor state of repair. Monica was responsible for overseeing the work of community development which was particularly successful. She usually began with house-to-house visitation in the immediate vicinity of the buildings to discover local needs and to make the project known among local people, many of whom were not even aware of the presence of the church as in Trinity with its large premises hidden from the road by a thick hedge.

The first activity there was to form a lunch club for the elderly, with lots of volunteer participation and a small grant from the local council towards the provision of food. This rapidly led to a thriving over-60s club, while at the other end of the age scale an after-school club gave much needed service to the local community where many children were coming home from school to cold unsupervised houses while parents were still at work. Volunteers from the Senior Citizens Group helped in the supervision of the children, which was the start of community development where local people were able to help meet different needs in their community and at the same time find fulfilment such as elderly people who were lonely and who enjoyed being with the children.

A youth club with a 'Gospel Disco' soon followed and, once again, community development principles identified those with natural leadership gifts and others with practical skills for repairing the buildings and painting and decorating. Once the premises had been repaired there was a sense of ownership among the young people who made up their own rules for guarding the place and for discipline in the use of the premises. With their 'ownership' of the hall we did not suffer any vandalism, which was rife in the area, and our small staff exercised guidance rather than having to enforce discipline. The gospel disco run by some keen Christians from various churches brought many others to faith in Jesus and was a practical demonstration of our ethos of being both fully evangelical and fully committed to social action.

Moral Dilemmas

Of course, there were plenty of problems, including some unexpected ones, such as when volunteers were all bringing gifts of one kind or another—and one man brought a box of electric light bulbs. We were initially grateful until we noticed that each one was stamped 'London Borough of Newham' and we discovered that he was a storekeeper employed by the Borough. It presented us with a unique moral problem involving some delicate teaching.

A similar problem arose when a small group of 15-year-old girls gave their lives to the Lord and confessed that they had carried out a series of housebreaking offences. We asked what they had done with their stolen goods and they said they were all hidden under the stage in the church hall! I had to use up a lot of my store of goodwill with the local police to agree a deal whereby they took responsibility for the loot and I took responsibility for the girls whose identity I refused to reveal (although they were probably 'known'!)

We loved the work in Newham and Monica and I both thought that we would probably stay there for the rest of our lives. It was not until we began getting invitations to speak about the work in other parts of the country that we saw the wider significance of what we were doing in London.

Wider Ministry

When the invitation from Archbishop Coggan came, we had to do a lot of hard thinking and much praying. In time, we both came to the point of believing that God was calling us into a wider sphere of ministry, although we were really reluctant to leave this work. We never lost our love for the community with whom we worked in the East End, especially for our team of dedicated staff and volunteers. Volunteers were particularly precious as many were local people who had not previously perceived their own potential abilities and had been nurtured through participating in activities that they thought they could never do, which for many resulted in quite amazing changes in their lives.

Although we knew the Lord to be calling us into a wider sphere of ministry, it was nevertheless with heavy hearts that we moved out of East London. For the second time in our lives we left behind the love and security of a place and people and work that we had grown to love, and we moved out into uncharted waters.

Postscript

In 2012 Monica and I were invited to the 40th anniversary of the Trinity Centre in East Ham which was the old Presbyterian Church that we had bought in 1972. It was a wonderful occasion with the Mayor and many of the Newham Councillors as well as the local MP, Stephen Timms, present. No less than five different Christian congregations now use the premises and so too do communities of other faiths for social occasions.

The Hindus presented us with a large scarf which they wrapped around us, saying that it had been blessed in their Temple. It was a beautiful silk scarf and it was the highest honour that they could bestow upon us. We both had hugely mixed emotions in receiving it, but we knew ourselves to be protected by the blood of Jesus from any form of spiritual contamination. So, we simply expressed our deep gratitude in recognition of the honour that they were paying to us, and we spoke of our love as Christians for them and their community.

Our emotions were even more entangled when the leader of the Muslim community described how he had first come to Trinity when he was five years old in 1973. He said there were no mosques in East London at that time and we Christians were the only ones who allowed them to meet on our premises. He embraced us warmly and said that he would be eternally grateful to us for enabling him to learn the Qur'an! We greatly appreciated the sincerity of this tribute, although in allowing them to use our premises we had thought it was for a community meeting, not for learning the Qur'an! It was another of life's difficult moments in the tangled web of race relationships! But it gave us the opportunity of lovingly declaring the gospel as did the leader of one of the Christian congregations. These are great opportunities for evangelism once the bridges of relationships have been built.

Notes
[1] This refers to the common practice of new Christians in inner-city areas moving out to the suburbs when their economic or social status improves.
[2] Chapter 1 p. 17.
[3] The account of the acquisition of Trinity Centre East Ham, a former Presbyterian Church will be told in a forthcoming book – *By Faith*, expected 2019.
[4] As described in chapter one.
[5] Children with working parents who were given the key to let themselves into their homes unsupervised after-school.

Chapter Three

THE NATIONWIDE INITIATIVE IN EVANGELISM

Formation of NIE

As already noted, the Lambeth Group was formed following the 'Call to the Nation' by Archbishop Donald Coggan in October 1975. It had 16 members and its first meeting was in June 1976, which was the time John Poulton came to West Ham to meet Monica and me. I did not start attending the Group's meetings until later that year and in January 1978 the Lambeth Group was replaced by a Council of Reference with 39 members. Already at this early stage the 'Call to the Nation' was being institutionalised by the appointment of this large Council with representatives from a wide range of denominational churches from Anglo Catholics to the Salvation Army. It was obvious from the beginning that this group could not have a shared vision because they represented such a wide variety of theological and doctrinal positions. John Poulton was appointed the Minute Secretary until he retired sick in October 1979.

It is interesting to read Roger Whitehead's account of events surrounding my 'non-appointment' in his book *An Unwanted Child*[1] which was written some 10 years later, drawing largely upon the minutes of meetings. Whitehead notes that members of the Lambeth Group had recognised the need for an Executive Secretary who would lead the Initiative and be its 'front man'. They were hoping that relationships with the churches at all levels from local to denominational leaders would be warm and willing in their cooperation. They were also hoping that the Initiative would primarily be active at the local church level in accordance with John Poulton's oft repeated statement that 'whatever is not happening locally, is not happening'. It was this local church involvement that was seen to be my strength and why many on the Lambeth Group were keen to see my appointment to lead the work. They were hoping that relationships with the denominations would be so good that I and any other members of staff employed by the Initiative would be seconded by their churches on short-term contracts.

Roger Whitehead notes this and he records:

In May 1978, the Rev Dr Clifford Hill of the Newham Community Renewal Project offered his services as Executive Secretary on the understanding that his church had agreed to second him to undertake this national ministry, but this offer was not accepted.[2]

It was true that I had agreed an arrangement with my church to second me to the Initiative, but to read that I had 'offered my services' was particularly galling in the light of my experience. I had made this offer because Donald Coggan wanted me to lead a national evangelistic outreach directly from Lambeth Palace with the backing of the Lambeth Group. He had no funds at his disposal, and to obtain Anglican funds he would have had to go to the Synod where he would have been strongly opposed by the liberal bishops. So I offered to find my own salary and to assist with support. I was convinced that the funds to support the whole enterprise would have poured into Lambeth Palace if the Archbishop had been willing to risk a battle in the Synod of the Church of England. When it came to the crunch decision, he gave way.

In my secluded environment in the East End of London I had been sheltered from high-level interdenominational politics and until John Poulton's visit I had not even heard of the Lambeth Group or the proposed Initiative. Monica and I were totally immersed in the work that we loved and we had never envisaged leaving it. Insofar as we had given any thought to the future, we expected to stay in the East End for the rest of our lives – that was the extent of our commitment.

Headhunted

We were deliberately headhunted by the Archbishop and the Lambeth Group, so to say that I had 'offered my services' could not have been farther from the truth. Our lives had been turned upside down for a period of more than a year whilst the Group drew me into their deliberations and planning until they got to the point of actually making an appointment. By then the original Lambeth Group was powerless. The liberals had taken control and I was told that my services were no longer required. This decision was a shattering blow to the earlier hopes of both Donald Coggan and John Poulton. But Roger Whitehead had no means of knowing what had taken place behind the scenes.

Whitehead gives his version of the reason for this decision:

> The committee's decision not to seek a front man was partly a reaction to forceful personalities like Clifford Hill who (it was thought) might stamp their own character on the Initiative and be difficult to control within the committee's thinking; and partly a positive decision that the committee needed to be serviced, but also wanted to go only at the pace of agreement among its members.[3]

Of course, Whitehead had no means of knowing of the Archbishop's intention and of his bitter disappointment at the institutionalisation of what he had envisaged as a simple movement to stimulate evangelism at a local community level. The enforced opening of his initiative to denominational representatives destroyed his hopes. The power of the liberal bishops in the Church of England left the Archbishop powerless, and once the small Lambeth Group of his own choosing had been forced to give way to the larger Council of Reference he knew that his vision of a national outreach in evangelism was doomed to failure.

Initiative Committee

An Initiative Committee was also established to work alongside the Council of Reference as its action arm. In July 1978, the Initiative Committee advertised for an Executive Secretary and among the applicants they selected a 51-year-old businessman, David Taylor. He was a man with no theological background and no experience of church leadership. No doubt the main criterion was to get someone who could establish the organisation on a sound administrative basis, as Kenneth Greet and Canon Craston had demanded. Once again, it is interesting to note Whitehead's assessment of David Taylor's four years' service to the Initiative. He writes:

> One of the tasks originally envisaged for the Executive Secretary was keeping in touch with the denominations and particularly their Home Mission Boards; many of them, with a lifetime's experience of the church, were not impressed with his naivete and lack of knowledge of the denominations' complex interrelationships. As one of the central reasons for ending the Initiative was its poor relationship with the denominations, this in retrospect was a serious weakness.[4]

The Initiative Committee, which was established in March 1978, had been given as its prime responsibility the organising of an Assembly in 1980, originally called a Congress. This was largely based on the missiological experience of Tom Houston, Executive Director of the Bible Society, who had been a key person involved in the 1973 South African Congress on Mission and Evangelism and the 1974 Lausanne Congress on World Mission. He introduced the terms 'modality' and 'sodality', the former being the church institutions including local churches through to denominational structures, the second being parachurch organisations. But in fact, this added a further complication by trying to combine those committed to maintaining institutions with those committed to programmes of action. The Assembly was to bring these two groups together, combining their resources in a major national campaign to communicate the gospel to the nation.

Disunity
Disunity became immediately apparent when conservative evangelicals asked for a definition of the 'gospel' and the response from the Initiative Committee was that they were unable to agree such a definition. This lack of clarity of basic belief was apparent throughout the life of the Initiative. An attempt was made to bring together and harmonise the theological understanding of three different sections of the Christian world:

- The papal exhortation 'Evangelisation in the Modern World';
- The World Council of Churches 'Confessing Christ Today';
- The evangelicals' 'Lausanne Covenant'.

A group of 15 theologians was appointed to produce a statement of belief entitled 'The Gospel We Affirm Together'. The difficulties they faced were clearly reflected in the text.

- In referring to **Jesus Christ** they were quite unable to say simply that he died for the forgiveness of our sins. The nearest they got was to say that Jesus 'Willingly bore the brunt of society's hostility to his goodness.' And 'He identified himself with us in our sins in order to reconcile us to his Father.'
- In regard to **the Bible** they were unable to say simply that the Bible is the unchanging word of God. Instead they said that 'its message has a unique authority'.
- In regard to **evangelism** they were unable to refer to 'conversion' or being 'born again': instead they said that evangelism is 'When we humbly but joyfully reflect God's reconciling love for all humanity, in friendship and mutual respect, the Holy Spirit uses our witness and service to make God known.'[5]

The Initiative Committee had difficulty from the start in defining its purpose and whether the Initiative should be activist or reflective. This meant that they were not able to agree on either a date or how to go public. Eventually, in 1979, it was agreed to have a National Assembly. There were constant arguments for and against a possible visit of Billy Graham. But a Billy Graham Crusade was never the intention of the Archbishop or the Lambeth Group. Dr Coggan had made it clear when addressing the National Anglican Evangelical Council in 1977 that the time was not right for a Billy Graham mission. Donald Coggan's focus was primarily upon *local community evangelism* and he had no interest in a big national crusade. But somehow rumours of the possibility of a Billy Graham mission persisted and increased the suspicion among non-evangelicals in the denominations that this was the hidden objective of the NIE.

Negativity

The deep divisions in the NIE Council of Reference and the Initiative Committee were reflected in the argument regarding Billy Graham, but the divisions went even farther. Gavin Reid who was a member of the Initiative Committee wrote a paper 'NIE – Taking Stock on the First Year' in which he complained about the negativity among those involved in the Initiative. He said:

> Negative thinking is built into the existence of NIE. The only definite advice we seem to have been given has been negative. For example, *not* Billy Graham; *not* a national campaign; *not* an evangelical takeover; official BMU representatives *not* to be evangelical; *not* to initiate action (or so the Evangelical Alliance are now saying!); *not* to identify with any brand of evangelism that proceeds from a definite, authoritative view of the gospel (so say some in BCC circles); *not* to bypass synodical oversight (so says BMU).[6]

Roger Whitehead reported in his account of the NIE that the relationships between the denominations and the NIE were never good.

> It was clear within the first year that the relationship between the Council of Reference and the Initiative Committee was neither as harmonious nor as creative as intended by the Lambeth Group... When it was clear that the Council of Reference had no useful role to play, it was decided to disband it... The denominations finally abandoned the attempt to understand and work along with the Initiative Committee. Having given NIE enough rope, the denominations shortly thereafter hanged it.[7]

Facing the Inevitable

Winding up the Initiative was first discussed in February 1980 – six months before the Assembly. The decision was delayed until after the Assembly. Its future was inevitably closely linked with Dr Coggan who, in the autumn of 1979, made his decision to retire as Archbishop of Canterbury, a very disappointed man – his efforts to reshape the nation had been thwarted. He continued in office for some three months until

January 1980. Those closest to him said that he was broken-hearted over the failure of his attempt to initiate an outreach of the gospel to the nation following the tremendously positive response to his 'Call to the Nation' soon after he reached Lambeth Palace.

John Poulton

John Poulton also left the archbishop's service at the same time, September 1979. As already stated, he had a breakdown. John's resignation was directly related to his failure to achieve my appointment to lead the national outreach of the gospel in accordance with the wishes of the Archbishop. He counted this as a personal failure which had a devastating effect upon his health.

Through Donald Coggan's influence John was found a post as a resident Canon in the quiet cloisters of Norwich Cathedral under the benign and friendly eye of Bishop Maurice Wood – a keen evangelical. It was there, sometime later, in his cloistered cottage that John confessed to me that he had always believed that it was God's intention for me to lead the NIE and he bitterly regretted having given way to the pressures of the hierarchy within the Church of England that caused him to act as he did. He was a victim of the same forces that govern all those who hold authority within the Church of England – *even the Archbishop of Canterbury!* – the drive to maintain unity at all costs – to accommodate all theological beliefs, however contradictory. This is the central weakness of the Anglican Church that guarantees its ineffectiveness and its inability to offer any biblically-based moral, spiritual or social leadership in the nation.

Although in the matter of my appointment John had gone against the Archbishop and paid the price by losing his job, he was never able to tell me why he had followed the instructions of the liberal bishops against the wishes of Donald Coggan. Even though he had recovered from his breakdown, it was all too tender for him to recount the detail of his experience of being caught between two opposing forces of authority. John evidently believed that unity in the Church of England was of supreme importance and he could not face the consequences of being blamed for causing a split in the Anglican Church.

Church Unity

Of course, unity in any organisation is good, both for personal relationships and for achieving its objectives. The Psalmist says *How good and pleasant it is when brothers live together in unity ... for there the Lord bestows his blessing, even life for evermore* (see Psalm 133). But if truth is sacrificed on the altar of unity, it not only becomes error but it becomes a form of institutional idolatry that triumphs over spiritual values. This was happening in the Church of England in Donald Coggan's time.

How can such a church be used for the work of the Kingdom? We will see, in the following chapters, this same conundrum regarding church unity faced by successive Archbishops. When institutional unity becomes more important than adhering to biblical truth or upholding spiritual integrity, the value of the institution should surely be questioned.

When an organisation becomes more important than the activity for which it was formed, the organisation has surely outlived its purpose! We will return to this subject in the Epilogue.[8]

Isaac and Ishmael

The Archbishop's 'Call to the Nation' which received such strong public endorsement was undoubtedly inspired by God. The small, informal organisation he began, in the Lambeth Group, was an 'Isaac' but forces within the Church of England and the liberal elements within the Nonconformist denominations forced their involvement and turned it into an 'Ishmael'. It was never right to have a mishmash leadership in which all shades of opinion drawn from all the denominations and different sectors of the church were represented. The resultant Council of Reference was a group that could never agree even on the objective of the Initiative! Clearly, it was impossible to agree on a *policy* to achieve what they could not agree as a clear *goal*.

The Initiative was finally wound up in March 1983. But, even before that happened, the two main protagonists who had opposed the Archbishop and any form of evangelism through the NIE were taken out of public ministry. Bishop David Brown collapsed suddenly, in July 1982, with a heart attack and died. Dr Harry Morton was also taken out of ministry. He suffered a stroke in 1981 that robbed him of the power of speech at the height of his ministry. He lived for another seven years, but he never spoke again. He died in 1988. The deaths of these two men greatly disturbed me and I still think back to those days and wonder why it happened. Did they suffer some kind of divine judgment for their part in the ecclesiastical power-struggle that I had witnessed so clearly? There is no easy answer to such a question.

The Legacy of the NIE

Despite the negative views of those within the denominations and their representatives in the Council of Reference, the Assembly at Nottingham University in September 1980 did some good. It broke down a lot of negativity. It brought together people with different views who were able to listen to each other and were excited at discovering a measure of convergence not previously thought possible. Lewis Misselbrook, a leading Baptist and Church Growth leader, said "What NIE did very well was to get together people who would not normally have met at all from the BCC (British Council of Churches) and Evangelical Alliance. There was within NIE a tremendous sharing, and a sense of caring for and listening to one another."[9]

Another positive outcome from the Nottingham Assembly was the setting up of County Support Groups, although this was criticised by some of the denominations, particularly the Methodist Home Division. There had never been anything quite like this bringing together representatives of local churches in each region with a specific task of seeking united ways of sharing the gospel. In many cases local churches welcomed this and, despite their other commitments, local representatives attended the meetings with enthusiasm. Roger Whitehead described personally attending one of these County Support meetings in North Wiltshire where he was surprised not only at the level of enthusiasm and commitment, but also at the wisdom and experience that was brought together to focus upon evangelism in the county. This surely was an indication that local churches were ready to cooperate if there were to have been a co-ordinated lead given by national church leaders.[10]

NIE Demise

The whole enterprise began to collapse soon after the retirement of Donald Coggan. Dr Runcie, the new Archbishop of Canterbury, was invited to become chairman of the Council of Reference, but he declined, giving his reason as his 'other commitments'. The real reason was probably his lack of commitment to anything remotely linked with evangelism, although he did offer help in making contact with the Orthodox Churches. Dr Stuart Blanch, Archbishop of York, became chairman of the NIE in November 1980. But the beginning of the end of the Initiative can be traced much earlier.

The General Synod of the Church of England had agreed to support the Initiative with considerable reluctance. It had been hard for members not to agree to give their support in view of the considerable enthusiasm of their Archbishop. But the pressures to widen the scope of the Initiative through the inclusion of people who could not agree even to define the gospel was a considerable setback to Dr Coggan. When the Lambeth Group was disbanded to make way for the Council of Reference, he knew that the writing was on the wall for the kind of outreach to the nation that he had envisaged. Donald English, who chaired the Initiative Committee, is reported as saying that Donald Coggan never played a strong role in the Initiative once the Lambeth Group was disbanded. As mentioned earlier he had said,

> Although he chaired the Council of Reference, Dr Coggan quite deliberately distanced himself from our activities; we did not meet between those meetings and he made no attempt whatsoever to influence anything we did.[11]

It was the Church of England who finally pulled the plug on the Initiative by withdrawing its financial support. The other denominations quickly followed suit and the whole NIE was dead.

The Timing of the Initiative

Looking back on the Initiative we have to ask if it was right in the timing of the Lord. This was a question never examined by the Council of Reference or the Initiative Committee. Clearly, what has just been quoted from the North Wiltshire County Support meetings indicates grassroots support at local church level. This was the shared vision of the original Lambeth Group who came together as a response to the national welcome given to the Archbishop's 'Call to the Nation'. The 27,000 letters received at Lambeth Palace were just the tip of the iceberg. The mood in the nation was right for reflecting upon the moral and spiritual condition of the nation. It was a time of considerable social unrest stemming from industrial problems. The post-war boom giving rise to full employment had now waned and waves of strikes were increasing the sense of anxiety and uncertainty in the Government which was reflected in the nation among ordinary working people. The general perception was that there was something wrong, and Dr Coggan's call touched a chord.

The outreach to the nation with the gospel that Donald Coggan envisaged, which was embraced by the Lambeth Group, was for stimulating grassroots action. It was never intended to be a top down nationally directed ecumenical outreach – a campaign hierarchically imposed upon the nation.

There were many other indications that the time was right for a locally based national outreach of the gospel linked with social action that could have had a significant effect in changing the history of the nation. The decade had begun with the publication of the New English Bible, the unprecedented demand for which took the Oxford and Cambridge publishers by surprise. All 1 million copies were sold on the first day of publication. Reprints were running at 20,000 per week which reflected a massive increase in interest in the Bible.

Was the Time Right?

Of course, we can never know how the history of our nation would have changed if the intention of the Archbishop and the original Lambeth Group had been implemented. The time was right in the nation, but obviously some influential church leaders were not ready for change. It would be a fair assumption that the majority of the 27,000 letters written to Lambeth Palace would have come from churchgoing Christians spread right across the country. It is obvious that there was a faithful remnant eagerly looking for a lead from church leaders — a lead that never came.

A true reading of the situation in the late 1970s shows that there was a strong enough body of Christians in churches of all denominations throughout Britain to have supported and enthusiastically embraced a co-ordinated locally based movement for sharing the gospel with friends and neighbours alongside an imaginative and creative movement of social activities designed to meet local needs. This was Archbishop Coggan's vision and this is what he discussed with John Poulton and me and that he wanted Monica and me to lead. Of course, there is no way of telling how successful we would have been, but the lasting record of our work in the East End of London that is still continuing today bears some testimony. At the 30th anniversary of the Newham Community Renewal Programme in 2001 its annual budget was over £1 million and at the 40th anniversary of the Trinity Centre in East Ham ten years later the work there was still thriving.

We cannot be certain that people in the local churches would have responded positively, but all the evidence shows that there were Christians in churches throughout the country who would have welcomed the Archbishop's Initiative. The biblical record of God's dealings with his people in the past shows that he loves to work with small numbers like Gideon's 300 – God is not a democrat who waits for a majority before acting! There was certainly a sufficiently large committed remnant in the churches in the 1970s to support a major outreach into the nation. The community-based evangelism that we were practising in the East End provided solid evidence of its effectiveness, and it was this same community-based concept that was at the heart of proposals from Donald Coggan and John Poulton.

Undoubtedly I believe that the time was right and I have many times reflected upon the reasons why Donald Coggan did not simply go ahead and direct a national outreach from Lambeth Palace as was his original intention when he sent for Monica and me. I believe the answer is that he feared that it would have split the Church of England. This was a risk that, as Archbishop, he was not willing to take. In hindsight, I think he was wrong about fears of a split. I do not believe that the liberal bishops would have gone so far as to split the church — it was a challenge for leadership and a battle for power. But it is the liberals who value unity at all costs, far more than evangelicals.

The 1970s was also the early days of the Charismatic Movement that was beginning to impact all the mainline denominations of the Christian churches in Britain. There was clearly a genuine move of the Holy Spirit among Bible-believing Christians across the country. God's timing is always perfect. But, in order to achieve his purposes, God has chosen to rely upon the discernment and obedience of human beings. When church leaders are like the religious leaders in Jesus' day whom he described as, *"Though seeing, they do not see; though hearing, they do not hear or understand"* (Matthew 13.13), they not only fail to give effective leadership but they actually miss the timing of the Lord.

Jesus wept over Jerusalem when the leaders failed to perceive the time of God's coming among them. *"If you, even you had only known on this day what would bring you peace – but now it is hidden from your eyes"* (Luke 19.42). He referred to the disaster that would befall the city and the nation because they did not recognise the times of the Lord.

I have no doubt that it was not only Archbishop Donald Coggan and Canon John Poulton and Monica and I who were weeping over Britain in 1978.

Notes

[1] Roger Whitehead and Amy Sneddon, *An Unwanted Child?* The story of NIE, British Council of churches, London, 1990.

[2] *Ibid.*, p. 16.

[3] *Ibid.*, pp. 16-17.

[4] *Ibid.*, p. 17.

[5] *Ibid.*, pp. 117 and 119.

[6] Quoted by Whitehead. *Ibid.*, p. 93.

[7] *Ibid.*, p. 36.

[8] See p. 331.

[9] *Ibid.*, p. 96.

[10] *Ibid.*, p. 95.

[11] *Ibid.*, pp. 49-50.

Chapter Four

THE EA AND THE NATIONAL CONGRESS

Joining the EA

As soon as the decision was made that I was not to be appointed to lead the NIE, the Council of the Evangelical Alliance (EA) met and sent an invitation to Monica and me offering us a joint appointment putting together 'Evangelism' and 'Church Growth'. We were invited to share responsibility for a new national outreach under the auspices of the EA as Secretaries for Evangelism and Church Growth. They asked us to do under the EA banner what we would have done through the NIE.

It was not really what we wanted — we didn't want to work purely under an evangelical banner. In the East End we worked with churches of all denominations and different theological positions but with a common vision for reaching out with the gospel to those normally beyond the reach of the churches. In praying about the situation and consulting with our friends we could see no valid reason for refusing this invitation although we were not wildly enthusiastic. The EA Council knew about our work in Newham, and Gordon Landreth,[1] as one of the original members of the Lambeth Group, was well aware of what Donald Coggan had asked us to do. On that understanding we accepted and pledged to do our best.

We both have high levels of the Protestant work ethic so we plunged with all the energy at our disposal into a hectic round of speaking engagements up and down the country, under the banner of the Evangelical Alliance. It involved much travelling, while at the same time having to attend committees and do a lot of organisational work, as well as caring for our three children.

Our attendance at Council meetings led to an interesting discovery — that to many of those present Evangelism and Church Growth were synonymous, so any reports on Church Growth issues were dealt with at the end of the meeting – if there was time! Church Growth became the poor relation of the Evangelism Committee much to Monica's dismay (and others). This led to those who were interested in Church Growth meeting with Monica separately which led to the eventual setting up of a separate national organisation – the British Church Growth Association, with the EA as a member!

We were never really comfortable working with the Evangelical Alliance. Its conservative evangelical atmosphere was quite foreign to us, so too was the predominantly middle-class conservative social group with whom we found ourselves working.

We were the first charismatics they had had in the EA and I was also laughingly referred to as the first 'Marxist' member of staff. I hasten to add that I was never at any time in my life a Marxist,[2] but my previous appointment as a Senior Lecturer in Sociology, my links with the London School of Economics and my deep concern for the poor and powerless appeared radical to middle-class Conservative evangelical minds! This was reinforced by our many years of working among Caribbean and Asian immigrants, and our involvement in inner-city ministry which contrasted starkly with the suburban conservative white middle-class image of the Evangelical Alliance as it then was. That later changed under the more forthright leadership of Clive Calver, but that was after we had left.[3]

Our own plans were already under way to move away from the East End to a more central location, provided for us by a church in Cheltenham whose leaders had been pursuing me to be their minister for nearly a year. We had told them of the Archbishop's invitation to us and they were quite happy with the possibility of their minister being involved in what they perceived to be a high status national position and promised to engage an assistant minister so that I could do the two jobs. When they learned of the change to the Evangelical Alliance most of the leaders and many in the congregation were not so happy as the very word 'Evangelical' was not popular with them. The previous Minister had preached a liberal gospel and they were more used to hearing from the Reader's Digest than the Bible. I didn't last long. We had no experience of living and working among upper-middle-class Cheltenham Conservatives, so there were cultural problems as well as theological. We didn't share their values. Although I spoke the Queen's English (except when I was in the East End!) our children had Cockney accents. They threw me out after six months. We began in September 1978 and our last Sunday was Easter Day 1979. It was a painful experience. By this time I was not a stranger to the experience of rejection and I was beginning to understand more of what Paul describes as the 'fellowship of Christ's suffering' (Phil 3.10).

Nevertheless, many in the congregation liked to hear the Bible expounded and they liked to hear my exegetical biblical preaching which was usually applied to contemporary issues. They were unhappy with the action of the church leadership and they got together and generously rented a house for us to move into for 18 months to maintain our children's education when we had to vacate the church house. We were already renting a redundant school for our EA work (which Monica had renamed The Church Growth Centre) and a small congregation began to meet there on Sundays, asking me to preach for them. I was very reluctant to do this as I had no wish to cause a split in the church but they had already left the church and showed us so much loving care and support that we could not refuse. Their decision to begin a new fellowship was entirely their own initiative. The congregation grew rapidly and today it is a thriving church with their own premises in a different part of Cheltenham. We only stayed 18 months before moving back to London, where we were invited to join the Ministry Team of St Mark's Kennington in Lambeth. We were back in the smog with ordinary working people — it was great!

Plan for the 1980s

Despite many misgivings, Monica and I jointly set about the task of organising a nationwide evangelistic outreach under the EA. With only the support of the evangelical churches, we knew that it was only second best and it was not really the work to which we believed we were called. Towards the end of 1978, while we were still in Cheltenham, we outlined a plan for the 1980s which was to be designated a 'Decade of Evangelism'. The EA Council were delighted with the concept and warmly endorsed it.

The plan was to begin with providing resources to local churches to enable every believer to know how to share their faith with their neighbours and friends. The second step was to encourage groups of local churches to carry out small-scale evangelism in their locality. The third step was to move this outward to regional-based evangelism, and finally towards the end of the decade there was to be a large-scale national outreach. This was the vision that had been agreed with Donald Coggan and the Lambeth Group. It was to be launched with a nation-wide 'National Congress on Evangelism' which we linked with Spring Harvest that had been formed the previous year and held at Prestatyn in North Wales.

National Congress

The Congress took place in April 1980 and we prepared a programme drawing together a wide range of evangelistic projects that represented many different aspects of evangelism at that time. We ourselves were still in the early stages of learning about the wider church scene from which we had been insulated throughout our years of pastoral work in London, so we were only vaguely aware of the tensions and divisions within evangelicalism, especially between conservative evangelicals and charismatics. This became one of the highlights of the Congress. Dick Lucas (a Conservative Evangelical) gave the morning Bible studies and David Pawson (a Charismatic) spoke at the evening meetings. Lucas found something anti-charismatic to say in the morning to which Pawson robustly responded in the evening, which certainly added to the liveliness of the Congress!

The Congress attracted over 2,000 people from all over the UK and there were an additional 4,500 in the associated Spring Harvest. There had been many negative comments from members of the NIE Initiative Committee that the EA Congress would split loyalties in evangelism and could upstage their National Assembly which was at present in the early stages of planning. Dr Donald English, chairman of the NIE's committee, was invited to speak at the Congress in Prestatyn. He later reported to the

Initiative Committee that good relationships had been built up with the NIE. He said, "The EA Congress has been the most open, questioning, EA gathering I have ever attended, with a lot of tension held together in love, and an open receptive atmosphere."

The five-day Congress had 15 major addresses, 15 seminars, 38 workshops, 22 demonstrations of tools for evangelism and 53 regional groups discussing strategies for evangelism. The Congress not only had plenary sessions with Bible study in the mornings and inspirational gatherings in the evenings, but throughout the day there was a range of workshops with speakers tackling issues in reaching the unreached in society. These looked at problems faced by small rural churches, inner-city urban outreach programmes, and a range of social and political issues, analysing the socio-political environment for evangelism in the 1980s. In this, the Congress was tackling issues rarely discussed or even recognised by evangelicals. We harnessed our own many years of experience of living and working in tough inner-city working-class areas in addressing these subjects, and we brought in as speakers a number of urban mission practitioners from different regions around Britain who made valuable contributions to the Congress.

We took the opportunity of introducing a number of Church Growth concepts which were just coming into the British church at that time, and the small group of Council Members who had been meeting separately had expanded and been working on the first issue of the *Church Growth Digest*, which was also launched at this event. 'The British Church Growth Association'[4] had not yet been officially established and Church Growth was still under the aegis of the EA. But, as noted, it was usually placed at the end of the agenda for Council meetings, so it was regarded as something of an optional extra instead of a major new discipline studying the factors that inhibited or promoted growth. We also took the opportunity of organising seminars on inner-city mission based upon urban sociology and urban theology concepts. We introduced our concept of 'community-based evangelism' with its theological roots in New Testament teaching on a 'community of believers' and the 'priesthood of all believers'.

EA Report

A report to the EA Council prior to the Congress said that it would play a major role in helping the church to move from maintenance to mission. The four themes of the conference were 'Lifestyle', 'Culture', 'Renewal' and 'Strategy'. By the end of the Congress three major concerns emerged:

- a recognition that the nation was in a critical period of social change to which churches must adjust in their presentation of the gospel to the nation
- a concern for spiritual unity in the church
- a commitment to prayer for repentance and renewal

It was recognised that the nation stood on the brink of economic and social chaos and that the secularisation of society was accelerating. The church was divided and ineffective in influencing social change. There had to be radical change in the mission of the church if the gospel in Britain is to survive the coming days of trial. The churches lacked the vision for this and without vision there can be no strategy for the fulfilment of objectives.

Some quotes from speakers

Dick Lucas said the spirit of our age rejects certainties and praises open-mindedness. Our temptation is to trim the message in order not to offend, which will not lead to national repentance or spiritual growth.

David Watson said that greed is our western world's biggest weakness which will lead to severe economic decline. The church has lost credibility for preaching a message which calls for seeking first the kingdom of God but its members seek first material comforts in a consumer society. The church is lacking a prophetic voice in the nation.

Clifford Hill said three alternatives were facing Britain in the future: (a) political revolution from the far left; (b) social chaos leading to oppression and persecution of Christians; (c) Christian revival through the renewal movement. Of these three he believed that a period of social and economic chaos was the most likely.

Donald English said church leaders need to confess that Christians have followed the values of society rather than those of the kingdom of God.

The churches are driven by a passion for instant solutions and we need to seek the merciful forgiveness of God.

David Pawson said that God is weeping over the pitifully weak state of the church that has led to tragic results in society where one in three marriages break up leaving half-a-million children without both parents; and in the UK we have killed more babies since 1968 than Jews killed in Hitler's gas chambers. He warned that we are on a slippery slide into chaos in the nation.

Luis Palau, South American evangelist, said he was surprised and disturbed by the 'destructive cynical negativism' which pervaded the United Kingdom and had seeped into the churches. He said that Britain is now as ripe for harvest as Argentina had been 20 years earlier, but churches were not ready to reap the harvest.

The Congress agreed that repentance in the church should be the primary objective, recognising three prime areas of national life from which Christians had abdicated responsibility:

- Politics – there needs to be much greater positive Christian involvement
- Mass Media – using the media for propagating the gospel
- Trade Union Movements – working for justice and prosperity to combat greed and corruption

Many speakers saw the outlook for the future as bleak, unless there was repentance and radical change in the church that spilled over into the nation. The greatest problem in the church was disunity, lack of love and lack of vision. I told the Congress that I had found more love and concern for one another among liberals in the East End than I had amongst many evangelicals.[5] The hope for the future was that repentance in the church will lead to a caring, praying, active and powerful body of believers with a burden for the nation and a vision for change. In the final report I said:

Perhaps the most significant spiritual emphasis to emerge from Prestatyn was the recognition of our own powerlessness and of our responsibility as Christians for the state of the nation. God is longing to forgive us and to heal our land, but the precondition of being restored to a right relationship with him is our penitence. God is not waiting for the whole nation to turn to him before he will begin to pour out his blessings upon us, but he requires the penitence of us, his people ... Just as in former days 'the blood of the martyrs' was the seed of the church, so today the tears of the saints are the seeds of revival. The sacrifice acceptable to God is a broken spirit. *A broken and contrite heart, O God, you will not despise* (Ps 51.17). When we turn to God with empty hands he is able to fill us with the power of his Spirit. God was saying to the Congress at Prestatyn that Christians are now moving into a battle situation but the battle is his, not ours. The victory is assured: *Not by might, nor by power, but by my Spirit, says the Lord* (Zec 4.6).

Decade of Evangelism

The Congress also provided a launch platform for the 'Decade of Evangelism' but this had still not been thoroughly thought through with the EA Council, so we were not able to present it as a coherent programme. However, all those attending took away a full folder of ideas which Monica had coordinated. We spent many hours of discussion of our proposals in the EA Council, but while the concept of a 10-year programme was enthusiastically embraced, the programme we advocated was turned upside down. The Council could not envisage beginning with a grassroots programme mobilising ordinary Christians to share their faith with their neighbours: they wanted a big name professional evangelist to do it 'properly' and bring the gospel back into the public square!

The strategy we envisaged was to lay a foundation by stimulating evangelism at a local level by launching training courses designed to enable each individual churchgoer to be able to share their faith on a one-to-one basis. Once evangelism was happening naturally at a local level and each church was reaching their 'fringe' through a variety of activities, co-operation between churches at a local level would be encouraged. This would then be widened to regional activities and finally, towards the end of the 1980s, there was to have been a co-ordinated nationwide outreach.

The EA Council said that, although they liked the concept, they preferred to start with the big nationwide outreach and then move into locally based evangelism. We said that this was putting the roof on the building before the foundations had been properly laid. Sadly, there were strong pressures from EA supporters, especially those with the money, for an early invitation to Billy Graham. But we had no conviction that this was the right strategy for a national outreach.

We had very much embraced John Poulton's statement 'whatever is not happening locally is not happening' and this was confirmed by our own experience. Our many years of working in the community at a local level, meeting local needs and at the same time sharing the gospel, convinced us that the right start was at a local level. We believed this to be the right strategy, at the right time in the life of the nation. As noted above, this had been the concept agreed with the Lambeth Group as a result of much seeking the Lord in discussion and prayer.

Crusade Evangelism

Sadly, many of those who were influential in the EA (and their most generous financial supporters) could only think of 'crusade evangelism' as the right strategy for communicating the gospel to the nation. They wanted Billy Graham and they were quite unable to think outside the box. Their tunnel vision did not allow for God doing anything new, such as beginning with the mobilisation of ordinary people at the grassroots. They could only think in terms of hiring a professional evangelist from America to come and bring the gospel to Britain. They had learned nothing from the vast response of the British public to the 1975 Archbishop's 'Call to the Nation'.

Clearly, from our experience in London, the concept of beginning where people were at a local and personal level, helping people to understand and articulate their faith was the right starting place. It would have affirmed the worth of each individual and would have harnessed the mood of the nation and met the desire for change. It was probably the last opportunity for setting in motion a movement that could have resulted in a genuine revival of the Christian faith in Britain in the 20th century.

The EA Council, however, remained firmly entrenched in a traditional evangelical mould. They were convinced that the only way to do evangelism was with a high power international evangelist. We were quite unable to convince the Council that this was a new day, offering a new and unique opportunity to mobilise ordinary Christian believers – the sort of people Jesus chose to be his disciples. They were delighted with the success of the National Congress of Evangelism, but they learned nothing from the new concepts on evangelism that were presented. Neither had they learned from the radical concepts taught in the socio-political workshops or the practical reports from those with experience of inner-city/urban evangelism.

They were determined to go back to the old concept of 'crusade evangelism' with big-name celebrity evangelists. They remembered the success of the Billy Graham Crusade in the 1950s, and they were convinced that if Billy had been willing to stay a few more weeks at the end of that campaign, revival would have come to Britain. Their objective for the early 1980s was to do a repeat performance, only longer – to bring Billy Graham over to Britain and persuade him to stay for a period of about three months, with regional campaigns moved around the country which they felt sure would produce the longed-for revival. But they were quite unable to understand that Britain in the 1980s was a very different nation from the 1950s and the early post-World War II reactionary years of social conservatism. They just did not think in those concepts.

As already mentioned, we were quite unable to convince the Council that this was sociologically a new day and new methods of presenting the gospel were essential.[6] We said emphatically that to spend a lot of money and time and effort on the old-fashioned crusade evangelism was a waste of time and resources. It was not right in the timing of the Lord and would not be fruitful. They remained unconvinced. Invitations were duly sent to Luis Palau to do a London Mission and to Billy Graham to cover the rest of the UK. These became 'Mission London' and 'Mission England' 1982/83. As Director of Evangelism I had to sign the letters of invitation. It was the last thing I did on behalf of the EA. We resigned quietly with no public statements as to our reasons for leaving.

Missed Opportunity

We had no wish to be the cause of any harm being done to the preaching of the gospel in Britain and we personally had a warm regard and respect for both Billy and Luis. We knew that many people would be blessed by their preaching, but we were convinced that the timing of the Lord had already been missed for national revival. The momentum generated by the Archbishop's 'Call to the Nation' had already been dissipated in five years of wrangling between 1975 and 1980. We remained working with Luis Palau in the 'Mission London' group for some time helping to coordinate this work from the Leysian Mission in Old Street under the name of 'New Way London' and we built up quite a network of prayer and support.

We had only lasted three years with the EA from 1979 to 81. It was not a happy time as we were quite unable to open eyes to the situation in the nation and we faced the constant pressure of divisions within evangelicalism, particularly between those who had embraced the new emphasis upon the Holy Spirit that was gaining momentum in the 1970s through what was becoming known as the Charismatic Movement and those who were holding firmly to traditional conservative evangelicalism. Soon after the National Congress we organised a celebration on Pentecost Sunday 1980 in Trafalgar Square. We notified churches of all persuasions right across the Greater London area and the response was quite amazing.

Trafalgar Square was literally filled on a fine Sunday afternoon with Christians who had clearly come to enjoy a time of open worship, joining together in prayer and singing with great enthusiasm. The gospel was preached with strong, robust and forthright presentations from four speakers: Colin Urquhart, Jeremiah McIntyre, Ian Pettit and myself. Jeremiah McIntyre, who led a black majority Pentecostal church in Brixton, was particularly effective, with many passers-by around the Square stopping to listen.

Despite the great success of this event it was not appreciated by the EA Council and a number of churches withdrew their membership because we had invited Pentecostal and Charismatic speakers. A concern for some of the evangelical churches was that we had invited Father Ian Pettit, a charismatic Roman Catholic priest. He was in fact personally a Bible-believing evangelical who preached a forthright gospel of salvation in the Name of Jesus. I understood their hesitation, but others saw the opportunity of reaching a wider constituency.

Evangelism Scandal

A month after the National Congress I published a short booklet, *The Evangelism Scandal*,[7] which spoke about the disunity in the church that had been identified by most speakers at the Congress. I said that lack of love and concern for one another as a community of believers was at the heart of the disunity in the church. Until we recover the *koinonia* of the Early Church and the love of Jesus that bound believers together we would never experience the power of the Holy Spirit to evangelise the nation.

That same year, 1980, I published a book entitled *Towards the Dawn* which was launched at the Congress. It referred to the state of the nation and the weakness of the church. It said that the socio-economic forces of change and the spiritual forces of darkness that had been gathering momentum for several decades had reached a stage where they were virtually unstoppable. Only divine intervention could halt the progress towards the disintegration of the traditional social structure of the nation.

Warning

The book warned that revolutionary forces of social change were at work that would destroy the Judaeo-Christian foundations of society and that as a nation we were turning away from our core beliefs in a personal Creator God to a secular humanist worldview that would eventually destroy Western civilisation. At the same time, I spoke of the weaknesses of the church, of its divisions, and the unbelief that was being spread by liberal theology.

It may be that the Lord will bypass the institutional church. It may be that he has already written ICHABOD – 'Glory Departed' – over our denominations. It may be that our traditional denominational structures must fall into the ground and die in order that a new church may arise out of the dust to bring salvation to the nation.[8]

Monica and I left the EA with a mixed sense of relief and release, although once again we were walking away from a situation where we had security, into the unknown. We were no strangers to living by faith. We had done it before in the East End, but then we were part of large community where we prayed together daily and cared for each other. This time we were really on our own but, amazingly, a small group quickly formed around us, led by Crispin and Gill Brentford,[9] who understood what we were saying about community-based evangelism and encouraged others to come around us as a prayer support group. A number of Christians who were interested in the radical things that I was saying through *Towards the Dawn* and in various journal articles, began to meet with me to explore these concepts which were recognised as being in line with the message of the biblical prophets. This developed into meetings for Bible study in the context of facing social issues in Britain and on the international scene. It paved the way for the start of Prophetic Word Ministries (PWM), and the magazine *Prophecy Today*.

Church Growth Association Founded

Monica, meanwhile had found opportunities to continue her Church Growth work drawing together a group of church leaders who were keen to explore the new Church Growth concepts that were being developed both in Britain and in the USA. She led a group of several strong leaders in positions of responsibility in the mainline churches – Anglicans, Baptists, Methodists and others. Together they decided to organise an official launch of the 'British Church Growth Association' as a registered charity in 1981. This was done at a ceremony at the headquarters of the London Baptist Union which was then in Southampton Row, London.

Monica became Executive Secretary, Derek Tidball from London Bible College became the first Chairman, and Eddie Gibbs, an Anglican vicar working with the Bible Society, became the first President, although it was not long before he moved to California, taking up a Church Growth lecturing post in the Fuller Institute which was becoming a leading international centre for the subject. A strong Council of leaders from all denominations came together, membership soon spread through the country and the *Church Growth Digest,* its quarterly journal, expanded as many new books and resources on the subject began appearing.

The BCGA Council met regularly to discuss new concepts that

were being developed and research into the circumstances that aided numerical, spiritual and fellowship growth as well as those that impeded growth. They ran national conferences bringing concepts like 'Church Planting' into the national parlance as a mission concept needed as much in the UK as overseas, and coordinated a Church Planting Network supporting church evangelists. Their first book of the talks given at the Conference, *How To Plant Churches*,[10] sold out in record time and is now out of print. Their second conference on the various aspects of conversion, *Entering the Kingdom*,[11] is still in print. They were in touch with all the researchers and analysts of the actual growth of the church worldwide, but they resisted being only involved in what they called 'number-crunching' — simply counting numbers — and took a greater interest in the trends shown and the *quality* of fellowships involved.

A 'Small Church Network' developed, showing how the growing number of smaller churches could grow healthily, and an interest in the subject of Church Growth grew nationally.

This led before long to growing interest on the Continent, which resulted in the formation of the European Church Growth Association. Monica served as President of the ECGA for a period and helped to develop their resources. She then carried out a research project with Christian Schwarz[12] among churches of all denominations in Britain, studying the health of each congregation. This was followed by the adoption of 'Natural Church Development' principles, with its emphasis upon Healthy Churches.

The BCGA was a 'think tank' where leaders, researchers and practitioners of all denominations could share their insights with each other. They had a Council of 18 drawn from leaders in England, Scotland, Wales and Northern Ireland, representing most denominations. This included the Pentecostals, Brethren and the Salvation Army and also embraced some of the newer churches that were being formed at that time. They used to meet regularly three times a year to plan and debate issues and explore different concepts. These meetings were always well attended. Peter Bisset, of St Ninian's in Perth, Scotland, held the chair for a period and used to say that it gave him a wider vision and he would never miss a meeting no matter how far he had to travel. The Council developed a number of smaller subcommittees and many of their findings appeared in the *Church Growth Digest*[13] or in papers, books and booklets from which church leaders benefited over the years.

Notes

[1] Gordon Landreth was General Secretary of the Evangelical Alliance.

[2] In fact, I have never been a member of any political party.

[3] The Evangelical Alliance was so dominated by conservative evangelicals at that time that it did not admit Pentecostals as members. Charismatics, like Monica and myself, broke the mould.

[4] The BCGA was officially formed in 1982.

[5] See Clifford Hill, *The Evangelism Scandal*, Evangelical Alliance, London, 1980.

[6] See p. 63.

[7] Clifford Hill, *op. cit.*

[8] Clifford Hill, *Towards the Dawn*, Collins, London, 1980, p. 174.

[9] Viscount and Viscountess Brentford. Crispin was a London lawyer and he set up a Trust for our support – 'C and M Ministries', that became 'Issachar Ministries'.

[10] Monica Hill ed., *How to Plant Churches*, BCGA with MARC Europe, London, 1984.

[11] Monica Hill, *Entering the Kingdom*, MARC Europe, Bromley Kent, 1986.

[12] Christian Schwarz was a German Church Growth specialist who introduced the concept of 'Natural Church Development' and the eight 'quality characteristics' necessary for there to be healthy growth in a local church. These are empowering leadership, gift orientated ministry, passionate spirituality, functional structures, inspiring worship services, holistic small groups, need-orientated evangelism, loving relationships.

[13] Church Growth Digest, published by the British Church Growth Association from 1979 to 2006.

Chapter Five

REVIEWING THE SEVENTIES

Social and Industrial Unrest

The 1970s proved to be a decade of considerable social unrest. It began with the highest level of strikes seen in Britain since 1926 and the decade ended with even more. Large strikes with national ramifications involved dockers, postmen, newspaper workers and printers. But there were many other industries involved, not least car manufacturers at Dagenham and Oxford. I was lecturing in London University at the time and there were certain lecturers in the LSE who were occasionally missing and other members of staff would say, "There will be a strike at Dagenham tomorrow." Invariably this was the case, which confirmed the view that much of the social and industrial unrest emanated, not from the shopfloor in industry, but from the Sociology faculties in academia.

In June 1970 a Conservative Government was elected, the British public no doubt feeling that in a time of severe economic problems the Tories might have a better grasp of financial matters to deal with the nation's troubles. Edward Heath became Prime Minister and made it his objective to get Britain into the European Common Market, an objective that had been firmly opposed by General de Gaulle and the French delegates for a number of years. In 1972 the nation joined the EEC following a parliamentary vote which was widely regarded as a personal triumph for Heath although it later emerged that he had not told the whole truth when he assured the nation that the sole objective was to join the Common Market with no loss of national sovereignty.

In later years he admitted that he had always known that the ultimate objective was the formation of a single European state.

The strikes in industry grew steadily throughout the decade and by November 1972 the Government was forced to declare both a wages and a prices freeze, due to severe economic problems. The economy, however, did not recover quickly and by the end of 1973 Britain was on a three-day week and struggling to contain industrial unrest. It was economic problems that brought down Heath's Government and in April 1974 Harold Wilson became Prime Minister in a Labour administration.

Religion

The 1970s saw a serious decline in church attendance. This had begun in the 1960s which reversed the growth of the social reactionary period of the immediate post-World War II era and the 1950s, which had seen the highly successful Harringay meetings led by Billy Graham. There were a number of reasons for this decline in the 1960s. The end of petrol rationing in the late 1950s had significantly increased motoring and seen the beginning of weekend travel, particularly families visiting on Sundays. But it was the 'Swinging 60s' that had the greatest long-term impact upon church attendance, with the beginning of the secularisation of Britain when major movements of social change coalesced. We will be outlining these in Chapter 6.

The Effect of the 1960s

The movements of social change generating secularisation were undoubtedly aided by changes in theology in the training of clergy and ministers in both the Anglican and Nonconformist churches. These theological changes had been in the teaching offered in most theological colleges and universities for many years, but it was during the 1960s that liberal theology reached new pinnacles of scepticism in regard to biblical analysis.[1] This ultra-liberal theology was not only to be seen in the cloistered seclusion of university faculties and college lecture rooms, it became open to the public through the publication of such books as John Robinson's *Honest to God* in 1963,[2] which marked the beginning of the 'God is Dead' movement. In 1977, John Hick, Don Cupitt and others published *The Myth of God Incarnate*[3] which challenged much of traditional biblical thinking, particularly in connection with the divinity of Christ.

This ultra-liberal theology had an inevitable impact upon theological students preparing for the ministry of churches of all denominations. Its effect was to reduce confidence in the veracity of the Bible, which of course affected the preaching of the word of God at the time when secularisation was hitting every part of society. Without confidence in biblical truth to challenge the concepts of Marxism and humanism, church leaders and preachers were unable to stand against the tide of social change that was sweeping across the nation. Sociologist Jeffrey Hadden did a survey of ministers of a mainline denomination in the USA that showed some startling levels of unbelief among church leaders.

Hadden conducted a survey of all those attending a conference of the National Council of Churches of Christ in the USA in 1963 where he found that only 62% of ministers in pastoral charge and 60% of administrators could affirm that they had no doubts about the existence of God. A mere 18% believed that Jesus actually walked upon the water. The results of his survey are reproduced below.

Basic Beliefs of Clergy and Laity[4]

	ORDAINED MINISTERS		LAITY
	In Administrative Positions	In Pastoral Charge	
BELIEF IN: (No doubts)	%	%	%
God	60	62	78
Divinity of Christ	54	60	71
Life After Death	58	70	70
Virgin Birth	22	27	46
The Devil	18	28	7
Original Sin	11	22	17
Miracles	16	24	33

There was no similar research carried out in Britain at that time, but my own experience of what I was taught in theological college and university in that period affirms that the situation in Britain among preachers and church leaders in most of the mainline denominations would have been very similar to Hadden's findings. Unbelief, which was generated in the 1960s, spread among church leaders in the 1970s and escalated subsequently. The secular values of the world crept into the church. Instead of the church counteracting the secularisation of the nation it actually aided and encouraged its advance, through leaders who lacked confidence in its message.

Moral Issues – the Backlash
At the beginning of the 1970s there was a growing backlash in the nation against the libertarianism of the 1960s. The 1968 Theatres Act had abolished censorship in the theatre, allowing nudity and all kinds of explicit sexual acts to take place on stage in British theatres. The Act also eased restrictions upon publications and films which opened the floodgates for the use of sex in advertising and entertainment.

There were many references in the press and comments by well-known personalities that the moral values of the nation were collapsing. It was in the context of this concern that a grassroots movement arose to defend traditional morality and, among its more evangelical supporters, to declare the truth of the gospel and spread the light of Jesus, the light of the world. This was the vision behind the September 1971 Festival of Light that attracted enormous support from Christians of all denominations. Although it began as a grassroots movement it attracted much high-level support, including even a goodwill message from Prince Charles.

The Festival of Light
The Festival of Light attracted not only Christians but also large public support, with a huge rally in Trafalgar Square followed by a gathering of at least 100,000 people in Hyde Park. Some two weeks before the Trafalgar Square meeting, a packed meeting in Westminster Central Hall had been attacked by members of the newly formed Gay Liberation Front. The Front had been formed the previous year with just 250 members and this was their first opportunity to demonstrate

their strength. They were objecting to one of the Festival's objectives which was aimed at curbing sex and violence in public entertainment, which was depicted as a threat to personal liberty. Despite the strength of public support for the Festival there was no noticeable reduction in the increasing secularisation of the nation and the spread of sex and violence in the entertainment industry.

Monica and I were not involved in the Festival of Light. We were still quietly tucked away in the East End of London where national movements, and especially things emanating from the West End of London, rarely penetrated. Yet, strangely enough, within the next 10 years almost all of those who led the Festival we counted among our personal friends – Mary Whitehouse and Malcolm Muggeridge were the two dominant personalities in the Festival. Monica and I often visited Malcolm and Kitty in their comfortable oast house home in East Sussex which was near to our family home. We were very fond of them and I prayed with Malcolm on the day that he died.

Col. Orde Dobbie was another dear friend. He became Warden of the Garden Tomb in Jerusalem and I often stayed in his home. Other Festival leaders were: Eddie Stride, Rector of Christ Church Spitalfields, who worked with Monica on Church Growth issues; Gordon Landreth, who was General Secretary of the Evangelical Alliance; Jean Darnall, who had an office in St Mark's Kennington, where I was on the pastoral team and Monica based the BCGA central office for a number of years, and Steve Stevens, a former World War II fighter pilot who was a great enthusiast and committed evangelist.

Marriage Breakdown

The 1971 National Census showed a steep rise in marriage breakdown which was a result of the 1969 Divorce Reform Act which made the 'irretrievable breakdown' of marriage the ground for divorce, in practice removing the need to prove particular circumstances where the divorce is uncontested. It opened the way for easy divorce. Family breakdown rapidly escalated from this time, with a multitude of social problems particularly affecting children and vulnerable adults. This inevitably affected all the major social institutions in the nation and increased the sense of insecurity caused by economic problems and rising unemployment. As mentioned earlier in this chapter there were severe economic problems. By November 1972 the Government was forced to declare a wages and prices freeze.

The World Scene in Context

Riots in Ulster in 1971 led to the January 1972 'Bloody Sunday' during which some civilians were killed by British troops. This triggered IRA atrocities on the mainland, in the first of which, in March 1972, the IRA succeeded in bombing the Aldershot base of British soldiers. On the world scene many things were happening to sharpen the sense of insecurity. The war in Vietnam was being extensively covered in the Western press. TV news brought terrible scenes of violence right into our living rooms. In September 1972 the Israeli team of athletes at the Munich Olympics was attacked by Palestinian terrorists, while at the same time Amin was expelling 50,000 Asians from Uganda many of whom headed for Britain, especially to London.

Many of these refugees came to the East End of London where Monica and I were working. This had great effect upon our area and we took on additional staff to meet the very practical needs of the penniless migrants: dealing with housing, clothing, food and language problems. 1973 brought the Israeli Yom Kippur War, the Watergate scandal in the USA, and even more problems for the British economy. By the end of that year the nation had gone on a three-day week and was facing considerable industrial unrest. In April the following year, Harold Wilson became Prime Minister with a Labour administration replacing the Conservatives; Nixon resigned as a result of Watergate and Gerald Ford became President of the USA. The great shaking of the nations had begun to produce political as well as economic upheavals.

Economic Woes

Halfway through the decade, further economic woes saw the pound shrink to an all-time low. In May 1975 inflation was running at 22% and unemployment reached 1.25 million. With this bleak background it was not unexpected that the British people, in June 1975, voted overwhelmingly in a national referendum[5] to join the Common Market, no doubt hoping that this would solve our economic problems and calm the industrial and social unrest in the nation.

This was the situation that greeted Donald Coggan when he became Archbishop of Canterbury, and this was the background to his decision to broadcast to the nation in September 1975. As we noted in Chapter One, the response to his 'Call to the Nation' was overwhelmingly favourable, with a postbag in excess of 27,000. It seemed clear at the time to Donald Coggan and John Poulton that God was opening the door for the gospel to be heard among ordinary people in the land. They wanted to explain why there were so many problems in the nation which they believed to be because we had turned away from the word of the Lord and put ourselves outside God's blessing.

If My People

It was the early days of the Charismatic Movement when there was plenty of enthusiasm for new forms of worship and new songs. The mid-1970s also saw the musical *If My People* gain enormous popularity. This charismatic musical event, written and produced by Jimmy and Carol Owens, came over from the United States and was greeted by huge crowds as it toured Britain. Monica and I took a number of our people from the East End of London to the interactive performance in the Albert Hall which was packed for the event. Its catchy biblically-based songs, its quotations from the Bible and its call for a commitment to a greater personal relationship with Jesus carried considerable popular appeal. If this event had been combined with the kind of grassroots evangelism in the vision that Donald Coggan and John Poulton shared with me and which Monica and I fully embraced, it could have made an historic nation-changing impact.

Evangelism

The 1970s was probably the ideal decade for nationwide evangelism as it was a time of considerable industrial and social unrest. In such times of uncertainty, in sociological terms, there is a greater openness in the public to a consideration of what has gone wrong in the national life and therefore a greater openness to truth. Although churchgoing had declined in the 1960s there was still a considerable minority of active Christians in the 1970s. Some 20% of the nation still went to church at least once a month, and biblically-based Christianity was regularly taught in schools, both state and private. Biblical values were still foundational in the life of the nation, but despite the positive response to Archbishop Coggan's 1975 'Call to the Nation' no lead was given by the churches and the opportunity was lost. The church was losing its grip in giving a moral and spiritual lead to the nation.

The depressed and anxious mood in the nation, due to its economic woes and a severe drought in the summer of 1976, gave a great opportunity for the gospel. The drought was so severe that water shortages were being caused throughout the country. Churches all around Bedfordshire organised a prayer meeting on Dunstable Downs to pray for rain in August 1976. Stanley Jebb, a local Baptist minister, and a friend of ours, was the only one who took an umbrella on a fine sunny day. Before the afternoon was over it started to rain. Stanley was the only one who didn't get wet! The lesson – if you're going to pray for rain, take an umbrella! Faith was still alive in Britain in the 1970s!

The opportunity for evangelism was increased due to the first wave of family breakdown that hit the nation in the first half of the 1970s. Britain was just beginning to be impacted by the Charismatic Movement which was enlivening churches of the traditional denominations and creating a new openness to the presence of God and the power of the Holy Spirit. If ever there were a time when revival could have swept the country it was surely the latter half of the 1970s and early 1980s when the Charismatic Movement was still in its fast-growing infancy, before deceptive teachings were introduced to muddy the spiritual waters and create confusion among Christians and division in the churches.

Mainline Churches

A major denominational change took place in 1972 with the merger of two churches: the Presbyterian Church of England and the Congregational Church of England and Wales. They had been in talks for a number of years and this merger was said to increase the economic viability of the churches. The Presbyterian Church in England was quite a small denomination but their congregations were often much larger than those of the Congregational Church who maintained a number of small village congregations. The Presbyterians tended to close a church if its membership fell below its financial viability. The Congregational Church had a greater emphasis upon community and they maintained ministry in small congregations through support from a central fund.

All the churches in the Congregational Church were offered a choice either to join the merger or to remain independent. All the churches with an evangelical majority saw the merger as motivated by secular interests rather than spiritual. They therefore voted to stay out of the merger. Smaller congregations in both urban and rural settings voted to stay independent, largely out of fear that the new Presbyterian influence would result in their closure. About 600 churches voted to form a new Federation of Independent Congregational churches (the Congregational Federation) while a smaller number of reformed evangelical churches had already formed a separate fellowship (FIEC).[6] The churches that were joined in the merger formed the United Reformed Church (URC). Although a theologically mixed church, the majority were non-evangelical and non-charismatic, remaining firmly in the middle-of-the-road nonconformist position, with the majority of ministers having been trained in theological institutions largely teaching liberal scholarship.

The Congregational Federation of churches was similarly mixed but had more of its leadership and congregations who leaned towards an evangelical position. The first two Presidents were women: Lady Margaret Stansgate (mother of the late Tony Benn MP), whose husband had been Home Secretary in a Liberal administration; and the Revd Elsie Chamberlain, who had served for a number of years as the leader of the BBC's religious department and was the first woman to be ordained in this country. I was the fourth President in 1976, which coincided with the bicentenary of the USA. I was the keynote speaker at the bicentennial celebrations of the Congregational Churches of the USA where they met in Harvard University in Boston in July 1976. They traced their roots back to the Pilgrim Fathers and the English Puritans, which was the same Reformation heritage as the Congregational Churches in Britain. They rented a large motorhome for us, and Monica and I and our three children went on a ten-State tour speaking at many of their largest churches, from Plymouth, Massachusetts to Minneapolis. It was both exciting and rewarding.

International Events

The second half of the 1970s saw massive changes on the world scene with Mao dying in China in 1976, that led, two years later, to his *Little Red Book* being denounced by the new Chinese leadership, creating a new openness to the West and the beginnings of a great spiritual awakening, bringing multitudes of new Christians into the 'unregistered' churches. In 1978 there were upheavals in the Catholic Church with two new Popes: John Paul I who died one month later, being replaced by the Polish John Paul II. American Christians were shocked in the same year by the Rev Jim Jones, an ex-Methodist preacher, who had led his flock to Guyana, then led 913 of them to die in a gruesome mass suicide.

Further upheavals on the international stage saw the Shah driven into exile from Iran in a revolution led by Ayatollah Khomeini, followed by the storming of the American embassy and a large number of American citizens taken hostage, creating an international incident that could easily have spilled over into war. On the home front economic woes continued into 1979 with the so-called 'Winter of Discontent' and wide scale strikes leading to rubbish piling up in the streets of London and the fall of the Labour Government led by Jim Callaghan, who had taken over from Harold Wilson some three years earlier. This opened the way for the May 1979 General Election, won by Margaret Thatcher, Britain's first woman Prime Minister, and the beginning of a new era in British politics.

There were many unsettling factors both in Britain and on the international scene that increased the sense of insecurity in the nation and created the kind of conditions that were fertile for the biblically-based message of the gospel that would give fresh direction in troubled times. The troubles in Ulster spilled over into the mainland, with terrorism atrocities in London, Manchester and elsewhere. The expulsion of 50,000 Asians from Uganda in 1972 caused social tension in London and other big cities. Britain and America's support of Israel in the Yom Kippur War brought a massive oil price hike by the Arabs in protest. This increased the financial crisis in Britain in 1973, with electricity cuts, a three-day-week in industry and disruption of the economy. By 1975, rampant inflation at 22% caused heavy falls of the pound which in turn created political uncertainty with strong left-wing pressures within the Labour Government.

All these social and economic difficulties created a mood of uncertainty and depression in the nation which undoubtedly had an effect in the nationwide response to the Archbishop's Call to the Nation. This mood of social insecurity increased the interest in the gospel as reflected in the massive demand for the Bible, and was yet another indication that Donald Coggan was right in his assessment of the mood of the nation.

The era of social change begun in the 1960s and accelerating through the 1970s increased the sense of insecurity in the nation and the desire for values that could be trusted. There was also a mood of lack of trust in the Government and political leaders, which made a grassroots movement of presenting the gospel attractive. A presentation of biblically-based values as an alternative to the social and political concepts that had got the nation into such a mess was additionally attractive; particularly if it was coming from locally based community leaders rather than from national figures, it was more likely to have been successful. All these considerations led to the conclusion that a national outreach in evangelism such as that envisaged by the Lambeth Group was rightly set in the timing of the Lord.

Notes

[1] It is important to distinguish between liberal theology and the scholarly study of the Bible. Scholarship is essential for a right understanding of the scripture, its origins, transmission and translation. When scholarship is taught in the context of faith in God it greatly contributes to our understanding of the Word of God; when it is taught in any context other than in the pursuit of truth it can be destructive. This is what is meant in this book when we use the term 'liberal' — it equates with 'unbelief'.

[2] John A.T. Robinson, *Honest to God*, SCM Press, London, 1963.

[3] Don Cupitt and John Hick, *The Myth of God Incarnate*, pbk, SCM Press, London, 1997.

[4] See *The Gathering Storm in the Church* by Jeffrey K Hadden, Doubleday, USA, pp. 228-230, 1969. Also, see table quoted in Clifford Hill *The Day Comes*, published as a Fount paperback by Collins, London, 1982, p. 309.

[5] This confirmed the parliamentary vote of 1972 which had been challenged by strong anti-European MPs in both Houses of Parliament and in the public domain.

[6] The Fellowship of Evangelical Christian Churches had been formed some years earlier and its numbers swelled when Dr Martyn Lloyd Jones from Westminster Chapel made his appeal 'come ye out of them' in 1966.

Chapter Six

FOUR MOVEMENTS OF SOCIAL CHANGE

Lack of Social Understanding

The lack of understanding by senior church leaders, in the 1970s and 80s, of the processes of social change had a fundamental effect upon the mission of the church. It was grossly exacerbated by theological error drawn from the Enlightenment in the case of the intellectual elite in the mainline churches and the lack of biblical scholarship among leaders in the independent churches and many of those involved in the emerging Charismatic Movement. These theological errors will be explored in the following chapters when we look at the influence of the Charismatic Movement that affected all the mainline denominations as well as the Independent Churches.

In this chapter we want to explore the processes of social change that were moving across the Western nations in this period and beginning to reshape Britain. Their effect was to initiate the most rapid and radical period of social change that the world had ever known —a process that is continuing until this present time. The intention in this chapter is to outline the processes of social change that hit the Western nations in the 1960s and their particular effect upon Britain. This exploration will be done in the context of the church and from the background of contemporary church history. It is, of course, an outline and not a comprehensive review.

Hopes of Revival

One of the greatest dangers facing the evangelical churches in the second half of the 20th century was the expectation of revival. Among traditional and liberal churches life went on as usual, with declining congregations, a struggle for survival, and an accelerating rate of closure of buildings. But among evangelicals for 50 years, stretching into the 21st century, there were prophecies of imminent revival. Since the heady days of Harringay with Billy Graham in 1954 these prophecies of revival brought disappointment and division among Christians.

Year after year the prophecies of revival persisted and many Christians, especially church leaders, were desperate to see the fulfilment of their hopes. This gave rise to the belief that as secularism advanced in the nation God would do something spectacular to answer the urgent prayers of his people by sending the Holy Spirit in power to change the nation. It was a thought that ran parallel to the 'Dominionism' and 'Latter Rain' teachings popularised by the Kansas City team and John Wimber in the 1980s and early 90s.

This desire for revival, which was widespread across churches of all denominations in the latter half of the 20th century, created an atmosphere of expectation that lowered the threshold of acceptance for new teachings that came in from various sources, often from the USA. This openness to new movements occurred at the very time when major movements in society were occurring that threatened to undermine the very foundations of Western civilisation with its roots in Judaeo-Christian spirituality and morality.

Attack upon Biblical Christianity

The attack upon the whole value system of biblical Christianity began in the early post-World War II days when the Western nations were war-weary and people were longing for a time of normality, peace and security. The post-World War II period was a time of dynamic social change. People in all the Western nations were looking for a radical new social order that would not only bring peace, but justice and equality of opportunity for all. In Britain, despite the fact that Churchill won the war, he and the Tory party he led were spectacularly defeated in the first post-war national parliamentary election in 1945.

Churchill was replaced by Clement Attlee, an atheist and strong anti-Semite with far-left wing socialist views, but little understanding of the principles of socio-political and economic change that began to drive the Western nations at that time. His leadership at this critical time of reconstruction was seen by many as weak and inept. His Foreign Secretary, Ernest Bevin, and others in the Cabinet were anti-Semitic which had a major impact on British policy in the Middle East, undermining the Balfour Declaration to found a Jewish State. The Government also supported the pro-Arab bias in the British Foreign Office that persists today.

Challenging the Social Order

The demand for change inevitably meant the rejection of traditional institutions which, in Britain, were rooted in the principle of 'ascribed status' that had been a major characteristic of the established social order since the days of the Tudors. But the social order was not simply rooted in *social* traditions, it also had strong *moral values* which were rooted in biblical truth. They provided a powerful foundation upon which the traditional 'Establishment' was built, giving it a strong element of divine sanction. It was these foundational values of Western civilisation that were challenged by the new movements of social change. They represented a paradigm shift of historic proportions that would significantly shape the Western world.

The inevitable end result of the processes of social change that were set in motion in the 1960s is a society dominated by moral and social anarchy which we have yet fully to see. They began to coalesce in the 1960s, heading towards the fragmentation of the structures of society and the dissolution of social cohesion. This would be the outcome of family breakdown and the inadequate socialisation of children resulting in physical and mental health problems, the increasing breakdown of law and order, the widespread practice of paganism, witchcraft and Satanism — leading towards the end result of the legalisation of paedophilia and all forms of sexual perversion and personal indulgence — so far only partially fulfilled.

In Britain, with the ongoing progress of these social processes, we are likely to see major structural changes in the institutions of society.

They could include the dissolution of the monarchy, the dismantling of the House of Lords, the disappearance of the traditional aristocracy, the disestablishment of the Church of England and the official declaration of Britain as a secular society where all forms of religion are tolerated on the basis of equality, but none is favoured.

These are the ultimate aims of the movements that were generated in the post-World War II period. Judging from the recent rate of change, they will probably have achieved their major objectives by the middle of the 21st century, unless other revolutionary forces arise (such as an Islamic revolution or Christian revival) or the British people awake from spiritual atrophy and recognise the danger to Western civilisation and to their own personal self-interest.

Four Social Movements

Four major social movements coalesced in the early post-World War II period to produce a dynamic period of social change that first came to the notice of the general public in what became known as the 'Swinging 60s'. Each of these four social movements have an occultic base. We will take a brief look at them. They are:

- **The Cultural Revolution**: led by rock 'n' roll music
- **The Spiritual Revolution:** led by the New Age Movement
- **The Political Revolution:** led by atheist Marxism
- **The Sexual Revolution:** led by the LGBTQ Movement

The Cultural Revolution

The first signs of major socio/cultural change in Britain came in the 1950s with the appearance of rock 'n' roll music. The film *Rock Around the Clock* with Bill Haley triggered disturbances among teenagers in cinemas such as the Odeon, Elephant and Castle, in London in 1955, where young people danced in the aisles and ripped up the seats. It was the beginning of the rise of the youth culture that dominated the next decade. But it was not the music with its DJs and Skiffle bands that brought the youth culture — that was only an outcome. The major cultural change of the 1960s resulted from a change in the *economy* in the immediate post-World War II period and through the 1950s.

It was a period of full employment as the nation set about the task of reconstructing its shattered buildings from the heavy bombing of our cities. This produced a high demand for labour. For the first time in British history, young people could earn high wages in the construction industry and many allied industries. So a new group of consumers came into the market — young people with money to spend and few social responsibilities. A free-market economy rapidly responds to such a change in the market, and before long the economy moved from age-domination to youth-domination particularly in the fashion world and in the world of entertainment.

Rock 'n' Roll was the defining characteristic of the 1960s' culture and it was Elvis Presley 'the King' who was the principal superstar. His gyrating hips introduced the eroticisation of music that had a strong sex appeal to young people and paved the way for the sexual revolution of the 'swinging 60s'. Presley came from a Christian family and regularly attended the local Assemblies of God church and remained, at least nominally, in fellowship through to his death in 1977. His recording of the Christian hymn *How Great Thou Art* showed something of his spiritual heritage.

It was not generally recognised at the time that Presley was heavily into the occult and was following the teaching of Helena Blavatsky and her Theosophist New-Age teaching, actually believing that he had the power to heal. At his concerts, he would sometimes read from Blavatsky's book *The Voice of Silence*, which emphasised the occultic links of rock music with its particular beat. He was introduced to drugs during his Army service and became increasingly drug dependent. He was also heavily into occultic Martial Arts and had a personal Karate instructor. His performance in the 1957 film *Jailhouse Rock* propelled him to stardom and it became a defining moment for the 'new morality' of the 1960s.

The 1960s also saw the rise to stardom of the Beatles, who were similarly involved with the New-Age Movement. The Beatles went to India to pursue their interest in Eastern mysticism and they were credited with promoting Transcendental Meditation in the West which was popularised in different forms by some churches and Christian teachers in America. Roy Livesey says,

The Rock beat, long used for calling up spirits by the pagan tribes of the world, was now unknowingly applied on a vast scale in the music of the West. Apart from the message and the lyrics, both significant though mostly not recognised, the evil element peculiar to Rock music is found in the beat. The effect is optimised in conjunction with the strobe lighting and other effects in the Disco, and truly what we have, even though Elvis, the 'King of Rock 'n' Roll', no longer lives, is a counterfeit worship...What we see is not the worship of God through Jesus Christ, the King, who is the Rock. What we have is pagan deceptions hung on Hindu philosophies and based on the worship of false gods seen in the East for thousands of years.[1]

The 1960s saw the beginnings of the cultural revolution affecting the social values of the nation. The earliest landmark was the Race Relations Act 1965 which outlawed discrimination in the workplace. It was a very limited piece of legislation that primarily affected private businesses rather than local government or international corporations. It had limited teeth and offences only led to civil prosecution rather than criminal. But its significance in terms of culture change is that it represented the beginnings of *curbs to freedom of speech* which hitherto had been an essential bulwark of British social values. It led eventually to the equality laws and legislation on so-called 'hate speech' and the targeting of ill-defined 'hate incidents' which inevitably involve subjective judgements.

The Spiritual Revolution
The 1960s saw the rise to public prominence of the New-Age Movement although its roots go back thousands of years. Its elements of supernatural 'knowledge' are traceable to Greek Gnosticism and its meditation practices can be traced back to the early days of Hinduism. Its aims for world domination go back to Babylon and the building of the Tower of Babel.

The Theosophical Society was launched in 1875, combining the mysticism of Egypt with the Gnosticism of Greece plus some of the theology of Judaism and Christianity. Its aim was self-realisation: helping people to discover themselves as part of the whole creation and to become aware of their 'godhead' through their oneness with creation. The founder was Helena Blavatsky who was highly influenced by Hinduism and used 'masters' as her guiding spirits.

Alice Bailey, a Blavinsky disciple who died in 1949, was nevertheless responsible for launching the post-World War II New-Age Movement in 1960s Britain. She used a Tibetan monk as her guiding spirit and she left instructions in her writings saying that the Age of Aquarius was to begin in 1975, 100 years after the launch of the Theosophical Society. This effectively began the New-Age Movement with great expectations of a new age of peace and prosperity with ordinary individuals discovering their spiritual potential.

The interest in the New-Age Movement grew rapidly in the 1960s through to the 1990s. A new industry in various forms of occultism appeared. Horoscopes were published in many newspapers, giving their predictions from their readings of the stars, that were avidly followed by many people. At the same time, interest in crystals arose. Even Tony Higton, a prominent evangelical Church of England minister, installed crystals in his Essex parish church, advocating them for prayer and meditation.

The most outstanding church that got involved with the New-Age Movement was St James Piccadilly where they had yoga classes and a variety of occultic activities. The Vicar, Donald Reeves, hosted a wide range of activities under his 'Alternatives' programme. His programme for 1990 announced that on January 22nd there would be an evening of 'Spoon bending as a spiritual lesson'. It added a note: 'Please bring your own spoon'. The evening was to be led by a psychic therapist, 'who has been manifesting paranormal gifts for many years'.

In July 1990, St James hosted Matthew Fox, the American Dominican priest who was excommunicated from the Roman Catholic Church on the grounds of heresy but was accepted into the Anglican Communion as a priest.[2] Fox believed that human beings go through stages of advancement in spiritual maturity until they reach the ultimate stage of divinity, which the Catholic Church pronounced as heresy. His teaching on 'creation centred spirituality' was said to break new ground in enabling 'people of different religions and cultures to find their common roots in Earth and Cosmos and to release their creative energy for healing of the planet and creating dignity of life for all people'. His book *Original Blessing* was promoted by Donald Reeves as 'a brilliant and amazing introduction to lost traditions in Christianity about creation'.[3]

It is surely one of life's amazing anomalies that here was St James, Piccadilly, right in the heart of London's West End, openly promoting occultic activities with its Sufi Healing Centre, mysticism, multi-faith and creationist activities, while at the very same time, July 1990, another prominent Anglican Church, Holy Trinity Brompton (HTB), just a mile down the road in the richest part of West London near Harrods, was also promoting alternative spirituality, but with a very different theology. HTB was hosting the 'Kansas City Prophets' with John Wimber, Bob Jones and Paul Cain.

Donald Reeves was at the extreme liberal end of the theological spectrum while Sandy Millar, Rector of HTB, was at the far end of the charismatic evangelical movement where they were caught up in alternative spirituality of a very different kind. While Reeves was bending spoons, Cain, hosted by Millar, was offering words of knowledge (divination?) and personal prophecies – all attributed to the Holy Spirit. Four years later, 1994, HTB embraced the next wave of deception — the Toronto Blessing — with its uncontrollable laughter and animal noises, attributed to the Holy Spirit. Sandy Millar justified a group of women who were mooing as evidence that the Ark was coming back among God's people in the same way as the oxen pulled the Ark of the Covenant back into Israel from the Philistines. Londoners and visitors from around the world could take their choice between different forms of 'alternative spirituality' which were on offer in high status Anglican churches in the capital of the nation.

While charismatic Christians in the 1990s were falling about laughing, a social revolution was taking place in Britain and in the Western nations that would undermine the biblical foundations of Christianity and challenge not only the soul but the very fabric of Western civilisation. While Britain was being reshaped by powerful movements of social change, biblical truth disappeared from the public square in West London. The churches in Britain were either peacefully sleeping or actively involved in alternative spirituality of one kind or another!

The 1960s saw the beginning of migration from the Indian

subcontinent. Hindus, Sikhs and Muslims all began entering Britain without any regulations at the beginning of the decade. This created considerable public anxiety – more particularly over practical issues of employment and housing than religious issues. Public clamour reached such a pitch that could not be ignored in Whitehall and Westminster resulting in the first Race Relations Act since the time of Queen Elizabeth I in 1596, which had stated,

> Her Majesty understanding that there are of late divers blackmoores brought into this realme, of which kinde of people there are already too manie, consideringe how God hath blessed this land with great increase of people of our owne nation...those kinde of people should be sent forth from the lande."[4]

The Commonwealth Immigrants Act 1962 was the first restriction in the modern era placed on immigrants from the former British colonial territories with their largely black populations. The Act was predominantly brought forward because immigration from India and Pakistan was beginning to escalate from 1960. This was not aimed at restricting people of colour. The entire population of Jamaica was only two million at this time, but India and Pakistan represented vast potential of immigration that could not have been accommodated in Britain. Nevertheless, the Act and subsequent Acts left the door open to immigrants sending for their relatives and this began the practice of Asians sending their children back to India or Pakistan for a spouse when they reached marriageable age so that the migrant population increased with each generation. (The immigration and residency rules have become more complex in recent years.)

Demographically, with the falling white population the time will come when the non-white (black and Asian) population will exceed that of the native white, unless the immigration laws are changed. The most significant factor in this is the introduction of other religions into Britain, which had been a Christian country for more than 1,000 years, with virtually no adherents of other religions before the middle of the Twentieth Century. Since the 1960s, Hindus and Buddhists have built their temples in Britain. Those among whom our Victorian missionaries laboured on the mission field have come here and established their spiritual strongholds.

In the 1960s Muslims began building mosques in Britain and this has increased throughout the country. In one ward of Leicester in 2017 there were no fewer than 19 mosques and many of the local population did not speak English. Thus, the 1960s saw the beginning of Britain becoming a multiracial and multi-religious nation which has the potential to change the predominant religion of the nation with huge cultural, political and legal consequences for the future of Britain. At the present rate of social change, Sharia law will be recognised in Britain in the second half of the 21st century and the equal status of women, for which so many have struggled, will be lost. Britain will either be plunged back into the dark ages or enveloped in violent civil conflict such as that presently taking place in Nigeria.

The loss of social significance of Christianity in Britain since the 1960s cannot be blamed upon immigrants bringing their religions. White British people have not converted to other religions in significant numbers. They have simply abandoned their Judaeo-Christian heritage.[5] The decline in churchgoing began in the 1960s and has continued through to today. The decline has undoubtedly slowed, and significant numbers who have left the mainline denominations now attend new churches or alternative forms of church such as small groups for prayer and Bible study. Most of these small groups, however, cater for the needs of the older generation of Christians who are disillusioned with the traditional denominations.

The Political Revolution
In order to understand the post-World War II socio-political revolution that was birthed in the time of the Clement Attlee Government of 1945 with far-left thinkers such as an Aneurin Bevan, Ernest Bevin and Herbert Morrison, you have to examine its Marxist roots. Marxism was based on Hegelian philosophy. Hegel believed the dynamic of social change was to be found in the integration of the 'Divine Idea' into the physical world. He saw the pattern of this change in the dialectic — the thesis, antithesis and synthesis — which gave his understanding of history. Marx took this concept of history and turned it upside down by changing dialectical idealism into dialectical materialism in an atheistic

context as the key to reality. His theory of 'matter in motion' replaced the Hegelian interpretation of the world in terms of the integration of the 'divine idea' into human history.

The key to understanding Marxism lies in the fundamental dogma of 'Economic Determinism' which is the opposite of Hegelian Idealism. Economic Determinism is the application to the study of history of the fundamental principle that thought is conditioned by matter, because it is a product of matter in motion. Marx said that we can only understand history — that is, the culture, philosophy, art, religion and political life of humanity — by seeing it in the context of the material conditions in which human beings are living. In other words, human beings are the product of their environment.

It is this principle that underlies Marxist sociological theory which has been taught in most Western universities since the 1960s. It sees the transition from one social movement to another not as the result of the free decision of human minds to change the pattern, but rather as a fundamental shift in social structure that produces the conditions of change. Without such an understanding, human beings cannot exercise control over the processes of change. It is this principle that provides the key to the Marxist dialectic of historical analysis.

Marx sees the dynamic of social change not rooted in religious enlightenment or cultural development but in fundamental changes in the material basis of life. The Marxist sociologist sees the key to understanding all social change lying in the conflict between those who own or control the means of production and those who only have their labour to sell. The Communist Manifesto has this fundamental statement:

The modern bourgeois society that has sprouted from the ruins of the feudal society has not done away with class antagonisms. It has but established new classes, new conditions of oppression, new forms of struggle in place of the old ones. Our epoch, the epoch of the bourgeoisie, possesses, however, this distinctive feature: it has simplified the class antagonisms. Society as a whole is more and more splitting up into two great hostile camps, into two great classes directly facing each other — bourgeoisie and proletariat.[6]

According to Marxist understanding of history, capitalism contains within itself the seeds of its own destruction. Dialectical Materialism provides the key to understanding the historical process. Every society exists in 'unstable equilibrium' because it carries within itself the conditions of its own transformation — thesis, antithesis and synthesis. But each new synthesis is brought about by the class struggle, by power being passed from one class to another. Industrialisation produced a new class of ownership of the means of production which replaced the owners of the land who were the rulers who hired the labour of their serfs and used them in battle to defend their rights against the invasion of other landowners. Industry then created the proletariat who were uprooted from their rural occupations and became the new landless poor with no means of feeding themselves other than to hire their labour to the owners of industry.

Marx believed that the interests of the two classes in an open industrial society were inherently opposed. The interest of the workers was in high wages and low prices whereas the interest of the owners of capital was in low wages and high prices. The interests of the workers are in full employment whereas the interests of the employers lie in the maintenance of a surplus pool of labour so that workers can be hired at competitive rates. Unemployment and poverty are therefore essential to the maintenance of a capitalist economy.

Marx believed that 'the proletariat has nothing to lose but its chains' and therefore its interests lie in revolution to wrest power from the owners of production. The triumph of the workers' revolution would be to establish a classless society. But in order to do this there would have to be a period of transition in which a small group of workers would take total control of society, because throughout history no owners of power have ever yielded their power willingly. The revolutionary party must be prepared to take control and to exercise a period of 'dictatorship of the proletariat' until a fully democratic system is established.

Of course, the danger of this theory lies in Marx's own recognition that no group of rulers has ever willingly yielded power, and therefore under Communism the dictatorship of the proletariat is likely to remain for ever! This has certainly been borne out in the history of the USSR where the struggle to overcome the dictatorship of the Kremlin came from within the system, with an emerging anarchy of corruption through which large numbers of individuals acquired immense wealth through the redistribution of power in an unstable social system that is still in transition today. We are currently seeing a similar process in China where the Communist old guard are holding on to power despite the revolutionary changes in industry and production that have brought new wealth to the masses. The old guard are still determined to maintain their political power in a capitalist system, but for how long is a question yet to be answered at the time of writing.

In Britain, the Attlee Government, although Marxist, did not embrace Communism. Its Marxist ideology was atheist, anti-Semitic and aimed at destroying the Judaeo-Christian foundations of society which were seen as a tool of repression institutionalising the supremacy of the upper classes. Nevertheless, its programme of social reform was not revolutionary. In fact, most of its policies had been agreed during the wartime Coalition Government headed by Churchill and Attlee. Churchill was wholly dedicated to winning the war, allowing Attlee to issue a number of White Papers, including the welfare policy devised by William Beveridge, a leading Liberal politician of the 1930s. Even the broad programme of nationalisation of the Labour Government had been agreed under the wartime Government in order to guarantee employment for returning ex-servicemen after the war. The only exception was said to be the nationalisation of iron and steel which was an innovation introduced by Attlee's Government.

Despite the broad cross-party wartime agreement on social reform, the Attlee Government put their stamp of liberal socialism on measures that formed the basis of policy which was followed by all Governments until that of Margaret Thatcher. This policy contributed to the 'us and them' division of society that has persisted, despite the increased wealth of the working classes, and contributed to the continuing 'boom and bust' cycles in the economy.

The vast mountain of personal debt in the nation injects a massive element of uncertainty into the economy as even a small rise in interest rates could trigger a rise in bankruptcy and the inability of individuals to meet their mortgage requirements, which could trigger a fall in house prices and lead to a slump in the national economy.

The banking crisis of 2008 was a warning of the highly fragile state of the world economy, and vast levels of national debt in many countries present a continuous fear of sudden collapse. Most economists recognise this danger although they also recognise their inability to change the system, or to insure against economic disaster which they see as inevitable. This would appear to confirm the Marxist view that 'capitalism contains within itself the seeds of its own destruction'. There are many indications today that capitalism is nearing the end of its life-cycle.

The Sexual Revolution

The sexual revolution that hit Britain, America and Western Europe in the 1960s had its roots as far back as the Enlightenment, with atheist philosophers such as Voltaire, Rousseau and Kant, and the movement in the late Victorian era to reject the rigid prudery of the day. The 1960s, however, saw a different kind of sexual revolution that openly advocated total sexual freedom and the establishment of a permissive society in which all kinds of sexual expression and activity were permissible and all legal restrictions were to be abolished. The concept of free love caught the imagination of young people in particular, at a time of great social change, when traditional concepts and social values were being challenged.

In the summer of 1967, 100,000 young people from many different nations went to San Francisco in what became known as the 'summer of love' which was a watershed in the development of the counterculture of the 1960s. This was part of the social revolution symbolised by the 'Flower People', a generation of hippies linked with protests against the war in Vietnam in which many young people in the USA refused to participate. The flower children were part of the 'Flower Power Movement' that advocated making love rather than making war — a concept that spread rapidly through the Western nations in the mid-1960s.

The counterculture movement was linked with a number of other movements of that era such as the gay rights and the women's movement that led to the breaking down of barriers and social taboos in regard to the public display of sex. Many historians see Freud as the initiator of the counterculture movement through his teaching on the harmful effects of sexual repression, which led to many different expressions of exploring the body and mind free from moral and legal restrictions. The 1960s saw the rise of sexually explicit literature such as Playboy magazine and blue movies that were rapidly seized upon in a capitalist economy to become a multi-billion dollar pornography industry flooding the market with films and videos of explicit sexual activity.

The work of Alfred Kinsey was highly influential in the development of the sexual revolution in this period. His books, *Sexual Behaviour in the Human Male* (1948), and *Sexual Behaviour in the Human Female* (1953), paved the way for greater public awareness of human sexuality and certainly had considerable influence in encouraging homosexuality. His claim that 37% of adult men had experienced some form of homosexual activity is a gross exaggeration. The true figure for male homosexuals is still around 1.5% of the male population in Britain. But Kinsey's research, which has subsequently been shown to be fraudulent in almost every respect, was undoubtedly influential in encouraging the Gay Pride Movement which was kick-started in America by the Stonewall Riots of 1969 and in Britain in the early 1970s by the publication of a gay-rights manifesto.

The 1960s to 1980s was an era of massive social change with the legalisation of easy divorce, of abortion and the availability of the contraceptive pill on the NHS. These social changes initiated the relaxation of sexual mores and the reshaping of marriage and family, with fundamental outcomes for the future of the nation. Divorce rates soared and the breakdown of family life rapidly followed with the introduction of casual sex overcoming all previous taboos. Sex changed from being confined to the marriage bed with the primary purpose of procreation, to a leisure activity separated from family and marriage.

The rapid changes in society from the reactionary social conservatism of the immediate post-World War II era to the 'swinging 60s' led the way to new concepts of open marriage, wife swapping and communal sex that characterised the social revolution, all of which contributed to the breakdown of family and marriage. Rapid changes in society always produce a period of uncertainty and instability that affects all social institutions, and this was reflected in the late 1960s and in the economic instability of the 1970s which saw numerous industrial strikes and political tensions.

All these changes in the attitudes toward sexual mores took place alongside the feminist movement that had been growing since the beginning of the 20th century with the suffragette campaign for political equality and the vote for women that had not been fully achieved until 1928. Kinsey's contribution to female sexuality was not inconsiderable and it led to the widespread demand in the 1970s for the contraceptive pill to be available on the NHS, not simply to married women but to all females of any age, on demand. The slogan 'a woman's right to choose' was widely paraded among student populations in the universities and led to the growing sexual liberation from traditional restrictions. The social taboos against unmarried mothers, although still rigid in the 1950s, rapidly disintegrated in the 1960s with the consequent rise in teenage pregnancies and the demand for abortions. This persisted right into the 21st century when other factors began to influence sexual behaviour among young people — particularly forced upon them by the epidemic proportions of sexually transmitted diseases.

The feminist movement, which is usually defined as a movement for social, economic and political equality of men and women, also involved the rights of women over their own bodies and the recognition that their sexual participation should not be primarily aimed at giving pleasure to men. This sexual freedom helped to encourage the LGBTQ+ movement of sexual libertarianism that grew out of the Gay Pride Movement. The social significance of this movement can hardly be exaggerated. From the beginning, their stated objectives in the 1972 manifesto in Britain, was the destruction of the traditional family, which they said was the 'source of our oppression'.

Liberal social policies pursued by Local Authorities promoted homosexuality under their 'equal opportunities' and 'equalities' agenda. They began the serious promotion of homosexual lifestyles in the 1980s by making grants to homosexual groups. The Greater London Council was the most active in pursuing this policy when Ken Livingstone was the leader. The GLC Women's Committee declared heterosexuality to be 'an oppression'. They said:

> Like other oppressions, it is perpetrated by a dominant and powerful group, in this case heterosexuals. Like other oppressions it works both on an institutional level and through individuals.[7]

During the 1980s a number of local authorities, particularly in the London area, began actively promoting homosexual groups by handing out grants and supporting homosexual projects such as the London Lesbian and Gay Community Centre in Islington that received some £750,000 from the GLC. The Inner London Education Authority provided school libraries with a book *Jenny lives with Eric and Martin* depicting a girl living with her father and his male partner. When Margaret Thatcher heard of this she was said to be outraged and in 1988 her Government passed the Local Government Act which included Clause 28 which prohibited intentionally promoting homosexuality or publishing 'material with the intention of promoting homosexuality' or promoting 'the teaching in any maintained school of the acceptability of homosexuality as a pretended family relationship'. From 1988 to 2003, Clause 28 became a battleground between liberal-left politicians and those who supported traditional moral values and who wished to strengthen family life. Rachael Tingle, in a comprehensive study, did much to uncover the activities of Local Authorities who were using ratepayers' money to promote homosexuality in a book published in 1986.[8]

Since the early 1970s the LGBTQ+ movement has steadily gained in social recognition and political power. Its representatives have infiltrated all the major social institutions in Britain, the USA and Western Europe, especially influencing the European Union. In Britain, every political department in Westminster and in the broadcasting media, especially in the BBC, has been infiltrated by LGBTQ representatives. Their political influence grew considerably when David Cameron announced that he was espousing same-sex marriage when he led the Coalition Government in partnership with the Lib Dems. This led to the passing of the Same-Sex Marriage Act in 2013 which was passed with the support of the Labour Party despite opposition from more than half of backbench Conservative MPs.

The advance of the LGBTQ+ movement in gaining social power and influence since the beginning of the 21st century has been spectacular. An example of the increase in homosexual political power was seen in the rise of Justine Greening who became Member of Parliament for Putney in 2005. She was appointed Minister of State for Transport 2011–12; then

Secretary of State for International affairs 2012–16, when she became Minister for Women and Equalities. In June 2016, she announced that she was a lesbian in a same-sex relationship. Just one month later she was promoted by Theresa May, who appointed her Secretary of State for Education with responsibility for the education of all children in England and Wales.

This could hardly have been a more influential post for advancing the homosexual agenda in Britain. It shows the enormous influence of the movement in Downing Street and in the whole of Westminster. It was not long before Greening announced that she was in favour of lowering the age for starting sex education to the beginning of the primary school for five-year-olds. Greening resigned after refusing a different appointment in the New Year Cabinet reshuffle of 2018.

LGBT policy came directly from Peter Tatchell who made a speech in Wolverhampton University in 2013 which defined policy being followed by Greening:

What I propose — as a positive — is that all schools, from the very first year of primary education, should be required by law to have mandatory equality and diversity lessons ... throughout the rest of their school life — to combat prejudice — to promote understanding — to encourage acceptance — not just on LGBT issues, but also on race, gender, disability, faith and belief. The idea is to create an inclusive, compassionate society.

Peter Tatchell went on to make the following chilling declaration:

... Now I would say that having the lessons themselves, is not sufficient. The equality and diversity lessons need to be backed up with exams – because pupils and often teachers only take things seriously when there is an exam. Make them do the exam. Make those exam results go into their school report. Make it a mandatory requirement for all job applicants to produce the results of their equality and diversity exams.... I think you need exams sometimes to concentrate the mind and to get results.

This sounds very much like a call for a Big Brother Police State where every child is brainwashed to accept the same set of evolutionary atheist values and anyone who does not share those values would even be barred from obtaining a job. It sounds very much like the kind of society enforced by 'the beast' depicted in Revelation 13.16f. :

> He also forced everyone, small and great, rich and poor, free and slave, to receive a mark on his right hand or on his forehead, so that no-one could buy or sell unless he had the mark, which is the name of the beast or the number of his name. (NIV)

In April 2017 the National Union of Teachers (NUT) passed a resolution at their annual conference to press the Government for LGBTQ-based sex education to begin in the nursery with two-year-old children. All three mainstream political parties responded to this by including homosexual demands in their Manifestos for the June 2017 General Election. This is what we printed in *Prophecy Today* UK:[9]

The **Conservative Party** *'will introduce comprehensive relationships and sex education in all primary and secondary schools'* (p 79).

Labour will *'make age appropriate sex and relationship education a compulsory part of the curriculum'* (p 77).

Labour will *'ensure that all teachers receive initial and ongoing training on the issues students face and how to address them. We will ensure that the new guidance for relationships and sex education is LGBT inclusive'* (p 111).

The **Liberal Democrats** will *'include in SRE teaching about sexual consent, LGBT+ relationships, and issues surrounding explicit images and content'* (p 29).

As already stated,[10] the ultimate result of all this liberalisation of sexual mores in Britain could be the legalisation of sexual activity with children of any age. Similar moves to reach this end can be seen in the

USA and other Western nations where the breaking down of restrictions is being enforced under 'equality' regulations. The Trojan horse being pushed into the public arena is the demand of transgender people for unfettered access to public toilets of their choosing. The drive towards the breaking down of traditional sexual norms is also taking place in schools where children of any age can claim to be in denial of their birth gender. In Britain, they can claim treatment funded by the NHS to aid their sexual transition and when they are sufficiently mature they can have state-funded surgery. In the meantime, 'equality' regulations can ensure that they can use the school toilets and showers of their choosing, although this has not yet been enforced by legislation.

Back in 1981, Philip Vander Elst published a prophetic paper in which he said that both political and sexual revolutionaries had similar objectives. He said:

> They wish to destroy the present social order and build a new one upon its ruins, and that cannot be done unless the restraints imposed by morality, property and the family are swept away.[11]

In the same way as political revolutionaries see private property and strong family life as barriers to socialism, sexual revolutionaries see the family as the origin of sexual repression and enemies of the LGBTQ+ community. Strong family life is seen by their militants as the means by which the values of bourgeois society and male supremacy are groomed into children. Their objective is to gain political power to control education whereby they can counter the influence of Judaeo-Christian families as their children spend more time in school than at home. A combination of Darwinian evolutionary science and LGBTQ+ sex education is seen as a sufficiently powerful force to counter the biblical values taught in Christian families and to destroy Christianity in the Western nations, which is an ultimate objective of the sexual revolution.

Sadly, church leaders remain largely unaware of the revolutionary forces aiming to reshape Britain. That storm will suddenly break, when the secular humanists feel strong enough to strike, sweeping away the Judaeo-Christian foundations of the nation like a tsunami. But will the church or politicians or the public awake to the danger in time to resist?

In July and August 2017, the BBC, influenced by LGBTQ ideology, broadcast a series of programmes on radio and television marking the 50th anniversary of the legalisation of homosexual activity in England and Wales. These were widely advertised and many other programmes had references to homosexuality in one form or another. This was clearly following the objective of 'normalisation' which is at the heart of LGBT strategy. By this time gender had become the central issue, with a lot of publicity given to children wanting to change their gender. This reveals the central purpose of the LGBT strategy which is a battle against the God of Creation and the Judaeo-Christian heritage of Western society. Ever since the publication of their Manifesto in 1972, the destruction of family life has been the objective of homosexual activists. They recognise that the family is at the heart of God's creation. The Bible declares that God made human beings in his own image, both male and female. Destroying the difference between male and female genders is a direct assault upon God's act of creation.

The true nature of the homosexual battle is not sociological, it is theological. The vast majority of homosexuals who campaigned for same-sex marriage, were not interested in marriage as a covenant relationship between two people who love each other and pledge to be faithful to each other for life. Their interest was largely destructive – destroying the Godly institution of marriage that upholds the integrity of a love relationship and provides a secure environment for raising children. *Their primary objective was to defeat God.*

This has not been understood by many church leaders who suffer from sociological ignorance and a lack of spiritual discernment. By not understanding the nature of the battle, they have been not only unprepared but they have also failed to give biblically-based leadership. If present trends in the secularisation of society continue and the whole biblically-based Judaeo-Christian foundations of Western civilisation crumble, the primary responsibility will lie with the professional leadership of the Christian Church.

Notes

[1] Roy Livesey, *More Understanding of the New Age*, New Wine Press, Chichester, 1990, p. 87.

[2] The Anglican Church at that time boasted of being a 'Broad Church' that could embrace a wide variety of theological beliefs.

[3] Publications of St James Piccadilly held by the author and reports in *Prophecy Today*, Vol 5 No 3, May 1989.

[4] Acts of the Privy Council, 11th August 1596.

[5] In a 2018 survey of young people under 25 Dr Krish Kandiah found that 75% say they have no religion. But he found that more than half (51%) of this age group reported a positive experience of the church and Christianity. Krish Kandiah, *Faitheism: Why Christianity and Atheism have more in common than you think*, Hodder, London, 2018.

[6] Marx and Engels, *'Manifesto of the Communist Party'* chapter 1, 'Bourgeoisie and Proletariat' first published as a political pamphlet in 1848.

[7] Quoted in Stephen Green, *The Sexual Dead-End*, Broadview Books, London, 1992, p. 46.

[8] Rachael Tingle, *Gay Lessons*, Pickwick Books, London 1986.

[9] 19 May 2017.

[10] See p. 91 in this chapter.

[11] Philip Vander Elst, *Revolutionary Socialism and Sexual Politics,* 1981
http://selfeducatedamerican.com/2017/03/08/revolutionary-socialism-sexual-politics/

Chapter Seven

UNDERSTANDING THE TIMES

Social Unrest
The four movements of social change that hit the nation in the period 1960s to 1990s radically affected the culture of the nation, which impacted the whole social structure including its political and economic life. The significance of these movements is better discerned in hindsight, but even in the mid-1980s it was possible to discern many of the radical changes that had taken place in the past two decades and to see the direction in which the changes were heading and how the nation was being reshaped by the secular humanist forces that had been generated in the 1960s.

Home Office Teaching
For a number of years, beginning during our ministry in East London, I had been an adviser to the Home Office on inner-city issues. I had written seven books and scores of articles and newspaper reports, as well as radio and TV broadcasts, on immigration and the settlement of immigrants in Britain in the 1960s and 70s.[1] The Home Office had taken quite an interest in our work in Newham and we were in receipt of Home Office grants for our projects. I began getting invitations to speak to conferences of Senior Police Officers and Prison Governors. This was followed by invitations to lecture on in-service training courses for Senior Police Officers at regional police training establishments. It was a work that I enjoyed, enabling me to teach some urban sociology and to use

my own experience of working in inner-city environments and among people of mixed ethnic migrants. It gave me plenty of opportunities of bringing my own personal faith into the lectures, which generated plenty of feedback and canteen conversations.

In the early 1980s video recorders became very popular, with a wide range of video films available in local shops for purchase or hire. At that time, there were no regulations controlling any of these films. It was during one of my lectures in Derbyshire that a senior police officer who had responsibilities for youth offenders described an incident in which he had been involved where some children had committed a gross offence. He described how a little group of 10-year-old boys from a local primary school had been going at lunchtime to the home of one of the boys whose parents were at work but where pornographic videos were available. The boys had watched one of these video films that included a rape scene. They had then carried out the gang rape of a six-year-old girl, repeating the scene that they had viewed on the film.

This was discussed at some length by the other police officers who were attending the lecture and several of them said that this was not unusual as violent videos were commonly being viewed by school-aged children and were increasingly influencing their behaviour. All the officers agreed that this was a social phenomenon that was becoming of considerable significance in youth offending. It was agreed by the officers that this issue was something that ought to be investigated on a national basis as these explicit sex and violent video films were freely available in the nation, where video recorders were increasingly found in the homes of the general population and pornographic films were being seen by children of all ages.

Meeting MPs

Shortly after this lecture, I spoke to a meeting at Holy Trinity Brompton, where I referred to the new social phenomenon that was appearing and the widespread use of video-cassettes that were now reaching most people's homes in Britain. Among the video-cassettes were films depicting scenes of an explicit sexual nature and extreme violence. There were no regulations controlling the sale or hire of these films and in some households they were available for children of all ages to view. This was before the popular press had coined the term 'video nasty'. I related the incident that had been reported at my meeting with Senior Police Officers and I said that unless drastic measures were taken this would be the beginning of a cancer that would corrupt an entire generation of children.

Present at the meeting was a member of the House of Lords, Viscount Ingleby, who invited me to address a meeting of Members of both Houses of Parliament which he would organise. This was to have far-reaching consequences. The meeting decided that, before undertaking any political initiative pressing for legislation to curb the availability of video films, an Enquiry should be undertaken to provide the facts which would establish a case for legislation. It was decided that in the current climate of libertarianism in the nation it would be useless to try to curb pornography, but a case showing the harmful effects of violence (especially upon children) on the small screen could possibly be established. Many of the violent video films coming onto the market also had links with explicit sexual scenes. They set up 'The Parliamentary Video Enquiry' with the support of Members of all parties and both Houses of Parliament.

Parliamentary Video Enquiry

As a sociologist, I was invited to direct the Enquiry and to carry out a piece of research designed to show the extent to which schoolchildren were viewing violent videos and to discover what effect it was having upon them. I drew together a small team of senior academics, several of whom were university professors and heads of department. We designed a questionnaire and contacted a large number of schools selected at random from different counties across the country, ensuring a representative sample from urban and rural areas.

The response from head teachers was extremely encouraging, which indicated that many of them were already aware of the situation. This good co-operation from schools up and down the country resulted in thousands of children in primary schools completing a questionnaire in class time under the supervision of their teacher. Teachers were asked to collect the completed questionnaires and to select a few children at random to ask questions about their claims to have seen films named in the questionnaire. The children were asked to give a few details of the films to ensure that they were not just claiming to see something that they had not actually viewed.

The results, when analysed, were quite startling, showing that children of all ages were viewing violent films. Most children reported that their parents set limits upon what they were allowed to see but there were many ways in which they got around the restrictions. Most violent and obscene video films were watched at a friend's house where older young people showed them to their younger siblings.

In the research we used a list of video films provided by the Director of Public Prosecutions that they had judged to be 'obscene' under the Obscene Publications Act 1959. They were all films that were currently being seized by police who were bringing prosecutions against the distributors. We took the 10 films most watched by the thousands of children who took part in the research aged between 7 and 16 years. These film titles were:

The Evil Dead, Zombie Flesh Eaters, The Living Dead, The Bogeyman, The Burning, I Spit on Your Grave, Death Trap, Zombie Creeping Flesh, Zombie Terror, Driller Killer.

We gave brief details of the contents of each of these films, all of which contained scenes of violence and many of them also contained explicit rape scenes or multiple gang rapes. It was the violence that we were concentrating upon rather than the sexual content, but the research showed that significant numbers of all ages had seen these films that were highly unsuitable video films for children.

Front-Page News
Our findings were front-page news in all the national newspapers, and the tabloids especially highlighted the fact that millions of young children were watching scenes of sex and violence that were highly unsuitable for young eyes. Every national and regional newspaper in the country covered the story. It gave the press license to describe details of the films and to indulge in a multitude of stories about what the children had seen and the effects upon them.

We published the first stage of the Enquiry in November 1983. But before we could move into the second phase, which was to analyse the effects upon the lives of the children who had viewed scenes of horrendous violence, the video industry struck back. This was inevitable since our first report had been given a great deal of publicity in the media.

Attacks upon the Enquiry

The film industry saw the threat to their multi-million-pound pot of gold and they reacted with fury. During the following six months the attacks upon the research and upon me personally were intense. The police told us that the wealth produced by pornographic films of violence and explicit sex for 'entertainment' was as great as the drugs industry. A BBC reporter told us that the film industry had hired a top PR firm in London to find ways of publicly discrediting the research. It was before the days of social media and before the invention of the term 'fake news', but fake news was certainly used upon the Parliamentary Enquiry.

Press reports accusing the research of unreliability began to appear as the industry hired a variety of so-called experts, psychologists and sociologists, to try to prove either that the children had not seen what they claimed to have seen or that no harm was done to them anyway. With the co-operation of teachers, we ran a second piece of research that involved contributions from the teachers and parents.

The feedback on parental attitudes to what their children had been viewing provided powerful evidence, and the contribution from teachers gave additional checks upon what the children had seen. Even though we were able to prove the veracity of the research results, we were not only up against the huge vested interests behind the video film industry, but it soon became obvious that we were up against the powers of darkness – that this was a spiritual battle.

The secular humanist libertarians got together, no doubt with the backing of the film industry who were prepared to spend huge sums of money in an attempt to undermine public confidence in our research and to raise up opposition to the legislation that was already being framed in Parliament. The *Guardian* ran a full-page on the subject with a large cartoon ridiculing me, labelled 'Dr No'. And the BBC included me in their 'Spitting Image' programme. I was quite upset at the time but later

I decided to put my appearance on the infamous satirical programme on my CV! It was just another battle scar.

Report Publication

Both our first and second reports under the title 'Video Violence and Children' were presented to all MPs in the House of Commons and many Members of the Lords. The second report was published in March 1984 ahead of the debates in both the Commons and the Lords. The two reports were well received and gave a regional breakdown of children who had seen the highest number of obscene videos so that MPs were able to see what was happening in their constituencies. When the final vote was taken in the House of Commons there was not a single MP who voted against the restrictions imposed, which brought in classifications of all video films according to age suitability and completely banning as illegal those with explicit scenes of violence.

In the book of the same title, *Video Violence and Children*, published in 1985, Sir Martin Roth, Professor of Psychiatry, University of Cambridge, said,

It is a matter of grave concern that in the formative years, from the ages of 7 to 17 years, 45% of children should have seen one or more video films which would legally be classed as obscene in this country on account of the morbid, sadistic and repugnant nature of the violence they portray. The first knowledge of sexual life acquired by these children may come from viewing films in which sexual conduct is inextricably entwined with violence, hatred, coercion and the humiliation of women in particular.[2]

The book also described the attacks upon the integrity of the research that came from various sources in the film industry who saw a threat to their profits in the work of the Parliamentary Group and did their best to discredit the research. Opposition also came from ultra-liberals and social anarchists whose opposition came under the guise of defending freedom of speech. Professor Roth dismissed these objections, saying that the evidence of the harm being done by these violent films was overwhelming. It was evident that there was a powerful group ideology behind the film industry who were seeking to reshape the nation by indoctrinating children and young people to promote their ultra-libertarianism while at the same time making fortunes out of a vulnerable sector of the public.

Psychiatrists Professor Andrew Sims and Dr Graham Melville-Thomas provided valuable information for the book. They carried out a survey of over 400 consultant psychiatrists and senior registrars working in the field of child and adolescent psychiatry, to discover the extent to which psychiatrists were seeing the effects upon children and young people of watching violent films. They analysed the data which showed the harmful effects in anxiety symptoms, sleep disturbances, depression, as well as in behavioural disorders. Further evidence came from a survey of teachers who saw significant changes in children's behaviour since the introduction of violent videos in the home. There had been a significant increase in violence and aggression on school premises, especially in the playground.

Unexpected Outcome

A major outcome of the Parliamentary Video Enquiry that was to have long-term significance was the prayer support that rapidly grew during the video campaign. Members of the Lydia Prayer Fellowship who had heard about the Enquiry started praying for the MPs involved and the Working Party, and they contacted us for news. We responded with a regular short news bulletin that included items for prayer. This rapidly spread to other prayer networks and soon we had a mailing list of many hundreds. This was an unexpected bonus that proved a lifeline during the very difficult days when the Enquiry was under attack by the film industry.

When the Enquiry finished we expressed our gratitude in a final report that was widely circulated among intercessors and we invited feedback from which we discovered that people were hungry for information about what was happening in Parliament and for a biblical understanding of what was happening in the nation. Reports from many of these intercessor groups quoted the Bible and raised questions about biblical prophecy that appeared to be relevant to today. Inevitably, questions were being asked about the end times – were biblical prophecies of the end times being fulfilled in our lifetime?

Publication of *Prophecy Today*

It was this hunger for a biblical understanding of the times that gave rise to the determination of the small group with whom I was working to publish a magazine that would give a biblical perspective of contemporary news. We made lots of enquiries about publication, but none of us had any experience of publishing and we had no financial resources behind us. The whole matter was committed to prayer, but there was not long to wait for an answer. Only three months after the end of the Parliamentary Video Enquiry and the vote in the House of Commons, the chairman of our little group which was now going under the name of 'Prophetic Word Ministries', Michael Fenton Jones, a businessman working in London, had lunch with the Chairman of Marshall Pickering, the publishers. He told Michael that they had a strong desire to publish a magazine but they didn't have the right vision for it so they had set aside finance for it, which had been waiting for a year. Michael responded by saying that we had been sitting on a vision for a magazine for some time but we did not have the resources to publish it.

This conversation soon led to meetings between our groups and the staff of Marshalls and over the next two or three months the details were worked out. Marshall's generously promised to support the whole enterprise for the first year and they would take responsibility for all printing, publishing and distribution while we would take all responsibility for editorial content and contact with writers including appointment of editorial staff and an editorial board.

Prophecy Today was first published in March 1985 with a print run of 5000, produced by Marshalls and distributed free of charge to ministers of churches throughout the country. It grew steadily through the rest of the 1980s, and by 1990 it had reached a distribution of 20,000. Our research showed that many churches and house fellowships took copies which were passed around, and we estimated that each copy of the magazine was read by an average of five readers, which gave us a total readership well in excess of 100,000. It was not only evangelicals and charismatics who read the magazine, but Christians of all traditions who were eager to gain a biblical perspective on current events, which was the major emphasis of the articles we published. A copy of the magazine was sent regularly to 10 Downing Street and we were reliably informed that Prime Minister Margaret Thatcher used to read it.

As reported earlier in this chapter, it was in response to a growing hunger for a biblical understanding of what was happening in the world that the vision for the magazine *Prophecy Today* arose in the early 1980s. The magazine carefully avoided speculative articles on eschatology or biblical mathematics or offering dates for the fulfilment of biblical prophecy. In fact, it was the desire to counteract some of these wild pseudo-biblical teachings that resulted in the publication of *Prophecy Today*.

The 1970s had seen the rise of a number of false prophets and false messiahs. The world had been stunned in 1978 by the mass suicide of more than 900 men, women and children, followers of Jim Jones,[3] who was expecting the imminent return of Christ and the end of the world. He led his followers into the jungles of Guyana, South America, where they ended their lives. There were no survivors to report on the gruesome events that led up to this tragedy that engulfed the lives of those who put their trust in a false messiah.

Perhaps equally dangerous have been some teachers who take selective passages of Scripture, piecing them together to form a pattern that bears resemblance to events in the modern world and on this basis make predictions of future events. There were numerous 'prophecies' foretelling the date of the second coming of Christ and the 'Rapture'. An example of this kind of teaching was in *The Late Great Planet Earth* by Hal Lindsey, written in 1969 and published in 1970. His strongly anti-Communist line, and predictions of a nuclear holocaust and the inadequacy of American defences in the face of Russian arms, even gained him a hearing at the Pentagon, where he was invited to speak to high-ranking military chiefs. His own account stated, "I noticed that the men were visibly moved by what I said... A few days before our meeting, their computer had predicted the same events and outcomes."[4]

Defining Prophecy

When we began publishing the magazine *Prophecy Today* in the mid-1980s, our intention was to rescue 'prophecy' from the morass of false teaching that flooded the popular paperback market using wild interpretations of Daniel and Revelation. Typical of this kind of book was the bestseller *When Your Money Fails*, subtitled *The 666 System Is Here*. This was in 1981, where the writer stated,

> I unreservedly view the international usage of the number 666 by the present world system, to be presided over soon by Mr 666, the false Messiah, as the third most significant fulfilment of Bible prophecy in the church age [the past 2000 years].[5]

Forthtelling the Word

The central objective of *Prophecy Today* was to present a biblically-based commentary on current affairs, but alongside this we also published a number of teaching articles on biblical themes. There were series of articles on the writing prophets, the major prophets of Isaiah, Jeremiah and Ezekiel, and the Minor Prophets from Hosea to Malachi. We avoided Daniel on the grounds that in the Hebrew Bible it is not included among the prophets but is regarded as wisdom literature on account of its apocalyptic nature. In every issue of the magazine we included a policy statement which defined prophecy as the 'forthtelling of the word of God'. We said that this was the task of the prophets of Israel and that the responsibility of the church today is to be the prophet to the world. We concluded the statement with the words, 'The most urgent need for the nations is not to hear the opinions of men, but to hear the word of God. It is as a contribution towards this prophetic task that *Prophecy Today* is published.'

The magazine became well known for its biblical teaching and for taking a clear stand that the major characteristic of prophecy was not *foretelling* events, but *forthtelling* or *declaring* the word of God— applying biblical truth to current events. We noted that only about 20% of the biblical prophets' writings were about future events. Their major concern was to deal with the contemporary situation in their times. We were able to judge the effectiveness of the message we were publishing in the magazine, not only by its circulation but also by the large numbers of people who came to the meetings where our team was speaking in different parts of the UK. It was not unusual to have in excess of 1,000 people in these meetings. At one meeting in Westminster Central Hall in 1987 there were a number of MPs, including at least one Cabinet

Minister, with a near capacity crowd.

People were hungry for the prophetic word of God in a day when secular humanism appeared to be triumphing. We applied biblical teaching to current events, and lessons were learned from how God dealt with Israel in situations that were similar to our own.

This use of biblical truth applied to current events enabled Christians to gain an understanding of what was happening today. Clearly, people were not getting this kind of biblical teaching in the churches and *Prophecy Today* and PWM Team Ministries were filling a gap.

Notes
[1] The first of these books was *Black and White in Harmony,* Hodder and Stoughton, London, 1958 and the second was *West Indian Migrants and the London Churches,* Oxford University Press, 1963, which was a research report that had been commissioned by the London Institute of Race Relations.
[2] Eds. Geoffrey Barlow and Alison Hill, *Video Violence and Children,* Hodder and Stoughton, London, 1985, p. 3.
[3] Also in Chapter 5 p. 86.
[4] Hal Lindsey, *The 1980s, Countdown to Armageddon,* Lakeland, 1980, p. 6.
[5] Mary Stuart Relf, *When Your Money Fails,* 1981, p. 59.

Chapter Eight

SEEKING THE WORD OF GOD

Unsettled Times

To the keen observer of social change in the 1980s, the signs of the reshaping of the nation were already clear. It was the effect upon family life that was the most alarming. Births outside marriage in 1980 exceeded 10% for the first time in 400 years of British history and the divorce rate had begun soaring. The small ministry team that I was working with were aware that something dynamic was happening, particularly in terms of secularisation. We could see that this was a threat to the Christian values embedded in the foundations of Western civilisation and we knew that these values were responsible for the stability of the whole social structure. If they were disturbed it could have monumental repercussions.

We were very aware of the widespread social and industrial unrest that had begun in the 1970s and continued throughout 1980s Britain. We also were aware of the international situation, particularly the tensions in the Middle East and the war between Iran and Iraq. We especially watched the situation regarding Israel and the additional tension caused by the murder of more than 200 American and French soldiers in Lebanon in 1983.

In our times of team prayer and Bible study we sought to understand what was happening on the world scene in a biblical context. We particularly wanted to know what God was saying to us today and what he required from us. Was there any word from the Lord? How should we go about seeking such a word? We wanted to be in touch with Christians in other parts of the world to know how they were thinking and what God was saying to them.

Seeking Other Leaders

Finding Christian leaders around the world who had similar interests in what God was saying to his people today seemed an utterly impossible task. Our small group had few overseas contacts and I was relatively unknown outside the UK. Humanly speaking it was obviously an impossible task, but we all knew that with God nothing is impossible. At the height of the 'video nasties' battle when the forces against the Parliamentary Enquiry[1] seemed overwhelming, I had often read Jeremiah's prayer:

"Ah, Sovereign LORD, you have made the heavens and the earth by your great power and outstretched arm. Nothing is too hard for you..." (Jer 32.17, NIV).

We simply had to trust that God would bring the right people into contact with us. It was quite amazing how news spread far and wide about the possibility of men and women with prophetic ministries coming together to share their experience and to seek what God was saying to the nations. It was decided to have a leadership gathering at Mt Carmel in northern Israel, to be followed by a meeting for intercessors and any Christians interested in seeking the word of God for today. The larger meeting was to be in Jerusalem at the Israeli national conference centre, the *Binyanei Ha'Ooma*.

As the word spread about the proposed gatherings, several international Christian leaders made contact with us. God began to draw together those who were his watchman in different parts of the world. This all happened without any advertising or specific steps taken to find those who had a concern for the word of God for our times. They began responding as God put it onto their hearts. One spoke to another and gradually we found ourselves in contact with men and women exercising prophetic ministries in many different nations. Out of this came a leadership group of seven for the international gatherings which were to take place in the spring of 1986.

Prayer Support

The Parliamentary Video Enquiry had brought a large number of intercessors and supporters, most of whom opted to continue receiving information via the newly formed PWM Trust. They became our main prayer base, and there was considerable excitement when we announced that we were seeking to organise a conference in Israel at which we would be drawing together international Christian leaders. There was a growing interest in what was happening in the world and the need for a prophetic or biblically-based understanding and response. *Prophecy Today* was already beginning to meet this need since its launch in March 1985 as a bi-monthly magazine.

Carmel Gathering

The magazine played a significant part in giving publicity to the international gathering in Jerusalem which was to follow the Mt Carmel meeting. No fewer than 5,000 Christians from around the world signed up to attend the Jerusalem gathering. We were not looking for a large number at the Mount Carmel meeting as we were only looking for Christian leaders exercising prophetic ministries. Each one was allowed to bring an intercessor with them, which was particularly necessary if the leader was not proficient in the English language. The total leaders and intercessors from around the world gathered at Mt Carmel was 153. The meeting was at the 'Yaarot Ha' Carmel' in April 1986. The venue was a rehabilitation centre for the survivors of the Holocaust. It had been set up by the German Government as part of their reparations following the Second World War. The survivors were quite elderly and by 1986 they were few in number, so the decision had been made to open the facility as a conference centre.

We were the first Christians to occupy the buildings alongside about 20 elderly residents, some of whom used to come and sit in the conference hall with us when they heard us at worship singing Hebrew songs. Two of them accepted Jesus as their Lord and Messiah during the week that we were there. Both said that Jesus had appeared to them during the night and had spoken to them.

Following a 24-hour time of silence we all shared what we were hearing from God in our prayer times. All agreed that what we were hearing was expressed in Haggai 2.6–7:

"This is what the LORD Almighty says: 'In a little while I will once more shake the heavens and the earth, the sea and the dry land. I will shake all nations, and the desired of all nations will come, and I will fill this house with glory,' says the LORD Almighty". (NIV)

We also read Hebrews 12.26f where the prophecy of Haggai is repeated and an interpretation is given. Hebrews was one of the last books to be written in the New Testament. So we concluded that Haggai's prophecy was still in the future near the end of the first century A.D. and may be relevant for what we were seeing in our lifetime. There was already considerable evidence of the shaking of the heavens and the earth. It was only six months since an earthquake had destroyed the largest city in the world, Mexico City, with as many as 30,000 deaths. There was also plenty of evidence of the shaking of the nations—the social, economic and political systems of humanity.

God Speaks
Lance Lambert and I each read the words of prophecy that we had received on the theme of God shaking the nations. We were followed by ten others who each gave words that corroborated and were in line with the first two prophecies. Further words showed that God was calling for repentance and cleansing in the church. The word given to Lance Lambert was recognised as of special significance. Part of it is reproduced below:

It will not be long before there will come upon the world a time of unparalleled upheaval and turmoil. Do not fear for it is I the Lord who am shaking all things. I began this shaking with the First World War and I greatly increased it through the Second World War. Since 1973 I have given it an even greater impetus. In the last stage, I plan to complete it with the shaking of the universe itself, with signs in the sun and moon and stars.

But before that point is reached, I will judge the nations and the time is near. It will not only be by war and civil war, by anarchy and terrorism, and by monetary collapses that I will judge the nations, but also by natural disasters: by earthquakes, by shortages and famines, and by old and new plague diseases. I will also judge them by giving them over to their own ways, to lawlessness, to loveless selfishness, to delusion and to believing a lie, to false religion and an apostate church, even to a Christianity without me.

Do not fear when these things begin to happen, for I disclose these things to you before they commence in order that you might be prepared, and that in the day of trouble and of evil you may stand firm and overcome. For I purpose that you may become the means of encouraging and strengthening many who love me but who are weak.[2]

One of the leaders from China described what had been happening in that country during the long years of persecution since the Communist Revolution in 1949 and the banning of Western missionaries with their material resources which Westerners thought to be essential for evangelism. With no theological colleges to train leaders, the 'underground' church had grown from a mere half a million to somewhere between 50 million and 100 million believers. He noted that the great spiritual awakening in China did not start until the Christians ceased to rely upon human resources.

The Message from Carmel

Through a number of prophetic words, it was concluded that a time of great shaking was coming upon the world that would affect the natural creation as well as causing a time of political and social upheaval. This would lead to severe persecution of Christians in many parts of the world that would spread even to the rich Western nations, who would also suffer from forthcoming times of economic hardship and social breakdown. We believed we were receiving these warnings at Mt Carmel in order to strengthen and prepare the church for the coming days.

Jerusalem Gathering

The week at Carmel concluded on the Saturday morning and we made our way up to Jerusalem to the *Binyanei Ha'Ooma* where large crowds were already gathering. The stage setting was impressive with a huge gold lampstand in the centre with a bowl at the top and seven lights on it, with seven channels to the lights. On either side of the lampstand were two olive trees, exactly as described in Zechariah 4.2-3, with the words: *"Not by might nor by power, but by my Spirit, says the Lord Almighty"* (Zec 4.4). This was the central theme of the gathering, seeking God's word to the nations.

The morning seminars were in different locations allowing people the choice of subject. Most of them were repeated so that people could cover a range of subjects. The evening meetings in the Great Hall brought together the whole company of 5000 for worship and an inspirational message. It was Holy Week which coincided with the Jewish Passover that year. The worship on Maundy Thursday was special with the whole assembly humbling themselves before the Lord. The following day, Good Friday, was also special and the evening meeting was reserved for declaring the word of the Lord from Carmel for which people had been eagerly awaiting.

The Message from Jerusalem

Lance Lambert and I each read the words we had received at Mt Carmel and we spoke about the great shaking of the nations that was going to intensify, reading the prophecy from both Haggai 2 and Hebrews 12. I had received a further word that the Soviet Union would be the first nation to be severely shaken. In 1986 the collapse of the USSR seemed impossible to imagine; it was still a mighty world power. Moscow controlled not only Russia but half of Europe including East Germany. The Communist empire seemed impregnable: but the word of prophecy proved to be true.

Just three weeks later the Chernobyl nuclear power station near Kiev was destroyed by an enormous explosion that scattered radioactive dust for thousands of miles, even reaching the mountains of North Wales. Chernobyl in the Ukrainian language means 'bitterness' or 'wormwood' and many Russian Christians saw the link with Revelation 8.11 and its reference to *a third of the waters turned bitter*. The power station at Chernobyl had been built on the site of a mass grave of Jews from a 1930s' pogrom. Was this an act of divine justice following the murder of the Jews and the deliberate insult of building the power station on their graves? Perhaps it was even more significant as it led to the collapse of the Soviet Union. The pollution of the land in the Ukraine which was the breadbasket of the USSR was catastrophic. The Soviet army was just withdrawing from Afghanistan with thousands more mouths to be fed. The Soviet Union had to buy grain from the West which required dollars and severely impacted the Soviet economy leading them to practice an unprecedented openness which in turn led directly to the breakup of the Soviet Union just three years later.

The Berlin Wall was broken down and the Warsaw Pact Treaty was dissolved. The prophecy received at Carmel saying that judgment was about to begin on the USSR, also referred to the fact that it was 70 years from the 1916 revolution. In the same way as Babylon had been given 70 years, according to Jeremiah 29.10, so God had allowed the Communist regime to last for a similar period.

Post-Jerusalem

It was in St Mark's Kennington in March 1986 that a new phase of ministry began for PWM. The team had just returned from the meetings in Carmel and Jerusalem and more than 1000 people gathered at St Mark's to hear reports of what had happened in Israel. There was a genuine eagerness to hear what God was saying in the context of the current world situation and the times of social unrest and economic difficulties that were being experienced in Britain. This same receptiveness was rapidly followed by invitations for the team to speak in many different parts of the UK.

From that time in May 1986 the team faced a packed programme that ran to the end of that year with just a four-week break in August. During these months we visited Brighton and Hove, Bath, Basildon, Shrewsbury, Newtown Wales, Swansea, Liverpool, Westminster and Lambeth in London, Birmingham, Trowbridge, Malmesbury, Kingston upon Thames, Leeds, Carberry Tower (for a conference), Edinburgh, Thirsk, Scarborough, Bristol, Coventry and Plymouth. We took a team of speakers and our own worship band. Large crowds gathered at every location, eager to hear what God was saying to his people today.

Team Tour

This new phase of ministry was described in *Prophecy Today* (May 1986) as having the primary purpose of presenting the message that had been received at Carmel and publicly declared in Jerusalem. The team believed that through presenting this message God would *"open eyes and ears to give understanding of the contemporary world scene in its biblical significance, and mobilise the resources of the Body of Christ for the outreach of the gospel."* This was summarised as:

- To understand the times in which we live;
- To warn of the great dangers facing humanity;
- To intercede for the church and the world;
- To offer hope through the gospel of our Lord Jesus Christ.

The announcement of the meetings in *Prophecy Today* stated:

> We believe that God has not only given us a message, but that he has been preparing us as a team to share this with other Christians in Britain. It has, therefore, been both an encouragement and a confirmation to receive invitations from a large number of Christian leaders in different parts of the country. We have done no advertising, but the invitations have come, and we see them as a sign of the fulfilment of God's promise. We are, however, deeply concerned lest we present ourselves in the wrong way. We are simply fellow servants of the Lord coming amongst the churches to share a message that we believe we have heard from God.
>
> We are not a high-powered team. We have no superstars and we do not wish to see our image projected in the ways of the world. Our only desire is that the Name of the Lord Jesus will be glorified. We have a sense of urgency that comes from the conviction that we are hearing from God concerning the times in which we live and what will soon be happening among the nations and in Britain. We believe God is giving us a boldness for the task that lies ahead, but

it is a boldness not of the flesh, for God is strongly reminding his church today that it is *"Not by might, nor by power, but by my Spirit says the Lord Almighty"*.[3]

A Word for the Times

The meetings were attended by people from churches of all denominations and we usually spoke on the theme 'THE WORD OF GOD FOR OUR TIMES'. Everywhere we went we used the scriptures from Haggai 2 and Hebrews 12 that refer to God shaking the whole natural order of creation and also shaking the nations in their social, political and economic systems. There was plenty of evidence of this in the daily news and we were never short of contemporary events to support the theme that God was shaking everything and it was clear that the pace of change was increasing rapidly.

Everywhere we went there was a ready response to the message which was not presented as tidings of gloom and doom, but as a message of both warning and hope. The warning was that the course upon which the nations, and Britain in particular, had embarked, would only lead to disaster — but there was hope. The hope lay in turning and repentance; turning to the word of God with a determination to follow his ways of righteousness.

Gideon's Army

We often referred to the account of Gideon's ministry during the period of the Judges in the history of Israel. This had come to mean a lot in our ministry since the early days of the PWM Team. At the first conference that we had organised (which was at Pilgrim Hall, Sussex in 1984) Jean Darnall had prophesied over our ministry, saying there were three stages in the message; and that these would be revealed to us in due time through the three trumpets in the story of Gideon.

It was a long time before we discovered the third of the three trumpets and saw something of their significance. It was easy to identify two trumpets in the story of Gideon where, in Judges 6.34, it is recorded that *the Spirit of the Lord came upon Gideon and he blew a trumpet summoning the Abiezrites to follow him*. He then sent messengers throughout Israel, mobilising all the fighting men to prepare to resist the Midianites and the Amalekites who had invaded the land. Another trumpet was blown when Gideon, and his three hundred men surrounding the enemy camp, each blew a trumpet which signalled the beginning of the battle.

The thing we had not immediately discerned was that God's initial action in sending a prophet to the Israelites represented the blowing of the first trumpet in the nation. *When the Israelites cried to the Lord because of Midian, he sent them a prophet, who said, "This is what the Lord, the God of Israel says"* (Judges 6.7- 8). The prophet explained to Gideon the reason why all this disaster had come upon the land, inflicted by the invasion by Midianites and Amalekites. It was because they had forsaken the Lord God. But God had heard their cry and was responding by calling them to turn to him, to forsake idolatry, to rebuild the altar of God and to worship him. Thus, in Gideon's time, the first trumpet was an interpretation of the signs of the times giving understanding of the contemporary situation, plus a call to return to the Lord. It was this prophetic mission that was PWM's calling from God to take to the nation at that time,

Shaking All Things

This theme took on a new meaning for us following the Carmel Gathering and the declaration that God was shaking the nations. There was much that was occurring throughout the world that illustrated this, which we used to explain what God was doing in the contemporary situation. Specifically, his call was for repentance — a turning to him and forsaking the gross idolatry of modern humanity which was to be seen, not only in the world, but also in the church.

The message was widely accepted by believers from many different sectors of the church. One tangible result was the coming together of a number of intercessory organisations to call a 'Day of Repentance' in 1988. Meetings were held simultaneously in cities, towns and villages throughout the UK, the largest being in Westminster Central Hall in London which was filled for a whole day of prayer and calling upon the Lord to forgive us for our share of responsibility for the state of our nation. Sadly, while there was good support from evangelicals of all denominations, a major sector of charismatic churches, the Restorationist churches, did not join in.[4] Their leaders said that they believed the Lord was calling them to prepare for *revival* rather than repentance, which revealed the lack of unity in the churches.

The Message

The message we were taking to the churches post 1986 was an elaboration of what had been received at Carmel and Jerusalem, that the world was entering a period of unprecedented instability that would shake all nations. We said that the shaking had begun in 1914 with the First World War. By the time that war ended some of the most powerful empires in world history had disappeared. Others were clearly in decline.

The entire face of Europe, Russia, the Middle East and North Africa had changed. The Prussian Empire went, the Austrian Hungarian Empire went, the dynasty of the Czar that had ruled Russia for more than 1,000 years was shattered and replaced by the world's first Marxist regime. The Ottoman Empire that had kept Palestine under Muslim rule for centuries was finally crushed and the way was paved by the Balfour Declaration in 1917 for the return of the Jews and the eventual establishment of the State of Israel.

The shaking of the nations had continued with the traumas of economic recession in the 1930s and with the bloodshed and destruction of the Second World War in the 1940s. This was followed by the rise of nationalism and the drive towards independence among many colonial nations such as India, Nigeria, Jamaica and others. The dismantling of the British Empire was a painful time of change, although most people in Britain were consoled with the establishment of the British Commonwealth of nations. But everyone knew that the days of Britain's ruling the waves with British power extending to all parts of the globe and the sun never setting on our Empire – those days were finished. Britain had to find a new *raison d'être* in a rapidly changing world.

At home, massive cultural and social changes were taking place as immigrants from the Commonwealth settled in the 'mother country' and competed with the native-born population for jobs and houses, creating tensions in inner-city areas and occasional outbursts of violence on the streets. Immigration laws controlling the numbers of newcomers changed the philosophy of people throughout the Empire, being British citizens with the right to travel anywhere. At the same time laws were introduced controlling race relations and regulating behaviour and language; eventually leading to the targeting of so-called 'hate speech'. The rapid social changes that began in the 1960s continued unabated for decades to come, with an additional driving force from technological development, the invention of the Internet, the mobile phone and social media initiating revolutionary changes, not only in the culture of the nation, but in the fundamental social structure of Britain. The nation was being reshaped in a very significant way.

But the future was still unclear. We saw three alternatives: Would political revolution reshape Britain? Or would social revolution sweep away the heritage of centuries? Or would a great spiritual revival take place, through which the gospel would reshape the nation?

Notes
[1] See Chapter 7 p. 115.
[2] This was first published in Clifford Hill Editor, *From Carmel to Jerusalem*, PWM Trust (now Issachar Ministries) 1998 p. 16. The remainder of this prophecy is reproduced in the Epilogue of this book.
[3] *Prophecy Today,* Vol 2, No 3.
[4] The Restorationist Movement began in the late 1960s in Britain although it had earlier roots in the USA. It resulted in the formation of 'new churches' such as, Harvest Time, Ichthus, New Frontiers, Pioneer and others. Their distinctive beliefs were in the restoration of the New Testament 'fivefold ministries' and that the gifts of the Holy Spirit that were practised in the Early Church, but neglected by the mainline churches, were available to Christians today. These beliefs were shared by many charismatic leaders and teachers in the mainline denominational churches, but they were the foundational beliefs of those who formed the first 'house churches' that later became known as the New Churches.

Chapter Nine

ARCHBISHOP ROBERT RUNCIE

The Most Revd and Rt Hon Dr Robert Runcie
Archbishop of Canterbury February 1982 – January 1991

It took two years to appoint another Archbishop following the resignation of Donald Coggan in January 1980. Finally, the liberal bishops succeeded in exercising their influence and managed to secure the appointment of Robert Runcie, probably the most liberal cleric ever to occupy the office of Archbishop of Canterbury. He was appointed in February 1982 and led the Church of England until January 1991. It was a critical decade of social change, which we will be covering in the next chapter, in which the state church was led by a man who in all my contact with him appeared to lack a personal relationship with the God of the Bible.

Liberal Theology

Runcie's liberal theology and lack of biblical conviction was publicly exposed at the time of the York Minster fire when, despite a newly installed state-of-the-art lightning conductor and an almost cloudless sky, the Minster was struck by lightning on 9th July 1984. It was only hours after the consecration in the Minster of David Jenkins as Bishop of Durham. Jenkins was renowned for his ultra-liberal views on the Bible, and in particular for his views on the resurrection, which he had referred to in the context of a 'conjuring trick with bones'. He later denied this, but nevertheless affirmed that he saw the resurrection of Jesus, not as an historical event, but as a series of experiences that built up the tradition that Jesus had actually risen from the dead.

Many people immediately saw the connection between Jenkins' consecration and the Minster fire. Even the secular media saw it as 'an act of God'. Runcie was interviewed on the BBC one o'clock news when he declared that God does not do such things and that God has no control over the weather. Met Office records for that day showed a clear blue sky over the whole of the British Isles and Northern Europe. There was just one tiny cloud to be seen travelling across Yorkshire. Out of a bright clear night sky, from that one small cloud there came a lightning strike of such power and ferocity that it overrode the sophisticated lightning conductor system and did immense damage to the Minster.

Even secular journalists could see the significance of what had happened, but Dr Runcie, defended the appointment of the new Bishop and dismissed the suggestion of this being an 'act of God'. It later emerged that if he had admitted this to be an 'act of God' the insurance might have been null and void.

No Clear Lead

Throughout his time at Canterbury there were calls for the Archbishop to 'give a clear lead' to the nation but Runcie knew that the theological and biblical divisions within the Church of England made this an impossible task, just as Donald Coggan had discovered. Clergy in the C of E at this time were probably evenly split on the subject of biblical truth, especially on the subject of miracles. There were those who leaned towards a fundamentalist view of Scripture and there were others who made no attempt to hide their disbelief in any of the miracles in the Gospels.[1]

Dr Runcie was continually at odds with Margaret Thatcher and his distinguished service as a tank commander in World War II, where he had won the Military Cross for bravery, should have made her more respectful of his views on the conflict with Argentina in the Falklands War. His sermon at the Service of Thanksgiving in St Paul's Cathedral grossly offended those who were banging a triumphalist drum in the Conservative Party because he remembered the Argentinian dead as well as the British. He was a man who had seen the dead bodies of both Germans and Britons in battle, and much of the pillorying in the press was unjustified.

Runcie's hiring of Terry Waite as his secretary for Anglican

Communion Affairs drew a lot of criticism from the popular press after Waite was kidnapped and held by terrorists in Lebanon. He was involved in further controversies throughout his time at Lambeth Palace such as the battles within the Church of England over homosexuals when Tony Higton called, in the spring of 1987 Synod, for a return to 'biblical standards of morality'. The issue was fudged, which led to Frank Field's epigram, quoted in the infamous Preface to *Crockford's Clerical Directory* as 'The Archbishop is usually to be found nailing his colours to the fence.'

It was probably his views on inter-church relationships, and particularly his desire for greater unity with Rome, that caused the greatest storm of Protestant outrage, when he said that the whole Christian church needed a primacy which could only be exercised by the Bishop of Rome. On his last visit to Rome he made overtures of unity which were firmly rejected by the Pope. But it was his uncertain theological convictions that caused the greatest offence to evangelicals, both within the Anglican church and among Nonconformists.

Interfaith Views

In March 1987, we published an article about Dr Runcie's lack of biblical convictions in *Prophecy Today* under the title *All Roads Lead To God?* [2] It is a long statement, but it is incredibly revealing of the character and beliefs of the man who led the Church of England for nearly a decade at a crucial time of social change. It needs to be recorded here:

In a remarkable speech revealing a dangerously misguided theology the Archbishop of Canterbury spoke recently of the need for interfaith dialogue and gave what he termed his **'own reflections on the encounter of Christianity with other religions'.** Dr Runcie was giving the Sir Francis Younghusband Memorial Lecture at Lambeth Palace on the 50th anniversary of the World Congress of Faiths.

In referring to other world religions Dr Runcie said that we need to **"recognise that other faiths than our own are genuine mansions of the Spirit with many rooms to be discovered".** Quoting Sir Francis Younghusband, Dr Runcie said, **"All the centuries that**

the Spirit of God has been working in Christians, he must also have been working in Hindus, Buddhists, Muslims and others". He noted that **"interreligious encounter and dialogue"** enabled people of different religions **"to share the sustaining insights and transforming treasures of their faith and to recognise an affinity of the human heart in the fellowship of the Spirit".**

This statement showed that Dr Runcie was a polytheist and certainly not a Bible believing Christian. He referred to his recent visit to India as **'a stunning experience'** that gave him first hand contact with other religions. He confessed that it left him **'dazed and uncertain of my bearings'**. He said he went to India with **'the certainties of an encapsulated Western Christianity'** but came away realising that **'there are new ways of thinking about God, Christ and the world'**. He spoke of his experience of God among Hindus at Madras ... where gods and goddesses take hundreds of different forms and images. The sheer diversity of the divine was disconcerting. God somehow seemed greater than Western monism... We have lost something that other faiths may help to restore to us.

One has to ask how any man holding the office of Archbishop of Canterbury can make such an incredible statement. How can the truth about the one true God revealed in the Bible – the God and Father of our Lord Jesus Christ – be enhanced by worshipping at the shrines of pagan gods and goddesses? It would seem that Dr Runcie did not believe the first and second commandments: *"I am the Lord your God, you shall have no other gods before me. You shall not make for yourself an idol in the form of anything in heaven above or in the earth beneath or in the waters below. You shall not bow down to them or worship them"* (Ex 20.1-4).

In his lecture, Dr Runcie spoke of **"a moving carving of Vishnu resting on the waters of creation"**. He did not seem to realise that he was speaking of a pagan idol. He spoke scornfully of a lady missionary who was driving to a hospital not far from Benares. They passed the shrine then she remarked, "I am always very sad to see the piety with which those Hindus worship at that shrine". Runcie asked why. **"Well" she said with a sort of simple finality,**

"there's no one there to hear". That 'simple finality' has no place today" said Dr Runcie.[3]

Runcie's statement revealed that he believed the pagan goddess was able to answer the prayers of those who worship her. It appeared that he was not only advocating idolatry but seeking to introduce into the Church of England the religious pluralism of which he spoke so warmly.

Dr Runcie apparently believed that God is at work in all the religions of the world and that none of them has a monopoly of the truth. He said, **"It takes humility and sincerity to concede that there is a certain incompleteness in each of our traditions", and that we need "to recognise the work of the Holy Spirit among us in other faiths."**

Clearly, he ignored the statement of Jesus in John 14.6, *"I am the way, the truth and the life"*. He stated, **"Ultimately all religions possess a provisional, interim character as ways and signs to help us in our pilgrimage to ultimate truth and perfection,"** which clearly dismissed Jesus' claim, *"No one comes to the Father except through me"* (John 14.6). In fact, Runcie specifically denied the words of Jesus by saying, **"Christians will have to abandon any narrowly conceived Christian apologetic based on a sense of superiority and an exclusive claim to truth."**

Runcie then made a statement that was pure New-Age teaching:

If we trust the life-giving power of the Spirit within us and amongst us, we can meet each other in openness and trust; we can learn to explore together the moments of revelation and the spiritual treasures which our respective faiths have handed down to us – a spark of divine life and a vision of holiness whereby the lives of countless people in past and present are nourished, sustained, transformed and sanctified.

To justify this Runcie added,

Christians recognise that other faiths reveal other aspects of God which may enrich and enlarge our Christian understanding.

Runcie went even farther in his Polytheistic teaching by saying that interfaith dialogue poses problems for Christian theology in terms of the 'mission of Christ' and 'the question as to the meaning and significance of the incarnation within the context of religious pluralism.' He stated:

In an age of radical historical consciousness, an understanding of the incarnation as the central Christian event must also be linked to an understanding of the historical circumstances in which this belief first took root and developed.

For the Archbishop of Canterbury, as leader of the Church of England, to make such a statement, casting doubt upon the historicity of the incarnation which is a cardinal statement of faith for the Christian church, was surely a major admission that he was no longer a Bible-believing Christian and he was totally unfit to be the most senior leader of the church in Britain.

Runcie's muddled theology was further revealed in his description of his visit to Mother Teresa's home for the dying in Calcutta. He said,

I had not realised before that her hospice is built on temple property – dedicated, appropriately enough, to the goddess Kali. Here was the love of Christ given and received by men and women of all faiths and of none alongside the goddess who symbolises a mixture of destruction and fertility.

One has to ask how the love of Christ can be given by men and women of all faiths and none who neither know the gospel nor acknowledge Jesus as Lord and Saviour. How can those who have never accepted the gospel, or experienced the redeeming love of Christ, reveal his love to others? Such a statement appears to be a denial of the necessity for new birth through Christ which is a fundamental denial of the gospel.

Dr Runcie concluded his lecture by reference to what he called **'a remarkable prophecy'** by historian Arnold Toynbee suggesting that future historians would look back upon the 20th century:

... not as an era of superpower confrontation or of the economic

and cultural renaissance of the Arabs, or the eclipse of Europe, but as the time when the first sign became visible of that great interpenetration of Eastern religions and Christianity which gave rise to the great universal religion of the third millennium AD.

We reported this incredible statement in *Prophecy Today* by saying:

Is this the policy the Archbishop wishes to see the Church of England pursue? In 1988, he hopes to lead the Church of England into a reunion with Rome, but it now appears that Dr Runcie's ultimate objective is union with Islam, Buddhism, Hinduism, Zoroastrianism and any other religion that will join forces to form a 'one-world-religion'. This may be a prophetic fulfilment of the false religion depicted in the Book of Revelation, but it should hardly be a policy advocated by the Archbishop of Canterbury!

In the early days of the Reformation, Dr Runcie would have been burned as a heretic. Neither Henry VIII nor Elizabeth I would have hesitated to have him sent to the stake for the statements he has made. Today, we are more tolerant, and so we stand back and watch him appoint 'unbelievers' to positions of power and influence in the church. But surely Dr Runcie has gone too far this time! He should either recant the statements he has made in this lecture, or resign as Archbishop of Canterbury and spiritual leader of the Church of England.[4]

Archbishop Runcie did not resign – at least, not for another four years. I met him shortly after publishing this piece when he visited the Evangelical Anglican Clergy Conference at a holiday camp on the east coast of England, but I did not take up the issue face-to-face with him. In fact, I felt sorry for him as he looked a sick man and he was clearly shaking nervously when he addressed the conference. Although there was a time of open questions to the Archbishop, none of the clergy cared to engage him in major issues of faith. It was all very polite, very British! No-one wanted to rock the boat that could lead to a split in the Church of England. Unity at all costs was the dominant objective.

New-Age Concepts

It is impossible to measure the immense amount of harm that Runcie did during his nine-year term as Archbishop of Canterbury. He was not only a liberal theologian, but he had actually embraced New-Age concepts as revealed in his statement, **"Ultimately all religions possess a provisional, interim character as ways and signs to help us in our pilgrimage to ultimate truth and perfection;"** and his further reference to the **"spark of divine life and a vision of holiness whereby the lives of countless people in past and present are nourished, sustained, transformed and sanctified."** That is pure New Age teaching.

He certainly had no concept of the 'God of Creation' as revealed in the Bible, who flung the stars into their orbit and who sustains the universe – the God who was revealed to Isaiah who *measured the waters in the hollow of his hand,* and, *held the dust of the earth in a basket,* who, *sits enthroned above the circle of the earth and its people are like grasshoppers. He stretches out the heavens like a canopy and spread them out like a tent to live in. He brings princes to naught and reduces the rulers of the world to nothing* (see Is 40.12 and 22 – 23).

Runcie not only lacked an understanding of the sovereignty of God but he also lacked a personal relationship with our Lord Jesus Christ who said, *"I am the way and the truth and the life. No one comes to the Father except through me. If you really knew me, you would know my Father as well"* (John 14.6-7). He could not accept the exclusivity implied in this testimony of Jesus to his disciples. Instead, he said, "All the centuries that the Spirit of God has been working in Christians, he must also have been working in Hindus, Buddhists, Muslims and others". But there is nowhere in the New Testament to support such teaching which undoubtedly would have been regarded as heretical in the apostolic age.

Having such a man at the head of the Church of England throughout the 1980s was tragic, not just for the state church, but for the nation. It was a decade of immense significance in the socio/political history of Britain. The effects of the Divorce Reform Act were just beginning to be seen in the rising tide of family breakdown. As already noted, the number of babies born out of wedlock hit 10% in 1980 for the first time in 400 years of British history. Abortion was being used as a form of contraceptive, which was never the intention of Parliament according to David Steel who had sponsored the original Bill.

If ever there were a time when a clear lead from the church was needed in both the social and political life of the nation it was surely the 1980s. But Runcie cared for none of these things. His foremost passion was to maintain institutional unity at all costs within the Church of England. He was also strongly committed to seeking greater unity between the Church of England and the church of Rome. Within a month of his enthronement at Canterbury he began preparing the way for such unity and he spelt out his proposals to the Pope on his visit to Britain. This brought highly vocal strong opposition from within the Church of England, especially from the Protestant evangelical wing. But Runcie persisted in this objective and in 1989 when he visited Rome he renewed his attempt at reunion which was firmly rejected by the Pope.

'Faith in the City' Report

In 1985 the landmark report *Faith in the City*[5] was published, which was immediately enveloped in controversy due to the political implications of its findings and recommendations. The report was dismissed by Margaret Thatcher's Government as 'pure Marxist theology'. This was unfortunate because the report accurately highlighted the plight of people in our inner-city areas who were caught in the urban poverty trap from which there was little or no opportunity for social mobility. Monica and I knew the reality of this from our many years' experience of living and working in inner-city areas of London.

It was unfortunate that the report placed the blame for inner-city poverty upon the monetary policy of the Thatcher Government, which was quickly labelled as political bias so that the serious situation described in the report was not given the attention it deserved. Its recommendations were too focused upon the need for state action and gave inadequate consideration to the kind of community development principles upon which we had been working in the East End of London, which identified the latent abilities of people and encouraged their development in the community. If the report had begun with some humility, admitting the failure of the church's mission in inner-city areas, its impact would have been greater. The report established the 'Church Urban Fund' which made a huge contribution to the support and development of inner-city mission. It raised more than £55 million to support the work of churches and faith projects in areas of considerable need.

If the Archbishop had not been so unpopular, not only with the Government, but also with the general public, the report might have made a strategic impact upon Christian mission in areas of social deprivation. If Runcie had been a man of faith in the mould of his predecessor, Donald Coggan, the report could have been commended to the public and given much more serious and favourable consideration, which could have impacted inner-city churches that had been in serious decline for two decades.

In Newham when we began the Renewal Programme less than 1% of the local population attended church. What was needed was a radical new policy based both upon a living faith in God and a commitment to transform society through creative policies of social change and community development. This would not only have affected mission in inner-city areas but also the presentation of the gospel nationwide. The opportunity for such a new policy had been there in the 1970s, but it died in the 1980s.

National Legacy
The vision held by the Lambeth Group was for a 'Decade of Evangelism' through the 1980s based upon stimulating local community activity. This could have been achieved if it had not been for the intervention of liberal church leaders who were totally opposed to any forms of evangelism while at the same time having no understanding of the powerful forces of social change that were already at work in society. Their liberalism, which came from the Enlightenment and Darwinian concepts of evolutionary processes of social change, left no place for the sovereignty of God and his activity in society. Their lack of understanding of the revelation of God given through the biblical prophets of the 8th to the 5th century BC was at the heart of their lack of understanding of the revolutionary nature of the gospel brought by Jesus and his revelation of the Fatherhood of God.

It was this crucial theological error combined with an ignorance of the processes of social change among church leaders that frustrated the

God-given opportunity of the Holy Spirit moving among the people in the 1970s and 80s. Instead of the church being re-energised and empowered with fresh vision to meet the challenge of secularisation and the demonically inspired onslaught of the secular humanist forces of change, the church was stripped of godly leadership and infected with biblical unbelief. This absence of theological and sociological understanding was destined to affect the history of the nation and have worldwide implications.

Not only was the opportunity of the 1970s and 80s lost through the intervention of liberal church leaders, but the appointment of an ultra-liberal Archbishop of Canterbury, combined with the 'trendy left-wing'[6] Archbishop Habgood in York, left a legacy of unbelief in the Church of England. This became widespread across the C of E through his appointment of church officials and senior clergy with little or no commitment to a biblically-based mission. His appointments of senior leaders in the Church of England such as David Jenkins to Durham and Richard Harries to Oxford are just two examples of such liberal clergy holding influential positions in the church. But it was not only liberal bishops who were Runcie's legacy to the state church; it was officials in all areas of the Church of England's administrative machinery including officials in Lambeth Palace.

Notes

[1] See survey of clergy beliefs by Jeffrey Hadden in Chapter 5 of this book on p. 79.

[2] *Prophecy Today*, Vol 3. No2. Pages 14-15.

[3] *Ibid.*, p. 14.

[4] Clifford Hill, *All roads lead to God?* – Published in *Prophecy Today* Volume 3 No 2 March 1987, p. 14-15.

[5] *Faith in the City* — A Call for Action by Church and Nation: Report of the Archbishop of Canterbury's Commission on Urban Priority Areas, Paperback, 4 Dec 1985.

[6] This was reportedly Margaret Thatcher's description of the Archbishop of York.

Chapter Ten

REVIEWING THE EIGHTIES

Decade of Evangelism

The 1980s was supposed to be a 'Decade of Evangelism' which was recognised by both the Evangelical Alliance (EA) and the Nationwide Initiative in Evangelism (NIE). These organisations were national institutions that called assemblies to consider plans for a programme of evangelism spread across the decade which took place in the summer of 1980. We have already referred to the 'Congress on Evangelism' organised by the EA at Prestatyn in North Wales in April, and the September Assembly organised by the NIE at Nottingham. Each of these events had some good outcomes, but neither of them led to the kind of long-term evangelism beginning at the grassroots in local churches that had been envisioned by the Lambeth Group. In fact, there was no nationally co-ordinated evangelism despite visits from both Luis Palau and Billy Graham. Both the London campaign, led by Luis, and the national mission, led by Billy, produced hardly a stir in the nation and certainly did not produce the nationwide revival that many people longed to see.

Social and Industrial Unrest

The industrial unrest of the 1970s continued and the 1980s saw some of the most bitter disputes of modern times, such as the long-running miners' strike. Margaret Thatcher's Government saw this as a crucial battle for the future of industrial relationships and deliberately rejected compromise, choosing confrontation with the Trade Union Movement. The economy also went through a torrid time in the middle of the decade with the pound falling to its lowest ever value and interest rates rising to 14% in an attempt to control inflation.

Social unrest in the 1980s took on a more distinctly racial character with riots that set the South London Borough of Brixton ablaze in April 1981, when black youths went on the rampage. Further riots took place later that year in the St Paul's area of Bristol, which had a large black immigrant population. Riots also took place in Wolverhampton, Birmingham, Reading, Luton, Chester, Hull, and Preston, the causes of which were a complex mixture of unemployment, racism, poor housing and police harassment. Such scenes were repeated several times later in the decade in different parts of the country, notably in Tottenham, North London, when PC Blakelock was brutally murdered in mob violence in 1985. The level of violence in the Tottenham riots actually shocked the nation and caused a lot of people to think seriously about race and community relations.

Terrorism also escalated in Britain during the 1980s, which saw the troubles in Northern Ireland spread to England with atrocities such as the IRA bomb in Hyde Park that killed a number of police horses in 1981, and in October 1984 when an IRA bomb breached security at a Brighton hotel where the Conservative Party was holding their annual conference and narrowly failed to kill Prime Minister, Margaret Thatcher. IRA violence reached its peak with the Iniskillin Remembrance Day atrocity in Ulster on 8th November 1987 that actually proved to be a turning point in community relationships that eventually produced the Good Friday Agreement.

Faith in the City Report

As mentioned in Chapter 9, the 'Faith in the City' Report[1] was also published in 1985. Although many saw its spiritual implications, particularly in the context of the growing violence in the inner cities, others did not, and it did not make the impact it should have done. It made the mistake of focusing upon political action rather than offering a vision of change through faith in God.

Public Morality

Standards of public morality were changing rapidly. In 1982 Mary Whitehouse used the Sexual Offences Act to take a theatre company to court on the charge of gross indecency for performing on the London stage a homosexual rape scene in a play about the Romans in Britain. Five years later she launched her 'Clean Up TV Campaign' particularly focusing upon the TV soap *East Enders* where two homosexuals had embraced, which she claimed to be deeply offensive. Although there were plenty of journalists and people in the media who scorned Mary Whitehouse and ridiculed her attempts to clean up the nation's morals, there was still considerable support from those who could see the direction in which the nation was going, and twenty years later many of her critics were saying she was right. They could see that the increased secularisation was adversely affecting the nation, as divorce and the effects of family breakdown upon children were becoming more obvious.

March for Jesus

Despite there being no outbreak of revival in Britain during the 1980s, evangelicals were nevertheless quite active. A group of charismatic evangelical leaders organised a *March for Jesus* in the City of London in the summer of 1986. This was based on a similar event that had taken place in Melbourne, Australia in 1983. Roger Forster, leader of 'Ichthus', Gerald Coates the leader of the 'Pioneer' group of churches, and Lynn Green of 'Youth with a Mission' (YWAM) were the main organisers. The march was intended to be an evangelistic outreach to the general public and from its small beginnings it spread rapidly to include churches of all denominations in the following years.

All the main cities in Britain participated in co-ordinated marches, with the support of mainline churches as well as charismatic evangelicals. By 1994 the *March for Jesus* had spread worldwide and the first Global March was estimated to involve over 10 million Christians from 170 nations. The final *Global March for Jesus* in June 2000 was said to involve more than 60 million Christians in 180 nations. It was certainly a major opportunity for Christians to witness to their faith, but there were no reports of widespread revival in any of the Western nations. This was in contrast to what was happening in other parts of the world, as Monica noted in her book *Rich Christians: Poor Christians*. She saw the significance of the spread of Christianity in the materially weak nations in contrast to the decline in the Western nations.

International Church Growth

On the international scene, there were reports of the Christian Church growing at an enormous rate in many regions, particularly in Africa south of the Sahara, and in Southeast Asia. Monica wrote about this 'Christian explosion' among the poorer nations which was exciting the attention of church leaders in the West. In a book published in 1989 she said:

> The developing nations with their new and vibrant faith in God and their rapidly expanding churches are coming of age and are now beginning to share in the worldwide task of spreading the good news.... The nations that were the missionary sending nations of the nineteenth and early twentieth centuries could soon be at the receiving end of mission.[2]

On the world church scene many new churches were being formed every week, and in Britain, with the spread of the Charismatic Movement in the 1980s, there was considerable expectation of national revival. In the September 1985 issue of *Prophecy Today* we noted that this spiritual awakening was happening in the poorer nations but not in the rich Western nations. We said:

> God is giving a special privilege to the underprivileged and new power to the powerless. He is bypassing the great nations of the West with their massive economies and their mighty armies, their overfed people, their sophistication, their proud traditions of academic learning and their all-embracing self-sufficiency.

We said,

> The Kingdom is not open to the proud and haughty, but to those who are of a humble and contrite heart. There will be no revival in the West until we are prepared for the *cost* of revival. The cost

of revival is repentance and brokenness, that breaks the chains of darkness that bind us to the earth.

We could see that the greatest stumbling block to revival in the nation was actually in the church and we continually warned that there would be no revival in the nation without repentance in the church. We said,

When we (the church) come weeping before God confessing our need, there will be such an outpouring of the Spirit of God that will cleanse the church, renew a right spirit within us and will overflow into the communities around us, cleansing and renewing the life of the nation.[3]

Warning Signs

During the 1980s there were a number of events which, in the magazine *Prophecy Today*, we saw as warning signs that something was wrong in the nation. We saw a close correlation with the six warning signs given by Jeremiah in his famous Temple Sermon (Jer 7). The six sins of Jerusalem were false religion, idolatry, immorality, injustice, oppression, and murder — the shedding of innocent blood.

The first sign in July 1984 was a warning to the church about false religion that came with the lightning strike upon York Minster following the consecration of David Jenkins as Bishop of Durham. The second was a warning about turning to other gods and abandoning our Christian heritage, when the Bradford City Football Stadium burnt down a few hours after Britain's first Muslim Mayor had been sworn into office on the Qur'an. The third sign which highlighted immorality was the Government campaign about AIDS which recommended the use of condoms instead of warning against sexual promiscuity. The fourth sign was a warning about injustice and greed with the capsizing of the cross-channel ferry the Herald of Free Enterprise, as she left Zeebrugge in March 1987 with the bow doors open to save time. Many lives were lost in an effort to maximise profit, demonstrating that the pursuit of wealth was more important than human life.

On October 16 that year, 16 million trees were felled in south-east England by a hurricane force storm blocking roads and rail to the capital where the Stock Exchange was unable to open for the first time in its history. This led to world stock markets tumbling and millions of pounds being wiped off share values. 'Hurricane Friday' was followed by 'Black Monday' in the City of London as winds of panic swept through the financial markets of the world and judgement on the rich nations' economies began. The following month saw the King's Cross Underground fire that killed 30 people, and this was followed by the crash of a Midland Airways passenger plane on the M1 motorway when confusion among the pilots caused them to shut down the wrong engine. The following year, two disasters in nine days were the Clapham Junction train crash and the air crash on the Scottish town of Lockerbie when terrorists exploded a bomb in a Pan Am plane in the air over the town.

On the international scene, both the Pope and President Reagan survived assassination attempts. Britain fought a short but bloody war to regain the Falkland Islands from an Argentinian invasion, in which the 'Belgrano', an Argentinian battleship, was sunk with the loss of all hands. The USA bombed Libya and shots were fired from the Libyan embassy in London, killing WPC Fletcher. 241 US Marines and 58 French soldiers were killed by Islamic terrorists in Beirut in October 1983. Disturbances in Lebanon continued throughout the decade and an uprising in Gaza in 1988 increased instability in the Middle East. In South Africa a state of emergency was called as tensions between the white Government and the black majority increased. Natural disasters also occurred in different parts of the world with severe flooding affecting millions in Pakistan, Bangladesh and China. The shaking of the nations and the shaking of the natural environment was increasing.

This brief outline of significant events in the 1980s gives a picture of increasing disturbances on the world scene and at home in Britain, all of which increased social unease and the sense of uncertainty in the general population. Among Christians there was an increasing sense of frustration with the mainline churches. There had been great expectations aroused through the Archbishop's 'Call to the Nation' in 1975 and news that the subject of 'nationwide evangelism' was being discussed at a high level. When nothing happened on both the local and national level, church life drifted on without any apparent recognition of the increasing dangers on the world scene and the economic, industrial and social unrest in the nation. Throughout the 1980s the Church of England was led by Robert Runcie, one of the weakest Archbishops of modern times. His poor leadership stemmed fundamentally from his lack of confidence in the gospel. His liberal theology gave him no confidence in the Bible as the authoritative word of God, so he was unable to give a lead to the nation, not only in terms of a national outreach in evangelism, but also even in the application of biblical standards to the great social issues of the day.

The Social Scene

In the 1980s AIDS was spreading rapidly in Britain, among homosexuals in particular. At the 1987 General Synod of the Church of England Dr Runcie was asked for a statement on the moral implications of AIDS. He declined to do so, saying that the bishops were "waiting for guidance from the Board of Social Responsibility". In *Prophecy Today* we said:

> At the heart of Dr Runcie's dilemma there lies a deep uncertainty on the question of authority. Traditionally on all matters of belief and practice, or faith and order, the church has appealed to three sources of authority: the **Bible** as the authoritative word of God, **tradition** as the beliefs and practices of the Fathers of the church, and the guidance of the **Holy Spirit** as given to the church in solemn assembly. But Dr Runcie has presided over the demolition of all three. He has made it clear that he does not believe the Bible to be the authoritative word of God. So, when faced with a simple question as to whether AIDS is a sign of judgement on a promiscuous generation he is unable to quote Scripture as defining God's attitude toward sexual immorality.[4]

Church Decline and Growth

Runcie led the Church of England throughout the 1980s which was supposed to have been 'A Decade of Evangelism'. In fact, despite considerable evangelical activity which was largely uncoordinated, the 1980s proved to be the decade of the greatest decline in church attendance of the century. Half a million fewer people in England attended church during 1989 than were in attendance in 1979. Church attendance declined during the 1980s at the rate of 1000 per week. Even so, church attendance on Sunday 15th October 1989, the day of a national church census in England, was 3.7 million adults. That was 10% of the adult population in England. In addition, there were 1.2 million children, or 14% of the child population of England. The survey results were published by Peter Brierley in *'Christian' England*.[5]

The survey showed that the United Reformed Churches declined by 18%, the Roman Catholic Church by 14%, the Methodists by 11% and the Anglicans by 9%. At the same time, the Independent Churches grew by 42% which included 144% growth in the House Church Movement. The Pentecostals grew by 8% and the African-Caribbeans grew by 4%. The only mainline church to show an increase were the Baptists who recorded a 2% growth which reflected the greater commitment to biblical Christianity among the Baptists. The survey was important in that it revealed the greatest decline was among churches with liberal theology and the greatest growth was among those committed to biblical teaching. The report also noted that, in addition to just over 10% of the population who were regular in church attendance, a further 9% plus were occasional attenders, thus showing that nearly 20% of the population of England had active connections with the Christian churches. But the church leaders of the mainline denominations who set policy for the next decade, appeared to learn nothing from this report.

Among evangelicals in the 1980s there was a lot of talk about the possibility of revival, which increased the desire for the church to give a lead on evangelism. At the same time, the Charismatic Movement was growing both in America and in Britain, with many stories going around about exciting things happening in churches where the Holy Spirit was active. This increased the frustration especially among lay people who were in churches that were firmly rooted in tradition and refused any changes in worship or other activities. People began leaving the denominational churches in increasing numbers and gathered in house groups which often rapidly increased in size so that they outgrew domestic accommodation and they began hiring school halls and other venues. The House Church Movement that had grown slowly during the 1970s, increased rapidly during the 1980s as the statistics in the Church Survey demonstrated.[6]

The slow decline of the institutional churches was a factor in the increasing sense of insecurity in the public. It was the strong faith in God that had held the nation together in the dark days of 1940 following Dunkirk and the victory of Nazi Germany over the whole of Western Europe when Britain stood alone. The National Days of Prayer called by the King produced an overwhelming response throughout the country. Without faith and a solid foundation to the nation's belief system and social values there is little doubt that Britain could not have been mobilised to resist the threat of invasion in the way that Churchill was enabled to inspire.

By contrast, Britain at the end of the 1980s was reduced to 80% of the population having no connection to a Christian church, leaving many people viewing the future with increasing fear. The threat to world peace was seen in the rise of terrorism, coupled with the spread of weapons of mass destruction, more nations acquiring nuclear status, plus the growing awareness of international pollution of air, sea and rivers. These all resulted in greater support for organisations like the CND, the Greenham Common Women's protest and Greenpeace.

Turbulent Times

Among Christians and the more spiritually aware, socio-economic and political turbulence gave rise to an increased interest in biblical prophecy and speculation as to whether we were entering the 'end times', particularly as described in apocalyptic biblical literature. It was in response to this growing interest in prophecy, which often led to wild speculation and false prophecy, that the small support group that had gathered around me in the early 1980s, after Monica and I left the EA, recognised the need for a more academic approach to the subject of prophecy. It was this recognition that led to the publication of the magazine *Prophecy Today* and the formation of PWM (Prophetic Word Ministries). We particularly wanted to recover a biblical understanding of 'prophecy' as the word of God relevant for today and rescue it from writers such as Hal Lindsay.[7] The growth of the Charismatic Movement and the increased interest in prophecy, are subjects dealt with in other chapters. In 1989 I published a Study Book on biblical prophecy.[8]

A time of change is always a time of uncertainty and fear for the future. The 1980s saw an increase in social unrest and protests against nuclear weapons. There was a significant development of the Greenham Common camp where women chained themselves to the perimeter fence around the RAF camp. In 1983 some 70,000 protesters had formed a human chain all the way from Greenham Common to Aldermaston where there was an ordnance factory. In 1987 the women were still cutting the perimeter fence night after night. The protests continued around Greenham Common throughout the decade and beyond. It was not until 1991 that the last missiles were removed from the camp.

The proliferation of nuclear weapons around the world increased the sense of uncertainty for the future and this was the background for the message that we were taking to the nations. Far from adding to the uncertainty of the times, the message that God was active in shaking the nations was reassuring for Christians as it reaffirmed the sovereignty of God — that he was still in ultimate control; he held the nations in his hands *as a drop in a bucket* (see Isaiah 40.15). The tour of Britain that we began in 1986 continued for the next three years. But we also responded to invitations from overseas. In 1987, we did our first tour of the Far East that included Hong Kong, China, Singapore and Indonesia. At the end of the year we made our first visit to Nigeria, and in 1988 return visits to the Far East while continuing to respond to invitations from churches throughout the UK where we spoke to large meetings in Scotland, Wales and Northern Ireland – from where we also travelled south and spoke to a number of large public meetings in Dublin.

Notes
[1] See p. 65.
[2] Monica Hill, *Rich Christians, Poor Christians*, Marshall Morgan and Scott, London, 1989, p. 60.
[3] *Prophecy Today*, Vol 1, No 4, 1985, page 3.
[4] *Prophecy Today*, Vol 3, No 5.
[5] Peter Brierley, *'Christian' England*, a 240pp paperback and a larger format 416pp hardback, breakdown of the statistics; *Prospects for the Nineties: Trends and Tables from the English Church Survey*, both published by MARC Europe, London, 1991.
[6] *Ibid.*, Peter Brierley.
[7] See chapter 7 p. 79 for more on Lindsay.
[8] Clifford Hill, *Prophecy Past and Present: an exploration of the Prophetic Ministry in the Bible and in the Church Today*: Highland Books, London, 1989. Revised and Updated edition, Eagle, Guildford, 1995.

Chapter Eleven

THE CHARISMATIC MOVEMENT

Beginnings

The Charismatic Movement had no sudden commencement. It was, of course, birthed in the Pentecostal movement active from the start of the century, but Pentecostals in the UK were regarded as sects, not churches, until the 1980s when mainstream churches began experiencing the Holy Spirit. There were early signs in the 1960s when groups began exploring the gifts of the Spirit in house meetings in different parts of the country. Among the first in the traditional churches to come to national prominence were two Anglican priests: Trevor Dearing, a vicar in Hainault, Essex, and Colin Urquhart who was a vicar in Luton. Both attracted large numbers to their churches and they each began to respond to invitations to visit churches in other towns and cities. At the same time, residential communities began to be formed in different parts of the country such as Post Green, a country house near Bournemouth and Poole, founded by Graham Pulkingham and led by Jean and Elmer Darnall; and the Jesus Army in Bugbrooke, Northampton, led by Noel Stanton.

Additionally, and spontaneously, many Christians from the mainline churches began meeting in house fellowships which multiplied rapidly during the 1970s to become a distinct movement. Each of these house fellowships was composed of people seeking to explore the gifts of the Holy Spirit and to study the Bible together in order to understand the times in which we were living. Most of these little fellowships were led by enthusiastic Christians who were theologically untrained, and some of their teaching in the early days was more motivated by enthusiasm than biblical scholarship. Many of these house churches outgrew their premises and sought meeting places in local schools and community halls. In due time many of the fellowships sought links with each other and formed what became known as the New Churches.

Great Expectations

The theology of the new churches was very largely Restorationism, which was often expressed in a form of realised eschatology.[1] Its expectations were that a new movement of divine power was being poured out upon believers which would lead to the second coming of Christ and this was likely to happen soon. The expectation was that before the Parousia there would be a great nationwide spiritual revival that would transform the nation. When this was being declared in the 1970s and the early 1980s, no-one seriously believed that the year 2000 might arrive without much of this victory already well in place. The songs in Charismatic worship reflected the triumphalism that was sweeping whole congregations along with their imminent expectation of seeing signs and wonders around them. The songs spoke about marching to take the land and subdue the enemy, scattering the powers of darkness and seeing the light of Christ spreading across the country.

The expectations amongst the people of God were quite enormous and they would return in their thousands from the great Bible weeks fully expecting to see progress within the following months. Church leaders themselves expected to see a power and transformation which far exceeded anything that had been experienced in the previous 2,000 years of Church history. Attempts were made to show that throughout the years, certainly since the Reformation, the Church had become, by successive stages, more powerful and more beautiful, and now the ultimate was about to be achieved.

Restoration theology spoke of the biblical ministries in Ephesians 4 being restored to the church. They were Apostles, Prophets, Evangelists, Pastors and Teachers. Each of these ministries was expected to operate in the new churches, and with an increasing number of fellowships operating on a New Testament basis a 'New Reformation' would take place that would transform society through the exercise of divine power by the new apostles and prophets. Their authority would be recognised in the world through the signs and wonders performed by the Holy Spirit through their ministries. They would exercise 'Dominion' over secular authorities and take control of the airwaves to carry out a divine reordering of society in preparation for the Second Coming of our Lord to whom they would hand the Kingdom.

This theology is not supported by biblical teaching, and while most of the mainline churches either ignored or rejected it outright, some in the mainline churches recognised that a significant spiritual movement was taking place that had implications for the worldwide church at this particular time in world history. It was this recognition that gave an impetus to the prophetic ministry and to a renewed emphasis upon studying the ministry and message of the biblical prophets, to see what God had said and done in their times which were also times of great social and political upheaval.

Slowly the Charismatic Movement began to impact many mainline churches through their music and worship. The presence of new churches growing up alongside the traditional denominations was a challenge in many ways – not just through the loss of church members to the new churches but through the penetration of lively worship and biblical teaching. It was not just Colin Urquhart and Trevor Dearing who were affecting Anglican churches but people like John Collins at Holy Trinity Brompton and David Watson in York were also drawing large numbers to hear their teaching on the Holy Spirit and their openness to charismatic phenomena. The significance of men like Collins and Watson was that they could not be marginalised; they were respected leaders in the Anglican church, each with a following of middle and upper middle-class establishment-supporting Christians. They gave social standing to the Charismatic Movement and made it legitimate for respectable people to indulge in its free expression.

Trevor Dearing spoke at our Saturday night meetings for 'Prayer Praise and Healing' in the East End of London and I soon became friends with Colin Urquhart and David Watson, speaking at a number of meetings jointly with David and sharing with him a lot of the biblical teaching on prophecy that we were developing. In the early 1980s a fellowship of charismatic leaders developed with a small number of men who were exercising distinctive ministries and who came together once a year in December to share with each other new concepts and biblical teaching, leading to greater understanding of what was happening in our times.

I have many memories of the exciting early days of the Charismatic Movement when large crowds flocked to meetings, eager to hear biblical teaching which they did not get in the mainline denominational churches, and seeing evidence of the presence of the Holy Spirit. There was a strong sense of brotherhood and belongingness among the early Charismatic leaders, although in those days there were two groups: one composed of leaders of the house churches and another of theological-college-educated leaders who were in the traditional churches. At that stage the two groups of leaders did not mix although there was a coming together later. Initially, the meeting of charismatic leaders that I attended were all ordained ministers in the mainline denominations. I have many happy memories of working with each of them in different ways and sitting up late at night drinking coffee and deep in biblical and theological discussion, as we used to when we were undergraduates.

Lots of my most vivid memories are of these happy times some of which were quite amusing such as David Watson's story of spending the night in an old vicarage when speaking at a local church. David was always very health-conscious, and before he got into his bed he produced a small mirror and put it between the sheets to see if there was any dampness. He was quite used to old vicarages and knew what to expect. David had come prepared with a black plastic mackintosh which he put on over his pyjamas. But in the morning the vicar's wife came into the darkened room with a cup of tea which she almost dropped as she screamed in fright when David sat up like a black apparition appearing to rise up out of the bed!

A Timely Message

There was an important distinction between the message that was being delivered in the house church movement and that which was being taught in the mainline churches in the early days of the Charismatic Movement. The former already had strong elements of Dominionism, revivalism, triumphalism and the expectation of the soon return of Christ.

By contrast, the message from church leaders who had had a traditional theological training was more cautious and the primary message was a call for repentance in the church in recognition of the huge amount of biblical error, such as liberalism and replacement theology, that had robbed the church of spiritual power for centuries. It was not until 1990 when HTB promoted the Kansas City 'prophets' that Dominionism spread right through the Charismatic Movement.

The meeting at St Mark's Kennington immediately after our return from Carmel and Jerusalem in March 1986 was the beginning of an intensive period of ministry and widespread travelling both in Britain and overseas. The PWM team now included a number of preachers and teachers who grew in experience and ability. We were empowered by the knowledge of carrying a message from the Lord that had been received in Israel and endorsed by a large number of international church leaders. The reaction at all the meetings where we spoke was so positive that we were greatly encouraged. The message that God was actively shaking the nations could be seen in the daily news in the press and on television. It was a time of rapid change – social, economic, political – all combined with massive strides in technology and communications.

Watching and Praying
Everywhere we went the message was received with great interest and a positive response. The message we carried around the world was that God wanted his church to be a watching, praying people in order that they could understand what was happening in the world and how God was working out his purposes. There was also an important point in the message that God wanted his church to be a *prophetic people*, not just hearing the word but declaring the word of God to the nations through words and lifestyle in these most significant days. In this sense, the message was revelationary – explaining in biblical terms what is happening in our lifetime – and also evangelistic, equipping God's people with a message for their friends and neighbours.

This was part of what we had wanted to do with the 'Decade of Evangelism' on a nationwide basis when we were invited by Donald Coggan to lead an outreach to the nation. We believed this grassroots activity was the most effective form of evangelism, not from the top down, but from the ground up — equipping all God's people to be prophets, as Moses had wished when he said, *"I wish that all the Lord's people were prophets and that the Lord would put his Spirit on them!"* (Num 11.29).

We began using the term 'Issachars' for those whom God was calling to be his watchmen in their local area. This term comes from the account in 1 Chronicles 12:32 where men from each of the tribes came to Hebron to celebrate David becoming king over all Israel. Each of the tribes sent companies of fully armed men for David's army. But the tribe of Issachar sent something infinitely more precious. They sent a little group of those *who understood the times and knew what Israel should do* (1 Chron 12.32). This little group of intercessors would have been invaluable to David when seeking the Lord in his leadership of the nation.

Wherever meetings were held in the UK, little groups of 'Issachars' were formed. We saw these groups as forming part of a larger Issachar community — a community of watchmen for the Lord, whom God was raising, not only in the UK, but worldwide. Issachar groups had been springing up spontaneously in a number of nations, just as they had grown throughout Britain.

God was laying it upon the hearts of his people to be his watchmen, to declare his word to the nation. God was calling for a response from his people: to watch what was happening around us, to come into his presence seeking enlightenment, so that we could pray with understanding, and then to seek *his* way of declaring *his* word to the world. These Issachar groups in many places were feeding information to church leaders and to intercessors, and it was our hope that they would be the forerunners of a worldwide Issachar community, God's 'Gideon's army' within the church.

Defining Prophecy

One of the most significant things that these meetings, led by the PWM team in the 1980s, did was to call people back to the Bible for an understanding of contemporary history. The message we carried redefined 'prophecy' in its biblical context as 'declaring the word of God for our times'. Even a superficial study of the biblical prophets shows that the largest part of their message was not predicting the future but declaring the word of God to their own generation. It was the contemporary word of God dealing with the contemporary situation facing God's covenant people. This was the definition of prophecy that we used in the magazine *Prophecy Today*. In every issue, we carried the following statement:

We define 'prophecy' as the forth telling of the word of God. This was the task of the prophets in ancient Israel. It is the task of the Church today. The Church is the prophet to the world. Christ wants his Church to be a 'prophetic people' proclaiming his word to his world. It was for this reason that the Holy Spirit was given to the New Testament community of believers.

We believe that the root problems facing humanity are not simply economic, social or political, but spiritual and that the gospel is the only answer. We note that in times of crisis in ancient Israel, God used the prophets to alert people to danger, to correct their ways, to call them back to him and to direct their steps. So today, we believe God is longing to use his Church in this prophetic role in the world. The most urgent need for the nations is not to hear the opinions of human beings, but to hear the word of God. It is as a contribution towards this prophetic task that *Prophecy Today* is published.

The message that God wanted his church to be a prophetic people who understood the times and were able to present the gospel in a way that was relevant to the contemporary world situation, enabled people to make sense of what was happening in the world. It also took away fear, because it gave people the assurance that God was in control, and it equipped people with a message and a sense of purpose.

Sudden Intervention

Then suddenly, in 1990 everything changed. From being involved in a buoyant and enthusiastic movement which we believed was being directed by the Holy Spirit, suddenly we found ourselves to be on the defensive – defending biblical truth against false teaching. We were used to speaking firmly about the New Age Movement and exposing their lies and deception. But this new threat was not coming from out in the world.

It was coming from *within the church itself*, from men who claimed to be preachers of the word of God and appeared to be fine upstanding men of eloquence with a persuasive message. Suddenly our little world fell apart – confusion – we had to sort out the truth from deception – no easy task! Deception always appears attractive and closely related to the truth, otherwise it would fool no one!

John Wimber, a former rock band leader whose conversion in 1963 led him into evangelism and to an interest in church growth, came to Britain in the mid-1980s. He came with a message of power to the powerless. It was brilliant timing and could hardly have had a more seductive appeal to church leaders, especially evangelicals. The Luis Palau 'Mission to London' in 1983 and the Billy Graham 'Mission England' in 1984 had barely raised a ripple in the nation. Church attendance had been in steep decline for two decades. No one knew what to do to halt this downward slide.

The Charismatic Movement had been with us for 20 years, and while there were strong signs of growth in the House Church Movement, the growth was not being replicated in the mainline churches. There were exceptions: a few mainline churches had opened up to the Holy Spirit and recognised that the New Testament gifts of the Spirit were available today. Among those leaders, David Watson was a leading Anglican. I counted him among my friends and we did meetings together sharing a platform. I felt very much on the same wavelength as David, but I was unable to share his enthusiasm for John Wimber. It was the message of power that worried me. Of course, we needed the power of the Holy Spirit, but his trilogy of books on power concerned me. They were *Power Evangelism* (1986), *Power Healing* (1987) and *Power Encounters* (1988).They were all in a breezy American style with plenty of biblical content. But I was unhappy with their general thrust that did not appear to me to reflect sound biblical teaching. The message we had received at Carmel and Jerusalem was *Not by might nor by power, but by my Spirit, says the Lord Almighty* (Zec 4.6)), ensuring that all the glory in evangelism is given to Jesus.

Power and Dominion Theology

Wimber began speaking on power evangelism in the early 1980s. He came to Britain in 1984 at the invitation of the Bible Society to do a conference in Westminster organised by the Rev Douglas McBain, General Superintendent of the Baptist Union of London. Writing about this later, McBain said that Wimber's claim to an 'astonishingly high level of objective success' was not borne out in reality. He said "We did not witness such an encounter with the miraculous power of the Holy Spirit that revolutionised the whole concept of evangelism for us." He said that Wimber appealed to "the circus mentality to which charismatics and many evangelicals are so easily attracted ... Entertainment will not bring revival to London. It is healthy, earthed, practical, caring, converting revival that London needs." He said that Wimber's claim to 'power evangelism' was not borne out in practice although large crowds of church leaders were attracted to hear him, there were few, if any, miraculous healings.

The message of power to the powerless could not have come at a more socially significant time. The church was no longer held in high esteem as it was when I had begun my ministry in the 1950s. Preachers felt powerless. Suddenly here was a message of hope. You've been doing it all wrong, you've been appealing to the heads of the people instead of to their hearts. You've been doing everything in your own strength, not in the power of God. Power evangelism would solve all that. There was also power for healing, power for driving out demons, power for spiritual warfare, and power praise. Of course, there were elements of truth in Wimber's message. He was right in declaring that God was saying "Give me back my church!" But the Call should have been for repentance that the church had been infiltrated with so much unbelief.

By the end of the 1980s the message of power had been extended to 'Dominion Theology' – the power to subdue nations, power to exercise dominion over governments, power to conquer secular kingdoms and to establish the Kingdom of God on earth with, of course, the additional subtle attraction – the charismatic leaders themselves would be the rulers of the nations who, in due time, would hand over the kingdom to Jesus at his Second Coming.

John Wimber and the KCF

In 1988 Wimber became linked with the Kansas City Fellowship led by Mike Bickle, a former youth leader. He had already linked with Paul Cain who had announced that he was bound to Wimber for life. John Wimber had by now become attracted to 'prophecy' and was focusing upon prophecy more than on power evangelism or healing. He had a high regard for Paul Cain and his much claimed 'prophetic accuracy' although he probably did not know Cain's personal background or theology. Wimber was not a theologian or he would have recognised the Latter Rain teachings being given by Paul Cain, Bob Jones, John Paul Jackson and Mike Bickle. In his youth, Cain had been a disciple of William Branham and had never renounced Branham's heretical teachings which had caused so much confusion in the Pentecostal movement of the 1940s and 50s. The KCF leaders used to feed each other with so-called 'prophecies' and each one added to another although this practice was roundly condemned in the Bible (Jer 23.25-32). In this way, they developed a body of teaching from their own imaginations that became farther and farther divorced from the Bible and any link to reality. They spoke of God raising a 'new breed of men' in the latter days although there is no biblical basis for such teaching.

They said that the generation of children born since 1973 would be the last generation before the return of Christ and they would be endued with supernatural power, greater than that given to the Apostles in New Testament times. They built a doctrine on Jesus' words, *"I tell you the truth, anyone who has faith in me will do what I have been doing. He will do even greater things than these, because I am going to the Father"* (John 14.12). They said that Jesus was the 'Alpha Son' while the final generation would be 'Omega sons' and would be given even greater power than the Apostles because theirs was a more difficult task. Jesus and the Apostles only had to start things off by founding the Kingdom, but the Omega generation would have to round everything up by subduing the nations and establishing the worldwide reign of God. This teaching, that has no biblical foundation, became the basis of 'Dominion Theology' that is still embraced by many Charismatic churches today, particularly in America among those who have embraced the 'Emerging Church' concepts.

The KCF 'prophets' said that there would be a team of elders who would go out from Anaheim, John Wimber's church, and from Kansas City to exercise control over the churches of all denominations and to exercise governance over the nations. John Wimber was told by the 'prophets' that he would be the senior elder who had been chosen by God to exercise this world control. Sadly, Wimber believed it. And it was armed with this teaching that he was to come to London in 1990.

A New Breed
The promise of a 'new breed' was central to Cain's teaching, although it was purely a figment of the collective imagination of the KCF team. Wimber saw Cain as a divine messenger giving revelation, confirmation and support to his own teaching on 'power evangelism', power for healing and power for signs and wonders. Speaking on Wimber's platform in Anaheim in 1989, Cain said that there was going to be a worldwide spiritual awakening and the gospel was going to reach every part of the earth. He said: "God is going to reach them with the supernatural, with the power evangelism that John Wimber so eloquently speaks about. It's the power evangelism that is going to do it."[2]

Cain popularised Wimber's teaching on power evangelism. At the same meeting, he went on to give this crowd-rousing message:

God is going to raise up a people out of the people and there is going to be a bunch of nobodies from nowhere. They may not have a lot of degrees and they may not have a lot of clout and they may not have a lot of PR, they may not have a great vocabulary, they may not even be able to do more than groan in the Spirit, but if that's all they do, it's going to be power! It's going to be powerful and it's going to accomplish more than all the beautiful words of oratory in the world... The Lord is doing his new things in these last days. The gospel of the Kingdom is not just the Word, it's the Word and power! The Word will do you no good.[3]

More Power Waves
Cain did not elaborate on what he meant by saying *"the Word will do you no good"* but slips like this by a preacher usually show that something

is wrong. Cain's prediction that ordinary people with little education or status were going to be given supernatural power was highly popular and received with great acclaim. Amid much clapping, shouting, whistling and cheering, Cain told the crowd:

There's going to be something in the wave of power and evangelism in these last days. Little children are going to lay their darling little hands on the sick and heal multitudes... We're going to be just like the Lord in that respect. They're going to say, 'Here comes that dreadful, fearful army of champions. Here comes those with a word of knowledge, the word of wisdom, the working of miracles, with a healing ministry, with the power to heal the sick and raise the dead, with the power to know what's going on behind the Iron Curtain.' You're going to really be a fearful group before this thing is all over and I'm resting on that.[4]

All this was heady stuff, exciting the crowds who flocked to Cain's meetings under the patronage of Wimber. But it did enormous harm to the Charismatic Movement in the USA and Britain and other nations. It brought confusion and division to churches of all denominations that had opened up to the charismatic.

'Prophetic' Revelation
The KCF prophets all spoke of a new breed of people who would be 'dread champions', with words of knowledge and supernatural power enabling them to perform signs and wonders. They built a whole body of doctrine and teaching upon this concept. But where did the term 'dread champions' come from? It did not come from the Bible: it came from Bob Jones who had no biblical or academic training. Jones said that he had had 'a little visitation from the Lord' and that Jesus had told him a new version of Psalm 12.1. The NIV reads *"Help, Lord, for the godly are no more; the faithful have vanished from among men"*. But Jones said that God gave him a new translation. He said that Psalm 12.1 should read "Help, Lord, release the champions, the dread champions". Bob Jones is not a Hebrew scholar and he had no authority for this translation other than his claim to have had a personal visitation, giving him this

new translation by 'revelation'. But this is a man who was a highly dangerous false prophet who admitted to me in front of witnesses that he received visitations from demons in the night.

The source of this 'revelation' is unknown! But KCF teaching was based upon his so-called prophetic 'revelations'. This New Breed of children born since 1973 were said to be the final generation of believers endued with supernatural power. They would be the 'dread champions' with words of knowledge and unprecedented power. They would also be immortal. This also became part of Cain's teaching. He said:

> If you have intimacy with God, they can't kill you, they just can't. There is something about you; you are connected to that vine; you're just so close to him. Oh, my friends, they can't kill you... If you're really in the vine and you're the branch, then the life sap from the Son of the Living God keeps you from cancer, keeps you from dying, keeps you from death... Not only will they not have diseases, they will also not die. They will have the kind of imperishable bodies that are talked about in the 15th chapter of [1] Corinthians... This army is invincible. If you have intimacy with God, they can't kill you.[5]

It was on the basis of this teaching that Bob Jones developed his 'Joel's Army'. All the KCF prophets added to this and it became part of their basic Restorationist teaching. It was all based, not upon the Bible, but on a supposed 'revelation' given to one of the false prophets —Bob Jones.

Jack Deere, one of KCF's teachers said,

> This army is unique.... When this army comes, it's large and it's mighty. It's so mighty that there has never been anything like it before. Not even Moses, not even David, not even Paul. What's going to happen now will transcend what Paul did, what David did, what Moses did, even though Moses parted the Red Sea.[6]

Joel's Army

Wimber himself embraced this 'Joel's Army' false teaching and it became a central part of his message that he gave at the Excel Centre London in October 1990. But their whole concept of 'Joel's Army' being an army of Holy Spirit-filled servants of the Lord is a reversal of Scripture; it is turning the Bible upside down.

Joel brought a strong warning to Israel by means of a horror story about a swarm of great locusts eating every bit of vegetation on the land with a second swarm of young locusts eating any little bits that might have been missed by the great locusts. He used the story to wake up the nation to the danger of an invasion from a powerful army that would plunge through the defences without breaking ranks. They would rush upon the city and run along the walls climbing into the houses and shaking the earth. Joel saw this as God bringing judgment and destruction upon the nation. He said, *The Lord thunders at the head of his army; his forces are beyond number, and mighty are those who obey his command. The day of the Lord is great, it is dreadful. Who can endure it?* (Joel 2.11).

Joel foresaw God allowing this enemy army to come upon his people in the land of Zion as judgment for their sinfulness. So, he called upon them urgently to repent and turn to the Lord who alone could defeat this wicked, all-destroying army. Biblical scholars argue over the date of Joel and are not sure whether he is warning against a Scythian invasion or Babylonian or even Greek. Some scholars believe that the dating of the Book of Joel comes from the 8th Century BC, while others think it is really late, around 410 BC. Whatever the date, the message is clear, Joel's Army of locusts is an evil army and part of God's judgement, not an army of Spirit-filled believers! Biblical scholars all agree with this.

Kansas City

My personal introduction to the Kansas City Prophets came a year before their first visit to Britain. I had heard that there was a group of men exercising prophetic ministries in the USA and I was naturally keen to know them and what was happening there. I discussed it with the PWM trustees in September 1989 and it was agreed that I and one of our trustees, Bruce Pullman, should visit Kansas City to meet with these men. Quite unexpectedly, I was approached by Bishop David Pytches saying that he had just returned from Kansas City and he was writing a book about this group of prophets and he would be greatly honoured if I would write a Foreword to his book. I responded warmly saying that I too was shortly to go to Kansas City but I would like to see his manuscript before writing the Foreword.

Bruce and I duly went to Kansas City in November 1989 and linked with Bruce Yocum, one of the pioneers in the American Charismatic Movement and author of the first book on modern prophecy that I had read.[7] We had a number of meetings with the KCF leaders Mike Bickle and John Paul Jackson, and we attended a prayer meeting and one of their public meetings. On one occasion one of the leaders, Jim Goll, took us to Bob Jones' home to meet with KCF's 'senior prophet'. We spent the morning there listening to his stories of having been converted from a life of alcoholism, drugs and crime. He said that he regularly received nightly angelic visitations and he often battled against demonic visits.

Jones claimed to receive regular revelations, often four or five in one day or night. He then said he wanted to link hands with me and see what God would reveal to him. By this time, the warning bells were ringing very loudly in my ears and I sought to conclude the visit as soon as possible. When we had entered the house, I had sensed a demonic presence and I felt that I had to be honest with him and tell him this. To my surprise, he did not deny it but said that it was his wife who had a problem with demon possession — he and the KCF leaders had tried a number of times to cast it out but they had been unable to do so.

David Pytches' Book

As soon as I returned from meeting the KCF leaders in November 1989 I telephoned David Pytches and reported my experience. He was quite dismissive, so Bruce and I went to see him and gave him a more detailed account of our concerns about these men, but David was determined to continue with his book. He ignored my request to see the manuscript and he dropped his request for me to write the Foreword. I heard nothing more until the book was published in May 1990. John Wimber was due to bring a team from KCF to Holy Trinity Brompton in July and David Pytches wanted his book to pave the way for their visit.

I wrote an extended review of the book *Some Said It Thundered* in the July 1990 issue of *Prophecy Today*. I said:

It is with great sadness that I have concluded that this book is both dangerous and potentially damaging for the spiritual health and unity of the church in Britain... It gives story after story of what are best described as 'paranormal experiences'... It makes no attempt to describe genuine prophecy or give sound biblical teaching... It adulates men and does nothing to glorify the Lord Jesus Christ.[8]

In the same issue of *Prophecy Today* I said:

Last November David Pytches asked me to write a Foreword to his book but after returning from a visit to Kansas City in December I told him my serious doubts concerning this ministry. I strongly advised him not to rush into print commending men whom he had met only once or twice... I suggested the 'Gamaliel principle' (wait and see). Only harm could be done by hasty reaction to a new ministry and by sensationalising signs and wonders.

The book sold out the first edition in a month, but my warnings were fully confirmed when Ernest Gruen, pastor of a Kansas City church, published a 200-page document listing the errors in teaching and false prophecies of the KCF leaders. At the same time, I was contacted by Hodder & Stoughton who said that they might not have published the book had they known that I was unhappy with it. By this time, Mike Bickle had also issued a statement saying that there were many errors in the book, but Hodder had already printed a second edition which they pulped.

False Prophecy at HTB

The two-week visit of the KCF team under John Wimber's leadership at Holy Trinity Brompton in July 1990 was fully booked, having been popularised by some high-power publicity which generated much excitement due to the prophecies of revival beginning in London at that event. Paul Cain prophesied that the full revival would begin in October when John Wimber was due to lead large meetings at the Excel Centre East London.

My colleagues David Forbes, Nicholas Rivett Carnac[9] and I went to meet the KCF team in the Rectory at Holy Trinity Brompton at the conclusion of their two-week conference. We spent most of the day talking with John Wimber, Mike Bickle, Paul Cain, Sandy Millar and David Pytches.

The morning meeting began with Wimber strongly questioning what I had published in *Prophecy Today*. He said that I was damaging his ministry and he wanted me to retract the things that I had said in the magazine. I said that what I had written was the truth and could not be retracted. I had simply dealt with the false prophecies published in David Pytches' book. I also told him that the prophecies given by Paul Cain and Bob Jones of a great revival in Britain beginning in October 1990 were false: they would not happen and it was wrong to mislead the public with false promises. I had said this publicly in *Prophecy Today* where I had said that God was calling for repentance and was not promising revival. I affirmed that I could not retract it because what I had said was the truth. I pleaded with him not to go ahead with his proposed visit to the Excel Centre because the event was based upon false prophecy and it would do immense harm to the churches in Britain.

After an hour or so of discussion in which all present took part, Wimber said that if I were prepared to retract the things that I had published in the magazine he would be happy to invite me to America to do some teaching at his church in Anaheim, California. I thanked him for the honour that he was offering me but I said that it would not be possible for me to deny the truth of what I had said. Wimber then became even more emphatic, saying that unless I supported his ministry, judgment would fall upon me. I said that my greatest fear was in misleading the Lord's people and that I would rather God took me out of ministry if I was not speaking the truth.

Once again, I explained that there was a great deal of immorality, unbelief and false teaching in the churches in Britain which made them unready for revival. I strongly believed that *God was calling for repentance in the churches and not promising revival*. Sadly, my warnings fell upon stony ground. John Wimber would not listen, and he continued saying some very hard things of the judgment that would fall upon me unless I retracted my words and supported him and his ministry.

I related to John my own experience of visiting Bob Jones' home when I had discerned a demonic presence, which Jones had affirmed – attributing it to his wife. John said that he was aware of the demonic problem in Bob Jones' life, but he nevertheless was convinced that he was a genuine prophet with a high level of accuracy. He said that because Bob Jones had a problem he did not allow him to speak on the public platform with him. He only allowed him to minister to church leaders. I was shocked by this and I expressed my dismay because I knew some of the men to whom Jones had 'prophesied'. I said that I was very unhappy that this man had laid his hands upon ministers of churches in Britain.

In the afternoon we were joined by about 30 or 40 church leaders from different sectors of the mainline churches and Independent Churches. We met in one of the small halls at HTB. Nicholas Rivett Carnac chaired the meeting which was to consider the truth or falsity of what I had published in the magazine. It was not an easy meeting, although both Bickle and Cain admitted many errors in their ministry and the immaturity in the KCF leadership that had been exposed by Ernest Gruen and my article in *Prophecy Today*. They both said that many of the stories reported in *Some Said It Thundered* were not true, and John Wimber reported that he had strongly advised David Pytches against publishing the book because of the immaturity of the ministry. Nicholas called upon David Pytches to repent, and to acknowledge that he should not have published the book. This he refused to do. It was a sad and difficult day with huge implications for the future of the Evangelical/Charismatic churches in Britain.

David Pytches and Sandy Millar, with the backing of many Charismatic Church leaders, had already booked the Excel Centre in East London and they were determined to go ahead with the meetings in October. Wimber declared that Paul Cain was never wrong in his prophecies and they were fully convinced that they would see revival. The meeting in HTB ended in stalemate without even a time of prayer, so there was no seeking the Lord together for his word. The American group went back to the USA and the British leaders went their separate ways with major issues of the truth or falsity of the KCF teaching left unresolved.

The Excel Centre Meetings

The October 1990 meetings at the Excel Centre went ahead as planned, drawing large crowds every day. A number of leading evangelicals had issued a statement prior to the meetings stating their support for the KCF team and urging people to attend the meetings. The statement was issued as a press-release from HTB by Sandy Millar.

At the meetings, John Wimber and other members of the team affirmed their 'restorationist' teaching, speaking about 'a new breed of men' and an 'army of locusts' who would sweep across the country as Holy Spirit revival gathered momentum. It would reach Scotland and sweep across to the Continent. Wimber was so convinced that Paul Cain's prophecies were accurate that he brought his whole family including his grandchildren over to witness the beginning of the great revival that he was to lead.

But there was no outpouring of the Spirit of God. On the last day, John was commanding the Holy Spirit to come but, like the prophets of Baal on Mount Carmel trying to call down fire in the presence of Elijah, there was no response. He returned to America a bitterly disappointed man.

John Wimber's Repentance

It was not long after the Excel Meetings that John Wimber contracted cancer of the throat which virtually finished his ministry. He died in November 1997 but not before he had dropped Paul Cain and Bob Jones from his ministry team, and cut off the Kansas City Fellowship from the Vineyard group of churches.

Wimber also severed connections with the Toronto Airport Church where the so-called 'Toronto Blessing'[10] was in full swing. He gave an interview to *Christianity Today* that was published in the USA in August 1997, in which he made a lot of corrections to the teaching he had been giving and publicly repented of the false teaching for which he had been responsible in Vineyard churches and false prophecy which he had believed. In September that year he and I spoke on the telephone. John repented of the hard things he had said to me and we were able to express love for each other. I arranged to visit him, but sadly he passed away before that was possible. We were at least reconciled two months before he died, which I feel sure was important for both of us.

Aftermath of Excel Meetings

Inevitably there was a huge amount of disappointment and disillusionment after the Excel Meetings. False prophecy is highly divisive, but it is impossible to know how much harm it did among Christians in Britain who had fully embraced the promises. It was not just the hosting of the July conference by HTB and the hype of the October meetings that did harm, but their endorsement by so many prominent British church leaders. A ringing endorsement of the Kansas City Team had been sent out by Sandy Millar from HTB in July 1990 which was published in *Renewal* magazine[11] and elsewhere, naming a list of leaders who, it was claimed, had examined the teaching of the KCF team which they found to be faithful to Scripture and they warmly commended their ministry to the British people. All these men were well-known British church leaders.[12]

I am not aware of any of those who signed this endorsement of KCF repenting publicly. Of course, they may have repented quietly before God, but having gone public they surely should have apologised publicly. Americans are much more ready to confess error and seek forgiveness and move on than Brits. British leaders tend to hang onto errors doggedly as long as possible. Then, when their statements are shown to be totally untrue, they put their heads down, keep very quiet and hope that everyone will have forgotten the things they said.

I felt that there was still an unresolved issue between myself and Sandy Millar concerning what I had said in *Prophecy Today* — that prophecies which had been given at HTB were false. I hoped to meet Sandy and tried to do so several times, but sadly no meeting has taken place.

It is a strange anomaly that HTB, the church that has arguably done more than any other church in Britain in outreach activities — through the Alpha Course, which reaches a worldwide audience — should also have been responsible for doing harm to the gospel in Britain. Sandy Millar was largely responsible for the enormous expansion of HTB's ministry during his 20 years of leadership from 1985 to 2005. Yet he was also responsible for the invitation to John Wimber and the Kansas City 'prophets' to do two weeks' ministry at HTB in July 1990. And he was also the leading sponsor of John Wimber's meetings at the Excel Centre in October 1990. These two events did enormous damage, not only to tens of thousands of individual Christians who were misled by false teaching and false prophecy, but also to the hundreds of churches in Britain who embraced the false doctrine of Dominionism that prepared the way for the injection of the great deception of the Toronto Blessing in 1994 and the serious division which that brought between churches and between individual Christians. It pains me to record these things, but it is necessary to note the level of deception that entered the church at this time and the enormous harm that was done to the mission of the gospel in Britain.

There are sound grounds for believing that there was a genuine move of God in the 1960s to 1980s that could have impacted the nation, but false prophecy and false teaching were widely distributed in mainline churches as well as the new churches. HTB and St Andrew's Chorleywood, two of the most influential Anglican churches in the Greater London area, were at the heart of this movement, promoting and distributing false teaching that did immense harm to the gospel in Britain. Nobody likes to speak about this now. We are all very British and we keep quiet about our failures, but this means that we learn nothing from past error which leaves the church wide open to the next wave of deception that will undoubtedly come flooding in at an appropriate time.

Notes

[1] There is an extensive literature on 'Realised Eschatology' which is usually associated with liberal theologians rather than conservative evangelicals. The term was first used by C.H. Dodd in his work on the Fourth Gospel. But in terms of the early days of the developing New Churches it refers to their expectations that eschatological prophecy was actually being fulfilled in the contemporary world and that the second coming of Christ would be seen in their lifetime.

[2] This prophecy is based upon teaching that came from the Latter Rain Revival Movement that began in the Sharon Bible School, North Battlefield, Canada in 1948. It was roundly condemned as heretical by the General Assembly of the Assemblies of God in the USA in the autumn of 1949. The Latter Rain Revival taught that God was restoring the offices of 'apostle' and 'prophet' who would be the key to raising a glorious end time church to rule the world. This teaching became central to 'Restorationism'. It is still taught today by a church in Redding California led by Bill Johnson although there is no biblical basis for such teaching.

[3] Quoted in Clifford Hill et al, *Blessing the Church*, Eagle Publishers, Guildford, 1995, p. 128.

[4] *Ibid.*, p. 132.

[5] Sadly, it was only five years after this teaching that John Wimber died of cancer in the throat.

[6] *Blessing the Church*, p. 133.

[7] Bruce Yocum, *Prophecy: Exercising the Prophetic Gifts of the Spirit in the Church Today*, Servant Books, USA, 1973.

[8] *Prophecy Today*, Vol 5, No 4.

[9] Nicholas was the Rector of St Mark's Kennington and was also a trustee of PWM and a member of our Ministry Team. He had previously been a curate at HTB. David Forbes was my Colleague and Deputy.

[10] Dealt with in the next chapter.

[11] *Renewal* magazine, in the USA, August 1990.

[12] Some of the names on the list are in *Blessing the Church*, p. 204.

Chapter Twelve

FALSE TEACHING

Latter Rain Again

The Excel Centre London meetings in October 1990 left many Christians in dismay and disillusionment. Their leaders had promised so much and it had all come to nothing. But it was not long before the same teaching bounced back in a different guise. It was less than three years later that another group of leaders began to proclaim the same 'Latter Rain' teachings that a great spiritual harvest was coming and the excitement began all over again. This is Rodney Howard Browne 'prophesying' at a Kenneth Copeland meeting in 1993:

> This is the day, this is the hour, saith the Lord, that I am moving in this earth... This is the day when I will cause you to step over into the supernatural... For the drops of rain are beginning to fall of the glory of God... This is the day of the glory of the Lord coming in great power... Many shall rub their eyes and say, 'Is this the person we used to know? For there is a fire inside him.' For this is the day of the fire and the glory of God coming into his church.[1]

You see in this prophecy all the elements of the classical 'Latter Rain' teachings of Franklin Hall. You see the 'rain', the 'fire', the 'power' and the 'glory' falling upon an elite company of believers, enduing them with supernatural power.

Latter Rain Teaching

The basic 'Latter Rain' teaching given by the Kansas City prophets in the 1980s was that those who were born in the previous decade would be the last generation to be born prior to the Second Coming of Jesus and they would actually witness his arrival.[2] By 1990 Kansas City Fellowship had been incorporated into the Vineyard group of churches under the leadership of John Wimber. At that stage their teaching of dates appeared to be revised from the final generation being born in 1973, to saying that the world had entered into the last days in 1990 and that there were 40 years left.

During this time the elite believers of the 'Latter Rain' would perform signs and wonders, stretching out their hands to immobilise the enemies of Christ and gain power in the nations in order to prepare the way for the coming of Christ. They said that when the army of 'overcomers' had established the Kingdom, Christ would come again to receive it. They further taught that an elite group of 'apostles' was being founded, led by John Wimber who would exercise 'Dominion Power' over the world. They would control the airwaves and governments of the nations. This elite group would perform greater signs and wonders than the original Apostles. They gave the same teaching that had been given in the previous wave, namely that the original Apostles were the Alpha Apostles and today's generation of super apostles would be the Omega Generation.

Originators of the Movement

There is an observable connection between Rodney Howard Browne and the Toronto Blessing, but it is interesting to note that John Wimber also claimed to be the father of the Toronto Blessing in the early days, saying that outbursts of laughter and other uncontrollable physical phenomena were occurring at his meetings long before Toronto.

Whoever was the originator, Rodney Howard Browne, Kenneth Copeland, Benny Hinn, Kenneth Hagin, the 'faith/prosperity teachers', or Wimber, Vineyard, Kansas City — you come back to the same source — the *Latter Rain heresy of the 1940s* with William Branham, Franklin Hall, George Warnock, the Hawtin Brothers and *the North Battlefield Group* with their prophecies of an end time, glorious and victorious church without spot or wrinkle which would predate the Second Coming of Christ and arise out of the great spiritual harvest of the last days? But all this is totally unbiblical.[3] There is not a shred of biblical teaching to back it up. It is an invention of the human mind, with odd scraps of the Bible ripped from their context as pseudo-proof texts.

There is nowhere in the Bible that prophesies a time of great end-time harvest. Jesus certainly speaks of a great gathering of the nations in front of him at his Second Coming, but it will be a time of judgement when he separates the good from the evil. He said all the nations will be gathered before him, and he will separate the people one from another as a shepherd separates the sheep from the goats (see Matt 25.32).

As noted in Chapter Eleven, the October 1990 issue of *Renewal* magazine in Britain, carried a statement under the names of many prominent church leaders in Britain stating that they had 'examined the teaching and practice of the Kansas City Prophets' and could find no fault with it. They commended them as men of exemplary character. Less than a year later, Bob Jones was exposed for gross sexual sin, misusing his so-called prophetic gifts to elicit sexual favours from women. Clearly the British Church leaders had been deceived in more ways than one. The statement was sent out on Holy Trinity Brompton notepaper in July 1990 and issued as a press release. The statement was no doubt prompted by the document issued by Ernest Gruen denouncing the KCF teaching, to which we also referred in *Prophecy Today*.

As far as I am aware none of the British Church leaders who signed the statement commending the KCF team to the British people, and urging Christians to attend the Excel Centre meetings, later retracted their statements or issued apologies for having misled many people. Certainly, the predictions of a great revival starting in London and spreading across the UK onto the Continent were all proved to be worthless.

But the church leaders, particularly David Pytches and Sandy Millar who so strongly promoted Wimber and the KCF team, never repented publicly of the level to which they personally had been deceived, and, as far as I am aware, they never apologised to all those who trusted their judgement. As Douglas McBain, leader of the London Baptist Union, said,

So again, God's good people have travelled great distances and paid large conference fees in order to stand the chance of getting some personal revelation.[4]

This was a measure of the hunger in the hearts of church leaders in Britain at this time. It overrode their rational processes.

Toronto Blessing

Great was the disappointment and disillusionment left in the wake of the Excel Centre meetings in October 1990. This paved the way for the new experience which became known as the 'Toronto Blessing'. It began in the Toronto Airport Church in January 1994. People were hungry for revival that had been promised by the Kansas City Prophets, and the fact that so many church leaders had commended them left those church leaders vulnerable to deception because they were desperate to see the fulfilment of what they had publicly supported. There were strange phenomena of physical shaking, laughter and even animal noises. Whilst some Christians present at the meetings subsequently testified of blessing and good fruit in their lives, there was inadequate spiritual discernment by leaders, and many of the reported phenomena were unbiblical.

The Church of England Newspaper published a banner headline[5] – **REVIVAL BREAKS OUT IN LONDON CHURCHES** with a subheading **Church Leaders admit bewilderment as manifestations affect business and staff meetings as well as church services.**

Where was this great revival breaking out according to the C of E newspaper? It was in none other than Holy Trinity Brompton and Vineyard Churches linked with John Wimber – the very place that had hosted the KCF team just four years earlier. The opening paragraph of the report was:

A number of charismatic churches in and around London have been experiencing a sudden revival in the weeks since Pentecost, leading to dramatic and unusual scenes during Sunday services, which they say are due to the Holy Spirit.

This uncritical acceptance of the phenomena as being a 'revival' inevitably caused some more cautious observers to say that before regarding this as a genuine revival we should wait to see the fruit. This is, of course, one of the tests, but before waiting for the fruit we should examine the *root*. Jesus not only said *"By their fruit you will recognise them"*, but, *"Do people pick grapes from thorn bushes, or figs from thistles?"* (Matt 7.16). Of course, you cannot pick grapes from thorn bushes. If the root of the bush is a wild blackberry or a thistle it will not produce grapes or figs. Examining the root involves identifying the people who were the originators and propagators of the experience.

Kenneth Copeland, a well-known word/faith proponent, published a statement at the same time as the C of E Newspaper, in which he declared the phenomenon to be the herald of the last days:

The reports are coming in from every quarter. The glory is here! God is manifesting his divine presence among his people. These are no minor showers of blessings either. They are the first waves of the great and final outpouring of the glory of God upon this earth. The former and latter rain of the Holy Spirit has begun to flood this planet like never before in history. The King is coming! And you can begin to count his return not just in decades and years but in days. This is it. This is the last days... Can you imagine somebody walking around with the power that Elisha and Elijah had and the power that Peter and Paul had – all at the same time? It is about to happen! If you get your act straightened up and get yourself moving in the Spirit of God, it will happen to you. It won't matter whether you have been to Bible School or not, my friend. If you will dare to believe God, you can get in on this glorious event... You'd better have your glory bag packed because we will be raptured out of this place![6]

This statement contained the keywords of the Latter Rain movement with the 'showers of blessing' and the 'glory of God' with the addition of power to the people and the imminent expectation of the rapture.

In *Prophecy Today* we took a cautious line, not wishing to condemn out of hand what was happening. But the very fact that the originators of what was already being called 'the laughing revival' were people like Rodney Howard Browne and Kenneth Copeland made us nervous. The *Sunday Telegraph*[7] also gave publicity to the strange phenomena. It reported an Anglican bishop in Toronto rolling on the floor and roaring like a lion. A church in Brighton was reported to have had a three and a half hour service where there was screaming and shouting culminating in a growing crescendo of the whole congregation growling.

Jeremiah associated this kind of phenomenon with the occult spirit of Babylon. *Her people all roar like young lions, they growl like lion cubs* (Jer 51.38). This was followed by a declaration of judgment upon Babylon, *"I will set out a feast for them and make them drunk, so that they shout with laughter – then sleep for ever and not awake," declares the Lord* (Jer 51.39).

The Toronto phenomenon did not, as some thought, start in Canada in January 1994 with a visit from Randy Clark,[8] it began some time earlier with the South African evangelist Rodney Howard Browne, who toured the USA during 1993 drawing large audiences whom he would bring 'under the power'. Like Benny Hinn he would only have to blow on the audience for whole sections to fall down. Rodney's speciality, however, was to have those who fall down begin to laugh uncontrollably, supposedly with the joy of the Lord.

Many of those who fell down shook uncontrollably and cried out with various sounds or animal noises. Often those who fell down were unable to get up and were robbed of speech so that they were unable to describe what had happened to them or give a testimony. Browne used to describe himself as a 'Holy Spirit bartender' as he made people drunk – supposedly with the Holy Spirit – and videos[9] show him walking up and down in front of the audience chanting a mantra which prompted people to laugh. The laughter infected other people until the whole audience was falling about and laughing uncontrollably when asked for their testimonies. A young pastor and his wife were brought up onto the stage but became helpless and speechless. It seems inconceivable that the Holy Spirit would prevent someone from giving a testimony of faith that would glorify Jesus. Surely, any mature Christian in the audience witnessing such a phenomenon would have realised that Rodney Howard Browne was operating through an alien spirit – certainly not the Spirit of Truth that Jesus promised would come upon his disciples.[10]

Browne and Copeland

The following is a transcript from a video of one at Howard Browne's prophecies when he was speaking at a meeting in September 1993, hosted by Kenneth Copeland. We have already mentioned this at the beginning of this chapter: note the use of key words, 'rain', 'fire' and 'glory'.

This is the day, this is the hour, saith the Lord, that I am moving in this earth. This is the day when I will cause you to step over into the realm of the supernatural. For many a preacher has prophesied of old that there is a move coming. But it is even now, and even at the door. For the drops of rain are beginning to fall of the glory of God. Yes! Yes! Many of you who have sat on the threshold and have said, 'O God when shall it be?' Oh you shall know that this is the day, and this is the hour, when you shall step over into that place of my glory. This is the day of the glory of the Lord coming in great power. I am going to break the mould, says the Lord, on many of your lives, and on many of your ministries, and the way you have operated in days gone by. Many shall rub their eyes and say, 'Is this the person we used to know?' For there is a fire inside him. For this is the day of the fire and the glory of God coming into his church. Rise up this day and be filled afresh with the new wine of the Holy Ghost.[11]

These were heady words, especially when given in the context of an act of worship and in the presence of a large congregation where choruses were endlessly repeated and the thought processes of all but the sharpest minds were dulled. This prophecy sounds like a wonderful promise coming directly from God, but it is false prophecy. It appeals powerfully to a power-hungry generation of people who feel powerless to stand against the disintegrating forces of moral and social and economic decay which are driving the nations towards the brink of disaster. It is small wonder that many people responded with great enthusiasm to this false 'prophecy' and others like it, in the meetings where Howard Browne and other Latter Rain preachers held meetings.

There are few Christians who would not like to receive a mighty outpouring of the power of God, but this is a false hope based upon faulty biblical exegesis. The Bible says it is *Jesus* who will subdue the nations; before *Him* every knee shall bow, not the followers of Rodney Howard Browne, or John Wimber, or Sandy Millar. Moreover, it will not be through the exercise of human power. It will be when Jesus returns to the earth on the day fixed by the Father. Jesus himself will establish a reign of righteousness and he will get all the glory. It will certainly not be left to unrighteous human beings to subdue the nations and present the Kingdom to Jesus. This is not only false prophecy, but verges on the blasphemous.

Kenneth Copeland, whose platform Howard Browne was sharing when he gave the above prophecy, added a prophecy of his own saying that those present were receiving an outpouring of power and that they would go out different people. People would fall at their feet in the shopping malls and say, 'I see Jesus in you'. Then he added, 'and your table will be full!' So, the promise he gave was not only for power, but for *prosperity*!

At the same meeting, Howard Browne went on to exhort the people to submit their wills to him and not to weigh what was happening. He said:

Don't try to work it out with your natural mind for the things of the Spirit of God are foolishness to the natural mind. But just let it bubble out of your belly, for the Scripture says, *'Out of your belly shall flow rivers of living waters'* – rivers – go ahead – let it flow right out of your belly!

This instruction not to weigh a prophetic word is directly against New Testament teaching. Paul very clearly said that *all prophecy should be weighed*.[12] So, too, was the instruction not to work things out with the 'natural mind'.

Howard Browne soon had the whole audience falling about in uncontrollable laughter. Clearly none of them had any realisation that this was false teaching because if they were truly born again believers they should not be controlled by a 'natural mind'! Their minds would have been renewed by the Spirit of God. Paul's teaching on this is very clear. He says: *Those who live according to the sinful nature have their minds set on what that nature desires; but those who live in accordance with the Spirit have their minds set on what the Spirit desires* (Rom 8.5). The Holy Spirit also enables each believer to know when they are being deceived – provided they do not willingly submit themselves to charlatans and deceivers! No wonder Jesus warned that the day would come when *"...false prophets will appear and perform great signs and miracles to deceive even the elect – if that were possible"*.[13]

Lack of Conversions

There were very few reports of unbelievers being converted in meetings called for the propagation of the Toronto Blessing. There was no emphasis upon repentance and responding to the gospel and certainly no evidence of large numbers coming under the conviction of sin and turning to the Lord. Most observers agreed that the Toronto experience was not a revival and many of its supporters called it 'a time of refreshment'. But, as Chris Hand, a young Baptist pastor, reported in *Prophecy Today*,[14] the usual testimony by people who had received the Toronto experience was that their love for Jesus had increased. He said:

> In fact when a television company wished to include testimonies of people for a programme they were making on the 'Toronto Blessing', there was genuine difficulty in finding suitable candidates with a testimony that would carry any weight or intelligibility outside the confines of the church.

Chris said that after five months of much soul-searching and prayer he and his wife left his church in Richmond.

The first public mention of what became known as the Toronto Blessing was in a newsletter of October 1993 sent out by the Trinity Broadcasting Network USA, announcing:

> Many churches are beginning to explode with REVIVAL. God is sending missionaries from other lands to America, including Reinhard Bonnke from Germany and Rodney Howard Browne from South Africa. Thanks to these and many others, a fresh wave of revival and a new joy of the Lord is sweeping the land.

By the summer of 1994, the so-called 'revival' sparked off by Browne's preaching was spreading like wildfire, not only in America. There were reports from Argentina, Canada and Australia, that massive crowds were gathering at meetings where 'holy laughter' and other manifestations were breaking out. In Argentina, people were reported to be so drunk with the Spirit that they could not drive home after services lasting up to six hours, with hundreds of Pentecostal and Charismatic Churches throughout Argentina becoming involved.[15]

Great Division

Before I heard news of the manifestations, in the spring of 1994, I had been at my family home near Rye in East Sussex where I had witnessed a fight in a normally docile flock of sheep with ewes attacking each other, resulting in the death of one of them. Through this incident, God warned me that an alien spirit was loose among the flock which would bring about a great division. A short time later I was sent a video (referred to above) of Howard-Browne speaking at a meeting in Birmingham where a Scottish pastor and his wife were struck dumb and powerless to give their testimony, with Howard Browne mocking them and causing the audience to laugh uncontrollably.

It was just possible to hear a man at the back praying loudly, "Father let your will be done!" Howard Browne reacted strongly, calling for the bouncers to stop the man. He said "That man over there praying! Tell him to shut up!" Three burly stewards hurried to do his bidding. He continued, "You can do anything you like in this meeting; you can shout, scream, laugh, turn cartwheels, anything you like, but I am the only one who speaks!" Clearly the great deception had arrived. Howard Browne could not tolerate a godly man in his meeting praying to the Lord!

My colleague David Noakes went to Toronto in the autumn of 1994 to the *Catch the Fire* conference. He reported on a mixture of blessing and deception, saying, "I would identify a good deal of what I saw as proceeding from demonic spirits associated with occult practices, particularly voodoo." He said that John Arnott appeared to be a sincere and godly man but he made no attempt to distinguish between what was of the Holy Spirit and what was either of the flesh or demonic. It was simply assumed that everything that was happening was inspired by the Holy Spirit.

Johannes Facius, the Director of 'International Intercessors', also paid a visit to the Toronto Airport Vineyard Fellowship and he sent me the following report:

> The Toronto Blessing is a matter of personal renewal. There does not seem to be any significant corporate experience connected to it, such as is seen in Acts 4.23–31, where the entire church lifted up its voice to God in intercessory prayer. The pastor of the Toronto Vineyard himself compared the experience to 'children coming to the Father to play'. We therefore know what level of instruction we are dealing with, and it is the children's level. Wherever we find people running after blessings and personal experiences we know we are dealing with spiritual children. Paul encountered this in the Church at Corinth. He said he could not give them solid food but was obliged instead to provide them with milk. They were still babes in Christ. The pastor in the Toronto Church underlined the importance of being like little children according to Matthew 18.2-5, but he forgot to emphasise that this scripture deals with the attitude at conversion, and that 'child-likeness' is one thing, but 'childishness' is quite another.

Experiential

The great danger was that the whole emphasis was upon *experience* rather than the teaching of the Word of God. One video shows Rodney Howard Browne addressing an audience of thousands who cheer as he declares, "Don't try to understand this. Don't you know the natural mind cannot receive the things of the Spirit of God?" This is a dangerous misquotation of Scripture as Peter Fenwick pointed out in his contribution to *Blessing the Church*.[16] It is based upon Paul's statement in 1 Corinthians 2.14: but Paul does not say *the natural **mind***, he is referring to *the natural **man***. The NIV is a rather poor translation: the Greek literally says: *But the natural man does not receive the things of the Spirit of God, for they are foolishness to him and he cannot know them because they are spiritually discerned.*[17] Paul clearly is speaking about unconverted human beings, not mature Christians who know the Bible.

Browne's teaching was that people had to stop thinking about what was happening and simply submit themselves to it. His wife, Andronica, told her own experience. She said she was offended when she first heard her husband say 'I command you to laugh!" Eventually she let down her guard and 'stepped into another dimension', ceasing to think about what was happening.[18]

This command not to think about what was happening is clear evidence of a controlling spirit, and a denial of biblical teaching. Paul says very clearly that we are to test the spirit: *Test everything. Hold on to the good. Avoid every kind of evil* (1 Thess 5.21). The word of God is given to us so that we can know the truth. Jesus promised that he would ask the Father and he would give the Holy Spirit to be with us for ever — *"the Spirit of truth"* (John 14.17). He said that *"The Holy Spirit, whom the Father will send in my name, will teach you all things and remind you of everything I have said to you"* (John 14.26). We have to use our minds to search the Scriptures and to understand the word of God and the teaching of Jesus.

Maturity is not one of the gifts of the Spirit. It is available to all Christians all the time and comes through prayer and study of the word of God – the whole word, not just the Gospels or the New Testament. This is the 'solid food' referred to in Hebrews: *But solid food is for the mature, who by constant use have trained themselves to distinguish good from evil* (Heb 5.14). Ezekiel had foreseen this as part of the fulfilment of Jeremiah's prophecy of the New Covenant relationship between God and his people. He wanted the priests *to teach the people the difference between the holy and the common and to show them how to distinguish between the unclean and the clean* (Ezek 44.23).

Deception

Many church leaders, as well as laypeople, from all over the world began going to Toronto to 'catch the spirit'. This was highly dangerous because they believed that 'The Blessing' was something that could be passed on from one human being to another. There is no biblical foundation for this! In fact, the Prophet Haggai was asked a question about blessing being passed from one to another and he answered very firmly that human beings cannot pass on the blessing of God to another person.

Only God can bestow his blessings. But human beings can pass on corruption, Haggai said, even though we cannot transmit the blessing of God *we can pass on corruption* (Hag 2.10–14). This is a spiritual truth of immense importance – we can pass on an alien spirit, and there is massive evidence that this is what happened at Toronto and in the untold number of churches where people passed on the laughing spirit from one to another. The harm that this did in bringing a vast amount of spiritual corruption into the church can never be known.

David Noakes was a member of the PWM team at the time he went to Toronto to see for himself what was being widely reported in Britain. He said on his return, "I didn't want to go, but finally God told me that I must, on the basis that I could not speak with any authority from my perspective unless I had actually seen what was going on. What I saw was appalling. I saw unclean spirits manifesting in men and women. It was devastating. Then when I came back I was shown some videos which included one of Rodney Howard Browne and Kenneth Copeland doing their dual comedy act on the stage.[19] I have never been quite so appalled seeing a blatant misuse of what should be a manifestation of the Holy Spirit. I went away from that meeting in London, and the next day I received the following word from the Lord.

What you are now seeing is not the first wave of the deception that is to come, nor will it be the last. Satan is establishing an increasingly strong and broad powerbase in the churches of your nation in order to draw my people away after false hopes of a cheap and illusory glory of the flesh in this age. Do not look to the men who seem to be the principal instruments of the deception. They are false prophets who come and go like shooting stars. Their judgment is in my hand and I will execute in its season. They prophesy by Baal but I will surely vindicate my own Holy Name.

Be concerned rather with the faceless shepherds of the flocks of my people. For an illusion of glory and success they sell the sheep of my pasture into the hand of the deceiver. False and deluded, they do not know my voice, for they do not reference my word. Puffed up with selfish ambition and vainglory they lead my people into false ways. Thinking that they see in their blindness, they lead those who trust them into a ditch. They are the Pharisees of old who love the places of honour and applause of men, and they gain it at the expense of leading gullible men and women into ways which have an appearance of light but are in truth a highway into deepest darkness.

Beware of such men. False prophets and blind guides.... This wave of deception will recede and with it those who now falsely prophesy. But the false shepherds among my people will remain as a danger, ready to grasp hold of the next wave when it comes, for surely it will do so. Each wave will be deadlier than the last and will attract more of those whose feet are not firmly grounded on the rock of my word....

Pray that the deaf may hear. Pray that the blind shepherds may see. But remember that it is only my Spirit which convicts of sin and guilt and of judgement to come. The task of the watchman is to warn. If you will fulfil that task you will have served your Master well.[20]

After Effects

The effects of the Toronto Blessing went on for a long time and impaired the thinking as well as the spiritual life of those affected. There were accounts of people whose business and professional lives were affected as well as their personal lives. Peter Fenwick, who pastored a church in Sheffield, referred to what he called the 'Toronto twitch'.[21] He recounted an incident where a dentist had been infected with the twitch which made his hands shake uncontrollably. It was triggered by certain words such as 'praise the Lord'. His assistant was a Christian so this presented a particular danger for him – and no doubt for his patients also – especially if she said 'praise the Lord' when he was drilling!

Many incidents such as this were reported at a conference of church leaders held at Bawtry Hall in Yorkshire in January 1995.[22]

A Common Error

A common error that was current at the time the Toronto Blessing was at its height was that Christians who are filled with the Holy Spirit cannot be deceived. In fact, the reverse is probably true – that those who have been baptised in the Spirit are actually more likely to be deceived than conservative evangelicals or traditional orthodox believers who are steeped in the knowledge of the Bible but are cessationists who have no experiential background. The reason for this is that conservative evangelicals judge what is right or wrong by the use of their intellect, or reason. They form a judgement based upon biblical principles rather than experience or emotional reaction. The more the believer is soaked in the word of God, the more likely they are to be able to make sound judgements. Those who are in the greatest danger are believers who have been newly baptised in the Spirit but who lack maturity in the word of God. They have opened their lives to the manifestations of the Holy Spirit and, without a firm biblical foundation, they begin to judge all things on an 'experiential' rather than a 'rational' basis. If they lack the depth of sound teaching in the word they are an easy target for the enemy, open to deception.

More Errors

A common error that appeared in churches with Restorationist teaching who allowed free rein to the manifestations generated by the Toronto Blessing, was claiming the protection of the blood of Christ over a whole congregation in order to ensure that no alien spirit could affect anyone present. This is not biblical teaching. The blood of Christ cleanses from sin and gives us access to God, and the blood of Christ is also the ground of victory over Satan because of what Jesus did at Calvary (Col 2.13–15). But this is an *individual experience* and there is no biblical example encouraging us to believe that a whole congregation can be put under the blood of protection. If one person is present who is giving ground to Satan, this will leave the door open for his entry, and manifestations of an alien spirit will follow. This is not at all an uncommon occurrence in Restorationist churches.

Another common error among leaders is praying to the Holy Spirit, or calling upon the Holy Spirit to come down upon a congregation. John Wimber did this at the final meeting in October 1990 in the Excel Centre. But the Holy Spirit is the gift which the Father gives to the believer. Jesus did not tell us to call upon the Holy Spirit. He said, *"I will ask the Father, and He will give you another Counsellor to be with you forever – the Spirit of truth"* (John 14.15). When he speaks of the coming of the Holy Spirit it is the *Father* who will send him (John 14.26 and 15.26). Jesus says that if we are in tune with him, the Father will give us anything that we ask in his name (John 15.16 and 16.23).

Prayer should always be addressed either to Jesus or to the Father. So long as the worshipper's eyes are fixed upon Jesus his/her whole attention will be upon the Lord and they are safe. But if worshippers call out for 'the spirit' to descend upon them the response may come from anywhere in the spirit-world and the manifestations can be highly spectacular but counterfeit. That is the substance of Jesus' warnings in Matthew 7.15–23 and in Matthew 24.

It is essential to remember that not all spiritual manifestations or 'supernatural phenomena' are of God! Scripture teaches us that it is important to discern the 'source' which may be either of God, of the flesh, or of the devil. 'Distinguishing between spirits' is one of the manifestations of the Spirit listed by Paul in 1 Corinthians 12. Paul links it with 'prophecy' which shows the importance of discerning the source of any 'prophetic word' that is given in the church.

Something Wrong

At the height of the Toronto Blessing in 1995, I was asked to speak at a meeting in the Regents Hall, Oxford Street, London. Two other speakers were Rob Warner and David Pawson. At the end of an hour-long address I gave the following summary:

You know there is something wrong when new teaching is based upon contemporary revelation instead of upon the revealed word of God in the Bible.

You know there is something wrong when doctrine is based upon experience instead of experience based upon doctrine.

You know there is something wrong when people travel halfway round the world to get a blessing instead of falling on their knees where they are.

You know there is something wrong when people talk of imparting a blessing from one to another when the Bible says that the only thing that can be passed on is corruption, not blessing.

You know there is something wrong when people are told not to use their minds and not to test the spirits as the New Testament instructs.

You know there is something wrong when Scripture is reversed and its upside down meaning is given as new teaching.

You know there is something wrong when prophecies of imminent revival remain unfulfilled year after year.

You know there is something wrong when meetings are advertised as spiritual spectaculars.

You know there's something wrong when people chase after signs and wonders which is contrary to the practice of Jesus who said *"a wicked and adulterous generation looks for miraculous signs"*.

You know there is something wrong when people exhibit uncontrollable physical symptoms and the New Testament teaches that self-control is a fruit of the Spirit.

You know there is something wrong when those who introduce new teachings charge those who wish to test these teachings biblically with being divisive.

You know that there is something wrong when those who claim to have been filled with a new love for Jesus pour out the vilest abuse upon those who question their teaching.

The greatest danger in churches that experienced the Toronto Blessing was where the leaders failed to discern what was happening and to distinguish between that which was of God and that which was not. Where there is a departure from Scripture there is great danger of the enemy taking control. When God begins to move among his people the enemy is always active, seeking to deceive and to counterfeit the work of the Holy Spirit. This is not possible where the believers, and especially their leaders, are thoroughly grounded in the word of God.

Gnosticism

It is strange how centuries-old heresies come back into the church from time to time. The whole 'Restorationist Movement' with its 'Latter Rain' teaching has its origins in some form of Gnosticism that troubled the Early Church. It is extremely dangerous when leaders claim to have 'secret knowledge' such as the word-faith teachings of Kenneth Hagin and Kenneth Copeland. Their teaching is particularly dangerous because it became the basis for doctrinal formula, reading things into biblical texts that were never intended, and giving the impression that their special knowledge would actually give success. Jacob Prasch gave an example of this[23] when he said that David Shearman, pastor of a Pentecostal church in Nottingham, had invited people to come forward to touch the hem of his garment to get a 'double portion of the Spirit' from him.

Yonggi Cho introduced a new element into the Gnosticism of Latter Rain teaching by adding 'visualisation' techniques which he had learned from Korean Buddhist shamanism. He teaches that worshippers can enter into a closer relationship with God through visualisation. He recommends reading a story in the Gospels, such as Jesus in the boat with the disciples on the Sea of Galilee, and meditating upon it until it becomes visual and the worshipper is transported into that scene. For the technique to work the worshipper has to exercise the secrets of visualisation. A number of church leaders in the charismatic sector were responsible for bringing Cho to Nottingham in March 1995 for the 'Dawn 2000' Conference at the height of the Toronto Blessing phenomenon when he gave this teaching.

Other forms of Gnosticism were also used to give an understanding of biblical symbolism in accordance with the special knowledge revealed to those in leadership as, for example, when Bob Jones claimed to have had a special revelation giving him a different rendering of Psalm 12.1[24] which had nothing to do with the text. The usual method of interpreting difficult passages of Scripture used by biblical scholars is to compare Scripture with Scripture. In other words, to find other examples of the word or phrase being used in other parts of the Bible which helps to give understanding of their meaning.

In the magazine *Prophecy Today*, throughout the 1990s and the early years of the 21st century, we warned of the dangers presented by these various forms of Gnosticism that were common in the Restorationist Churches and among those who had embraced the Toronto Blessing. It was a time when New-Age teachings were fashionable and were making inroads into Christian teaching in churches where they were experiencing the manifestations which were spread from Toronto.

Revival Hopes

By the end of the 1990s most churches that had embraced 'The Blessing' were recognising that it was not a genuine revival. They were not seeing large numbers of new believers, neither was there any sign that people in the street were experiencing the presence of the Holy Spirit leading them to repentance and to responding to the gospel. The classic signs of revival were not to be seen and so most leaders in these churches said that God was giving a 'time of refreshing' to his people. They recognised that what they were experiencing was not reaching people outside the churches but they still clung on to their belief that revival would come. They said this was simply a time of preparation for the big event. Thus, they kept revival hopes alive among their people.

If this were a right understanding of the purpose of the manifestations it would surely also have been right to apply the final test of any spiritual phenomena: to examine the fruit. In this regard, the statement by Chris Hand, the Baptist pastor from Wimbledon has already been mentioned,[25] that amongst all the people in his church the most common expression was that their love for Jesus had increased. This, of course, is a highly subjective statement that cannot be measured.

Bearing Fruit

The fruit of the Spirit should be measured in accordance with the teaching of Jesus who told his disciples that he had appointed them *"to go and bear fruit – fruit that will last"* (John 15.16). This has to be taken in conjunction with Jesus' last words to his disciples: *"Therefore go and make disciples of all nations, baptising them in the name of the Father and of the Son and of the Holy Spirit, and teaching them to obey everything that I have commanded you"* (Matt 28.19). He also said, *"When the Holy Spirit comes on you; you will be my witnesses in Jerusalem, and in all Judaea and Samaria, and to the ends of the earth"* (Acts 1.8).

The fact that Jesus did not just tell the disciples to go and bear fruit but added *'fruit that will last'* is very significant. The fruit that we pick from a tree will either be consumed or it will rot: it will not last. *The fruit that will last is another fruit tree.* This is what Jesus meant when he said *"Go and make disciples"* and that the disciples would be his witnesses.

Discipleship does not mean promoting our own teaching but promoting the teaching of the Master — witnessing to all that he did and said. For subsequent generations of witnesses the task is the same — witnessing to our own first-hand experience of *the Master's* teaching and what he has done in our lives. If we apply this test to the Toronto experience, we have to ask, 'Where is the fruit that lasts?'

Dennis Wrigley, writing in *Prophecy Today*[26] in 1998, described some of the ways in which Britain had turned away from God. He said:

> The clearest evidence of this is the way in which we are treating our children. Every day there are 10,000 calls to 'ChildLine' from children seeking help. Every week 600,000 children and young people take illegal drugs. Last year 11,000 children were expelled from school and each year nearly 100,000 children run away from home. There are currently over 30,000 children on child protection registers and over 15,000 children in care. Over 750,000 children never see their fathers and in the past 30 years we have seen a 600% increase in marriage breakdown.

Referring to the church, he said,

> We must bear heavy responsibility for what is happening.... Far from proclaiming the good news of liberation we have expended our energies in fruitless debate, airing our doubts and confusing the people... Before we seriously consider revival, we must accept our responsibility as Christians for what is happening...There can be no revival of faith unless there is a fusion of our wills with the grace of God in the act of repentance. Revival starts, not with choruses, but with prayers of repentance.

In the next chapter we look at what Dennis Wrigley was describing – the plight of children in Britain in the 1990s who were the innocent victims in a flood of family breakdown.

Notes

[1] The full text of this so-called prophecy is printed on p. 185.

[2] See *Blessing the Church?*, p. 94.

[3] This teaching is very clearly set out in Chapter Four by David Forbes in the book: Clifford Hill, Peter Fenwick, David Forbes, David Noakes, *Blessing the Church?*, Eagle publishers, Guildford, 1995. The book has been serialised in the online magazine *Prophecy Today.uk* where it is still available; or directly from Issachar Ministries.

[4] Douglas McBain, in a personal letter to the author.

[5] *Church of England Newspaper*, London, 17 June 1994.

[6] *Church of England Newspaper*, London, 17 June 1994.

[7] *Sunday Telegraph*, 19 June 1994.

[8] Randy Clarke was a Vineyard pastor from St Louis, a friend of John Arnott, the pastor of the Toronto Airport Vineyard Fellowship who had been to meetings led by Rodney Howard Browne.

[9] The writer has a collection of DVDs and videos showing these meetings, copies available from Issachar Ministries.

[10] John 14.16.

[11] Referred to on p. 185.

[12] 1 Thessalonians 5.21.

[13] Matthew 24.24.

[14] *Prophecy Today* volume 11, number 6, November 1995. Chris Hand was the Assistant Minister at Queens Road Baptist Church, Wimbledon, London.

[15] Reported in *Renewal* magazine, London, April 1994.

[16] Peter Fenwick, The Roots of The Toronto Blessing, in *Blessing the Church?*, p. 50, Eagle Publishing, Guildford, 1995.

[17] This is my own translation, using the Nestle version of the Greek New Testament first published in 1904.

[18] Reported in *Mainstream*, published by Banner Ministries, Derbyshire UK, summer 1994.

[19] The video shows Howard-Browne and Copeland supposedly speaking to each other in tongues – laughing and clowning to the great amusement of a large congregation.

[20] This prophecy from David Noakes was never published, but it was given and accepted at a PWM Team meeting.

[21] *Blessing the Church?*, p. 53.

[22] PWM Team Report, Charismatic Crossroads PWM, London, 1995

[23] News and Prayer Letter, Spring 1995.

[24] See more on Bob Jones in Chapter 11.

[25] See also p. 187.

[26] Volume 14, number 3, May 1998.

Chapter Thirteen

FAMILY MATTERS

Importance of The Family

The central importance of the family for the health and prosperity of the nation has been established by numerous research studies. It was as far back as the early 1980s that in PWM we began to be concerned at what was happening to family life in Britain. It was not until the 1980s that the breakdown of marriage had begun making a national impact, but by 1985, when we published the third and final part of our report on the 'video nasties', the breakdown of family life was widespread. Our particular concern was with children and we set up a special department on the family within our ministry, with staff and volunteers reading newspapers, studying reports and writing articles that we published in *Prophecy Today*.

It was the Bulger case in 1993,[1] of two 10 year-old boys who violently murdered a toddler after they had been watching a violent video film, that alerted MPs to the significance of pornography upon behaviour. They recognised that these issues had not been eliminated by the classification of all films in 1984. By this time I was an active member of the Lords and Commons Family and Child Protection Group which was chaired by Jill Knight MP.[2] A group of four MPs decided to take an initiative. They were Jill Knight (Conservative), Michael Alison (Conservative), David Alton (Liberal Democrat) and Donald Anderson (Labour). They decided to set up an Enquiry and I was asked to draw together a research team for that purpose.

Pornography and the Media

Gordon Heald was part of the team and he was the MD of Opinion Research Business (ORB) which had conducted a survey in January 1979 on the links between pornography, violence and behaviour. The new research was carried out in 1995/6 and we re-ran some of the questions that he had used in the earlier research. Copies of the report *Violence, Pornography and the Media*[3] were presented to all Members of the Commons and many in the Lords on 25 June 1996. It revealed a significant shift in public opinion on the subject of sex.

Whereas in 1979 only 1% disagreed with the statement that 'sex is a private matter and should never be publicly displayed for entertainment', in 1996 31% disagreed with that statement, and those agreeing fell from 65% to 44%. A similar shift took place in regard to rape, with a jump from 46% to 69% of those who disagreed with the statement that 'women who get raped are often partly responsible themselves'. To the question about a link between screen violence and violent crime 71% agreed, with only 13% against; and a massive 87% of the population said that they believed pornography encourages sexual assault upon children. The report stated,

> The message coming from professionals who work in the community is a clear warning about the dire social consequences of the diet of sex and violence which is being fed to the nation through a variety of media outlets. This view is now being reinforced by a clear expression of public opinion which is saying, 'Enough is enough!'

The report also noted the steep rise in crimes of violence and in sexual offences including rape between 1981 and 1994, and it gave a strong warning about the effects of viewing scenes of violence on the small screen by children of all ages.

> When this generation of children carry into adulthood the norms of violence that have been fed to them, we will need a police state to control the levels of aggression and social disorder that will result. America currently has one and a half million people locked up in its prisons and it looks as though Britain is heading in that direction. Surely there has to be a better way!

Family Breakdown

There was also a section on family breakdown, its effects upon children and the need for strengthening family life and protecting children. It was partly the results of this survey that encouraged the all-party Lords and Commons Family and Child Protection Group (LCFCPG) to undertake a national enquiry into what was happening in family life in Britain.

The fact that family breakdown had reached the Royal Family[4] shook the whole nation and this was seen with great concern by the Parliamentary Group. It was recognised that there was a need for a factual national enquiry into the health and well-being of the family which could form the basis for Government strategy for strengthening family life. I was asked to undertake this.

Lord Ashbourne, who had now taken over the chair of the LCFCPG from Jill Knight MP, arranged for me to meet Jack Straw MP who was then Home Secretary. He promised considerable help from the Civil Service with the Enquiry and one of the Home Office staff was deputed to attend meetings of the Working Party. After a few meetings we were not sure if he was there to contribute positively to the Enquiry or to report back to the Home Office. Shortly after the Enquiry was completed, but before we published the report, the Government published a Green Paper[5] in May 1998 on childcare, announcing its policy of creating 50,000 additional childcare places and guaranteeing that from September 1998 every four-year-old child would have free pre-school education in a childcare centre. They also announced their intention of giving parents the right to 3 months unpaid leave after the birth of a child. These measures were as much to stimulate the economy as to strengthen family life. But there was nothing in the Green Paper which was a direct measure to strengthen family life.

Family Matters

Our Enquiry Report[6] was presented to the Home Secretary at a packed meeting in the Moses Room in the House of Lords on 15 July 1998. Copies had previously been given to Jack Straw so that he was able to respond to its statements at the meeting. The report noted the complex character of family structures. It stated that social analysts now refer to 'first marriages', 'remarriages', 'cohabiting couples', 'lone-mother families', 'lone-father families', 'step families', 'multi-parent families' [where children spend some time with one parent and some time with another], 'multi-sibling families' [where children from different unions live in a single household with one parent, or stepparent, or other carer]. It was noted that these re-constituted families not only placed a stress upon the adults involved, but their negative effect upon the children, in terms of health, education, and their peer group relationships, was dramatic.

The Report summarised the effects of family breakdown upon children in the following terms: Children who have suffered a broken home are more likely to be affected in one or more of the following ways:

- become parents at an early age
- divorce if they marry
- suffer a breakup if they cohabit
- have children out of wedlock
- be involved in domestic violence
- have low levels of education
- have no qualifications
- have low status employment
- have low wages
- be unemployed
- be in social housing
- be homeless
- be involved in crime

The Report concluded with dire warnings of the consequences to the nation if the present trend of family breakdown continued. There were strong recommendations for Government action to support marriage and to strengthen family life in order to avoid the inevitable social catastrophe that would follow if present trends continued.

Research for the Report found that 98% of children involved in youth crime came from broken homes. It concluded that if the present rate of marriage and relationship breakdown continued it would have catastrophic effects upon the lives of children and young people, and upon the future stability of the social structure of the nation. The future outlook was that there would be:

- an increase in sexually transmitted diseases among young people
- an increase in mental and emotionally disturbed children
- an increase in fatherless children
- an escalation of behavioural problems among schoolchildren
- an increase in stress among teachers and strains in the education service
- an increase in juvenile crime rates
- an increase in crimes of violence and sex crimes
- an increase in levels of social alienation and social disorder

The Report also noted that the present trend of family breakdown would increase the pressures on the Health and Welfare Services particularly with pressures for the State to take responsibility for the elderly.

In responding to the Report, Jack Straw, as Home Secretary, publicly promised a White Paper[7] in which the Government would set out its proposals to meet the challenges presented in the Report. He acknowledged the seriousness of the situation and spoke of the necessity of strengthening family and marriage. Sadly, no White Paper came from the Government. This was because there were strong anti-marriage voices within the Government that came against Jack Straw and ensured that his promises could not be carried out. This reflected the growing influence of the LGBT lobby in the Civil Service, as well as in the Labour Government of Tony Blair. In 1999 the Chancellor Gordon Brown even removed the 'married person's allowance' in income tax, thus further sending out anti-marriage vibes to the nation and further weakening family life.

Formation of Family Matters Institute

Immediately after the publication of the report *Family Matters* in Parliament, PWM trustees took the decision to transform its education division into an Institute as a separate organisation with its own trustees and charitable status. A new director and staff were appointed. I retained responsibility for research which enabled me to work for the Parliamentary Group with the backing of the new Institute. The Family Matters Institute (FMI) rapidly gained respect in its field with a number of significant research projects and later establishing 'Dad Talk' as an online advisory service for men, dealing with a wide range of personal problems related to family, marriage and children. Ten years later it had more than a million men on its database.

Teenage Pregnancy

In June 1999, the Social Exclusion Unit presented a report 'Teenage Pregnancy' to the Prime Minister, which stated that Britain had the worst record on teenage pregnancies in Europe. PM Tony Blair responded to this, saying, "as a country we cannot afford to continue to ignore this shameful record" and he pledged to halve the teenage pregnancy record by the year 2010.

Sexual activity among teenagers in the late 1990s was slowly becoming recognised as a national issue. There were nearly 50,000 live births a year to women under 20, 9 out of 10 of whom were unmarried girls. The Government's answer, however, was not to teach young people to abstain from sexual intercourse, but to increase the amount of sex education, coupled with the provision of contraceptive devices and condoms to young people on demand, without parental permission. Parents were advised to have a condom drawer available to their children. This experiment in social policy and provision had predictably disastrous consequences — it simply increased the number of teenage pregnancies.

In 1999 the Family Education Trust asked me to carry out a national survey on its behalf. The research included a representative sample of 13 to 15-year-olds, boys and girls, all of whom were involved in education. It was surprising to discover that despite all the publicity about teenage promiscuity, only 17% said that they were sexually active, 76% said they were not and 7% gave no answer. The majority of those who were active said that it was unintended or a result of being drunk. They also said that the greatest pressure for engaging in sex was from their peer group, and one in five of 13 to 15-year-old girls thought that the age of consent should be raised to 18 to give them greater protection. A surprising result was that the research showed that three quarters of the parents of sexually active 13-year-old girls did not know that their daughters were not virgins. The report was published in May 2000 and copies given to MPs.[8]

The Cost of Family Breakdown

By the year 2000 the Lords and Commons Family and Child Protection Group was now chaired by Gerald Howarth MP and family breakdown was its major focus. The group decided to call for a major enquiry into the cost to the nation of family breakdown. Once again, I was asked to lead a research team with a group of experts in different disciplines. The research covered:

- **Family** — marriage, taxation, divorce, lone parenthood and cohabitation
- **Crime** and drugs, where there were links to family breakdown
- **Education** and disruption in schools through behaviour and exclusions
- **Health** including mental health, domestic violence and child abuse
- **The Economy**, focusing upon absenteeism due to stress, anxiety and mental health problems resulting from family breakdown, low productivity and unemployment.

The report *The Cost of Family Breakdown*[9] was published in July 2000. The direct costs to the nation of family breakdown in the year 2000 was estimated to be £15 billion. This was estimated to have doubled by 2010 and the estimate for 2015 was £40 billion. There were also many other side issues such as by 2016 there was a housing crisis and the shortage of houses was blamed upon family breakdown. Every marriage breakdown usually results in the need for another house. Family breakdown was also seen to be largely responsible for the rise in mental health issues and depression that puts an increased burden on the NHS.

The Parliamentary Group ensured that copies of the report *The Cost of Family Breakdown* were given to all MPs and placed in the House of Commons library. It was recognised as a report of great significance and was referred to in numerous debates in Parliament in many subsequent years, and its figures were updated from time to time to account for inflation.

Sex Education

A further report was published by FMI and presented to MPs on behalf of the Lords and Commons Family and Child Protection Group in July 2001.[10] The report referred to the increasing incidents of sexually transmitted diseases among teenagers – up 300% in the past four years with chlamydia in girls doubling in that time. A quarter of the sexually active 13-year-old boys and girls claimed to have had four or more sexual partners. Sexually active 13 to 15 year-old children were twice as likely to come from broken families. The report recommended measures to increase parental awareness and urged schools not only to warn of the dangers of STIs but also to teach the importance of marriage and stable family life. Sadly, Government policy

- stubbornly refused to recognise the facts
- continued to teach more explicit sex education
- refused to teach schoolchildren that marriage is the ideal
- refused to teach schoolchildren sexual abstinence but advocated 'safe-sex'
- included all kinds of sexual practices in sex education
- recommended each child to make their own decision at whatever age they felt comfortable to begin sexual activity

Social Issues

The negative prognostications in our 1998 report *Family Matters* were already being fulfilled in the years since the research was carried out for that report. Yet our politicians continued generating more and more intractable social problems by blindness and refusal to recognise the fundamental source of the cancer in our social system – the breakdown of family life. Among the politicians there was a reckless disregard of the facts produced by hundreds of research studies, all showing the pain and emotional hurt and the vast amount of human misery created by the breakdown of family relationships.

Politicians of all parties since the 1980s have followed a policy of reshaping the nation by deliberately downgrading family and marriage, ignoring the mountain of research showing that only faithful marriage produces the kind of family life that results in happy and healthy adults who provide the most favourable home life for children. The level of political blindness to the facts indicates a spiritual element tantamount to a death wish that is driving the nation towards the disintegration of the structures of society.

The Labour Government that was in power throughout the Noughties was fixated upon the social policy of 'equality'. This led them to the ideological position that all forms of family are of equal value. They therefore could not recognise the value of marriage and were determined not to allow marriage to be taught in school as the ideal, on the grounds that this would discriminate against children who were coming from broken homes. This was a major reason why Jack Straw was unable to produce the White Paper he had promised and the measures to strengthen family and marriage.

In addition to personal suffering in marriage breakdown, there have been huge financial costs attributable to family breakdown. These are borne not only by the individuals concerned, but also by local communities, by the taxpayer, and by society as a whole. The report *The Cost of Family Breakdown* warned that we will never see economic prosperity, or solve the social problems in the nation, until we face the fact that faithful, loving relationships in marriage is the only form of family life that produces conditions that promote the health and welfare of the nation. The following is from the 'Conclusion':

Family breakdown has pervasive ill effects on children and the five major institutions of society: the family, the economy, education, religion, and the legal system. The family is the building block of society and marriage its foundation. However, over the past 30 or 40 years, this foundation has been weakened. Fewer adults now enter into marriage with an increasing number preferring cohabitation or single parenthood, and more adults get divorced.

Britain's children are suffering as never before, family fragmentation is a major cause of poverty, inequality and social exclusion. Yet there are few attempts to engage with ideas to strengthen family and marriage. Research shows that children are twice as likely to suffer adverse outcomes from broken families as those from intact families. This is a huge disadvantage in education, emotional and physical health, and in life-chances for employment and personal fulfilment. **But 'political correctness' produces a kind of conspiracy of silence to ignore the facts, the outcome of which is to institutionalise the disadvantage of children and to promote depression and mental instability among adults.**[11]

Church Responsibility

An Education Bill was going through Parliament at the time we published *The Cost of Family Breakdown*. It was being considered in the Lords. An amendment was added to the section dealing with what pupils should be taught about sex and child rearing. This would ensure that the information in the Green Paper would be included, which stated that marriage was the ideal form of family life. This was totally contrary to the politically correct views of New Labour and the Government opposed the amendment. There was a large turnout of peers and the amendment was narrowly defeated.

Nine bishops voted against the amendment! If they had voted for the amendment it would have been carried. It was a strange anomaly that the official representatives of the Church of England voted against faithful monogamous marriage as the ideal family type. This was probably the pivotal point in reshaping the nation in line with the secular humanist agenda and the desire of the social anarchists to destroy family life and to undermine the Judeo-Christian foundations of the nation.

The Church colluded with the State to destroy marriage and family in Britain.

Notes

[1] Further details on Chapter 15, p. 228.

[2] The LCFCP Group had been formed as an outcome of the violent video research.

[3] *Violence, Pornography and the Media*, published by CCM, Bedford, on behalf of the All Party Family and Child Protection Group, 25 June 1996.

[4] See report in Chapter 15 on the Nineties.

[5] A Green Paper is a discussion document inviting public comment.

[6] *Family Matters*, A Report to the Home Secretary, The Rt Hon Jack Straw MP for the Lords and Commons Family and Child Protection Group, Chairman: Lord Ashbourne, published by The Centre for Contemporary Ministry, Bedford, 15th July 1998.

[7] A White Paper is a document laying out proposed legislation. It often follows a Green Paper and is the outcome of public discussion.

[8] *Sex Under Sixteen*, Family Education Trust, London, 2000.

[9] Gerald Howarth MP (Chair) David Lindsay, Clifford Hill, Deborah Halling (Eds), *The Cost of Family Breakdown*, published by The Family Matters Institute, Bedford, on behalf of The Lords and Commons Family and Child Protection Group, House of Commons, London, 2000.

[10] *Does Your Mother Know?* A Study of Underage Sexual Behaviour and Parental Responsibility, FMI, Bedford, July 2001.

[11] *Cost of Family Breakdown*, FMI, 2000, p. 80.

Chapter Fourteen

ARCHBISHOP GEORGE CAREY

The Most Revd and Rt Hon Dr George Carey
Archbishop of Canterbury April 1991 to October 2002

Robert Runcie was followed by Archbishop George Carey who was an evangelical. He had earlier earned a good reputation as a parish vicar in his ministry at Durham where the church trebled in membership, and he wrote a book entitled *The Church in the Market Place*. He subsequently held lecturing appointments at Oak Hill and St John's, Nottingham, and then in 1982 he was appointed Principal of Trinity College, Bristol. Five years later he became Bishop of Bath and Wells. He had only been at Bath three years when he was nominated as Archbishop of Canterbury by Margaret Thatcher who was said to have had an aversion to 'trendy left-wing clergy'. This meant that she did not favour Dr John Habgood, the Archbishop of York, who was reported to have been favourite to go to Canterbury. Neither did she favour any of the others said to have been considered — David Sheppard (Bishop of Liverpool), Colin James (Bishop of Winchester) and John Waine (Bishop of Chelmsford). Instead she recommended the outsider George Carey.

Although he only had three years' experience of diocesan responsibilities, Dr Carey was no stranger to international ecumenical meetings. He had represented the Church of England at a meeting of the Pontifical Council for Promoting Christian Unity in Rome in 1976, and like Runcie he was a keen advocate of seeking closer links with the Roman Catholic Church. He held some surprising views for an evangelical, such as taking a liberal stand upon divorce, including the remarriage of divorcees.

Biblically Orthodox

By contrast, the position held by the Archbishop on homosexuality was in line with biblical teaching and he opposed homosexual relationships among the clergy. It was with contrasting views such as these that George Carey managed to upset liberals as well as those who would naturally be his friends among evangelicals. I personally always found him kind and helpful. He was always willing to step in to take the chair at meetings of the Lords and Commons Family and Child Protection Group when I was Convenor if there was an unexpected need. He also readily became one of the sponsors of special meetings in Parliament in which I had organising responsibilities.

Despite his friendly nature George Carey became the most maligned Archbishop of Canterbury in recent times, suffering more than an average amount of public criticism. The *Daily Mail* labelled him 'without question the worst Archbishop imaginable for a media age'. Writing in the *Daily Mail,* Michael Arditti said of Carey, 'His eleven years in office were marked by unprecedented public criticism. He managed to alienate many of his natural supporters on the Evangelical wing of the Church, as well as both the Liberal and Conservative opposition.' Nevertheless, those who knew George personally recognised that this criticism in the media was unjustified.

The media charged him with a lack of decisiveness which was probably because on some social issues such as divorce and remarriage he took a more liberal view, and in others, such as his concern over family breakdown, he took a more conservative position. He vigorously upheld traditional marriage, but despite his opposition to homosexual practices and lifestyle he admitted that he had consecrated two bishops who he suspected were in homosexual relationships. He supported women in ministry and he was Archbishop when the first women were ordained in the Church of England. This was an historic change that inevitably was controversial and gained him many friends while losing the support of others. It is strange that he gained a reputation for indecisive leadership and drew much criticism both from the evangelical and the liberal wings of the Anglican Church. It is hard to discern why this should have happened unless it is that in his good natured approach to decision-making he tried to please everyone — something that is impossible in the Church of England!

Church Growth and Evangelism

At the beginning of his term as Archbishop of Canterbury, George Carey declared the 1990s to be a 'Decade of Evangelism', presumably because the 'Decade of Evangelism' in the 1980s had clearly not been a success, but this aroused strong opposition from the liberals within churches of all denominations. The Anglican Church continued to decline during the 1990s although several policy-related factors are shown to have been positively associated with church growth (or at least reduced the speed of church decline) at the diocesan level. Policies on the number of non-stipendiary clergy, the number of female clergy and the number of planned subscribers were good. Overall diocesan income and charitable giving as a proportion of total diocesan expenditure showed some success and there was an inverse link with the number of church closures, suggesting that resisting church closures helped to boost diocesan performance.

Ever since his days as a parish priest, George had taken an interest in Church Growth and evangelism. Monica and I both had numerous meetings with him when he was Archbishop and earlier during the time he was at Trinity College Bristol. He spoke at a British Church Growth Association (BCGA) conference on *Conversion* and he wrote a chapter in the ensuing book that Monica edited: *Entering the Kingdom.*[1] Before he became Archbishop, George Carey had shown a lot of interest in church planting in this country following the publication of a book by the BCGA entitled *How to Plant Churches.*[2]

This was a new concept for the UK with its Anglican church in every parish. He supported Church Planting Initiatives (ACPI),[3] suggesting many ways in which the Anglican Church could embrace these concepts within its parish system and be actively involved. But when he became Archbishop he did not follow these through and the links were dropped, much to the disappointment of leaders of the BCGA. No doubt this was due to pressures within the Anglican Church to maintain the parish system which conflicted with his personal desires to embrace Church Growth principles and to encourage evangelism at a local level.

Inherited Legacy

A major part of George's problem was the legacy he inherited from his predecessor. Runcie had made a number of key appointments of clergy and other officials in the Anglican bureaucracy, including the Lambeth Palace staff. These were people who held strongly liberal theological views and shared Runcie's scepticism of Scripture. In the view of those who were familiar with the Lambeth ecclesiastical scene, George's major mistake was in not making changes to these significant staff positions although he may have been concerned that there could have been legal difficulties with staff contracts. But those who knew the Lambeth situation believed that changes could and should have been made which would have given him greater opportunities of exercising creative leadership during his period as Archbishop.

The Lambeth staff have considerable influence on an Archbishop, on his speeches, on the engagements he accepts or rejects, and on policy and administration, including the agenda for Synods and relationships with Anglicans in other parts of the world as well as international and interdenominational relationships. George was never able to break free of these liberal influences that surrounded him at Lambeth. So the shadow of Runcie's highly liberal leadership was continually hanging over him.

Problems

It was quite a long time after George Carey retired from Canterbury that some of his decisions regarding Bishop Peter Ball were revealed. This involved his actions in an alleged cover up of the gross sexual offences committed by Ball when he was Bishop of Lewes and subsequently as Bishop of Gloucester. According to a report published in June 2017,[4] after Ball's arrest in 1992 George had received seven letters of complaint from individuals or families of those complaining about the alleged sexual misbehaviour of Peter Ball. George only submitted one of these letters to the police. This was a letter dealing with the most minor offence. The letters alleging the most serious sexual offences were reported to have been withheld by the Archbishop, which inevitably led to the assumption that withholding this evidence could have affected the trial that found Ball to be innocent. Following a further trial in October 2015, Ball was sentenced to 32 months in prison for misconduct in public office and indecent assault. He had admitted the abuse of 18 young men between the ages of 17 and 25.

We cannot know what took place between George Carey and Peter Ball in private conversation. But Ball evidently succeeded in convincing George that he was innocent and that the letters of complaint against him were unjustified. Evidence of this comes from the fact that George wrote to Bishop Michael Ball, Peter Ball's brother, saying that he believed him to be innocent. It was no doubt this confidence in Peter's innocence that led him to withhold the letters which he believed to be false accusations. This whole incident revealed, in hindsight, that it was a wrong decision not to present these letters although he strongly denied any attempt to influence the administration of justice. Following the publication of the report in 2017, George was asked to resign his position within the Church of England as an assistant bishop in the diocese of Oxford. His Permission to Officiate (PTO) was removed but later restored.

I have always found George to be helpful and sincere. However, it does appear that he made an error of judgement in trusting Peter Ball, but he no doubt believed either that Peter had repented and would not commit further offences or that he was the victim of false accusations. This is an error of a kind that others have made in regard to dealing with sexual offenders before the development of present-day Safeguarding procedures. In the pastoral ministry this kind of situation is never easy to deal with especially if you have confessions of offenders and apparently sincere repentance with promises never to repeat the offences. I don't know what the particular circumstances were with Peter Ball, but I do know how difficult it is to handle this kind of pastoral situation.

Jerusalem

Despite our friendship I was disappointed in George Carey's actions on one occasion when I was in Israel in January 1999. As Archbishop of Canterbury he was scheduled to be the guest preacher at the 150th anniversary celebrations of Christ Church in the Old City of Jerusalem. The church has an important history and a unique position in Jerusalem.

It is the only Protestant Christian church in the Old City. The church building was originally the chapel of the British Governor during the time of the British Mandate. The present Rectory next to the church was originally the official home of the Governor as head of the British Consulate in Jerusalem, and the only reason the church was allowed to be built was because it was for his 'personal use' and for consulate officials.

Christ Church used to be the seat of the Bishop of Jerusalem until St George's Cathedral was built in East Jerusalem which has a large Arab population. In recent times St George's has seen a succession of Arab bishops, notoriously sympathisers with, or active supporters of, the Palestine Liberation Organisation (the PLO). One Bishop was even caught by the police bringing in bombs and weapons from Jordan for the PLO — a scandal that was hushed up by the Foreign Office and the Church of England. Relationships between the Cathedral and Christ Church have been strained for many years, the two major differences being theological and racial.

The Cathedral is very liberal in its attitude to the Bible whereas Christ Church has a strong evangelical tradition. When I was last in the Cathedral, I looked at the Bibles there and saw that the Psalms had been retranslated, removing all references to 'Israel' and replacing all 65 references to 'Israel' with 'the land'. This is in compliance with the PLO's ambition to annihilate Israel and remove it from history – perhaps this has links to the prophetic Psalm,

> See how your enemies are astir,
> how your foes rear their heads.
> With cunning they conspire
> against your people;
> they plot against those you cherish.
> "Come," they say, "let us
> destroy them as a nation,
> that the name of Israel be
> remembered no more"
>
> (Ps 83.2-4, NIV).

The Cathedral actively supports Palestinian ambitions, whereas Christ Church is active among Jews and has a large Messianic congregation of Jewish believers in Jesus as their Messiah. The latter meets on Saturdays whereas the English Anglican congregation meets on Sundays.

On the occasion of the 150th anniversary celebrations, Archbishop Carey went first of all to pay his respects to the Bishop of Jerusalem at St George's which was correct protocol, but there he was subjected to strong pressure. As a result, George declined to preach at Christ Church on that special Sunday although this had been booked for a long time. The honour of preaching at the 150th celebration service by default fell to me as George's substitute. I happened to be in the land at the time with a party of visitors from Britain. Ray Lockhart, the Rector of Christ Church contacted me, explaining the situation and asking me to be the preacher on the following Sunday.

I believe that Ray and his wife were quite hurt by what appeared to be George's refusal to use his executive authority and resist the pressure put upon him. Ray and George had been at college together and they were not only good friends, but so too were their wives. Eileen was with George on this visit to Jerusalem and they actually passed the front door of Christ Church on their way to visit the Armenians in the next building. It was obviously not meant to be a personal snub to Ray and his wife but some of the Christ Church congregation were disappointed that the Archbishop did not come to this significant anniversary. No doubt I was a poor substitute!

George Carey retired from Canterbury at the end of October 2002 although he continued to take an interest in current affairs and to make occasional public pronouncements. In fact, in some ways he appeared more active in the media after his retirement than when he was Archbishop. He caused considerable controversy and consternation among those who have a commitment to pro-life issues by declaring himself in favour of euthanasia. His statement that there were circumstances when enabling someone to end their life to relieve them of pain was justified lost him some of his friends. This was seen by some in the media as an example of his unpredictability. In some ways I think George liked to think of himself as a rebel. On one occasion Eileen referred to my forthright articles in *Prophecy Today* and jokingly compared him with me, saying that we were "a pair of rebels". I don't think that either of us received that too well!

Lambeth Palace

At the beginning of his term in Canterbury there were great hopes among many people in the Church of England that, as an evangelical Archbishop, George Carey would reverse many of the decisions taken by Runcie, that he would undo some of the harm that had been done by ultra-liberalism and lack of commitment to biblical truth. Those hopes were gradually dissipated as the all-encompassing power of the Anglican machinery of government ensured the impossibility of systemic change. Perhaps if George had succeeded in replacing the Lambeth Palace staff with men and women who were faithful, Bible-believing advisers, things might have been different. In my opinion he was never able to shake himself free from Runcie's influence and lead the Church of England to exercise a strong social, moral and spiritual influence in the nation at a crucial time in its history.

Notes

[1] Monica Hill, ed., *Entering the Kingdom* — A Fresh Look at Conversion, MARC Europe, British Church Growth Association, Harrow, 1986.

[2] Monica Hill *How to Plant Churches*, MARC Europe, 1984.

[3] Anglican Church Planting Initiatives.
http://www.acpi.org.uk/joomla/index.php-option=com_frontpage&Itemid=1.html

[4] Moira Gibb, *An Abuse of Faith*, June 2017, a report commissioned by Justin Welby, Archbishop of Canterbury, in February 2016.

Chapter Fifteen

REVIEWING THE NINETIES

Evangelism Expectations
The 1990s dawned with similar hopes among evangelicals to that of the 1970s and 80s that at last a great revival would be seen in Britain. The 'Dawn 2000' campaign estimated that some 20,000 new churches would be planted in the UK by the end of the 1990s. There were several other campaigns as well as the burgeoning Charismatic Movement that was spilling over into the denominational churches in addition to the New Churches and House Church Movement. Hopes were probably higher than at any time since the mid-1970s.

The Elim Pentecostal Churches in March 1994 launched their 'JIM Challenge' (Jesus In Me) through which they estimated that a quarter of a million people would come to know Jesus. In the same year Reinhardt Bonnke's 'Minus to Plus' campaign was expected to produce five million responses. Between them these two campaigns cost British Christians in excess of £6 million. Reinhardt Bonnke's idea was to deliver a booklet outlining the gospel to every household in Britain. At the end of the campaign they reported a mere 16,000 responses to the 25 million delivered. We were not told how many of those who responded were already Christians and what happened to new believers.

Meanwhile, churches infected with the Toronto spirit continued to roar with laughter. It seemed this was the decade of DIY evangelism – everyone doing their own thing, with no national coordination. Good ideas were put into practice but none made any impact in the nation and certainly they did not bring revival. In the September 1994 issue of *Prophecy Today*[1] we summarised the situation saying:

Over the past 25 years the Charismatic Movement has gone through a number of phases with a succession of different emphases upon the gift of tongues, healings, praise-worship, dancing, falling down, prophecy, words of knowledge and various spiritual manifestations.

Fear, loneliness and despair are in the lives of most people in Britain today and there is a longing for good news. The nation is ripe for the gospel.... The great desire to see revival creates great danger. When our prayers for revival are unanswered, instead of asking God what is wrong, we take matters into our own hands, and what we produce is usually counterfeit.

In the same editorial, we said that the key to the situation lay in the words of the prophet Haggai:

Now this is what the Lord says: "Give careful thought to your ways. You have planted much, but have harvested little... You expected much, but see, it turned out to be little. What you brought home, I blew away. Why? declares the Lord Almighty. Because of my house which remains a ruin while each of you is busy with his own house" (see Hag 1.5-9).

In the 1990s charismatic Christians were busy building their own houses, while building the true church based upon the word of God was neglected. In a four-page report on what was happening in churches in all the Western nations where the 'Toronto Blessing' was spreading, we ended with a solemn warning:

God's good purposes and his perfect timing can be missed if we are not sensitive to what the Spirit is saying to the churches today. The greatest danger is that we may try to do things our way and not allow God to do it his way.

Inter Faith

A major reason why yet another 'Decade of Evangelism' did not produce the fruit of revival in Britain was due to the unbelief, corruption and false teaching in the institutional churches of all denominations including the new churches – some more than others. The Church of England in particular had been infiltrated with New-Age teaching at a high level throughout the period of Robert Runcie's time as Archbishop of Canterbury. We have already noted some of the things he said in his speech in Lambeth Palace at the Sir Frances Young Husband lecture.[2] Towards the end of his time at Canterbury he presided over a 'Festival of Faith and the Environment' in Canterbury Cathedral which included a Sunday morning 'Creation Eucharist' with quotations from Hindu, Buddhist, Baha'i, Islamic, Confucianist and Sikh writings on the printed Order of Service paper.

The Saturday of the festival[3] coincided with the annual 'March for Jesus' in which hundreds of thousands of Christians took part in towns and cities throughout Britain. Some 4,000 took part in the March through the City of Canterbury. I was one of a group who delivered a letter of protest about the inter-faith festival to the Archbishop. We began singing songs of praise to the Name of Jesus in the grounds outside the cathedral where we were ordered to stop singing by the cathedral staff who threatened to call the police and charge us with 'creating a disturbance'. We were not allowed to exhort the Name of Jesus outside, while inside the cathedral a group of Indian musicians were singing Hindu songs in the nave![4]

New Age

On 20th April that same year, 1990, St James Piccadilly, an Anglican church in the West End of London, celebrated the birth of the Buddha with a celebration in the church. Their publicity stated:

For many people in the New Age Movement Wesak — the full moon when the sun is in Taurus — is the most important spiritual event of the year. It is an opportunity for the most intense and focused spiritual work. This particular full moon is celebrated in the East as the Buddha's birthday. There is also a living legend which states that at this full Moon the Buddha and the Christ join together with all other liberated beings and with the Communion of Saints to invoke a great annual blessing for the planet. We shall be celebrating Wesak this year with an inter-denominational meditation ceremony in the church. We invite people of all cultures, religions and belief systems to join us in this great inner celebration.

We wrote to the Bishop of London about the New Age activities in St James Piccadilly but he took no action, and we knew that it was pointless appealing to the Archbishop of Canterbury, Robert Runcie, who would have no doubt approved of linking the Buddha and Christ in a New Age meditation. In the same issue of *Prophecy Today* we gave example after example of apostasy in the Anglican Church which we described as the exposure of the adulterous bride of Christ. We said, "God is longing to use his church to proclaim his word to the nations. But how can an unholy, unbelieving and unrepentant church call the nation to repentance?" We also referred to the unbelief of the Bishop of Durham (David Jenkins), saying, "There are thousands of clergy who secretly share his unbelief." This level of unbelief, once it gets into an institution the size of the Church of England, can take generations to eradicate.

Promiscuity

But it was not only unbelief that assailed the church in the 1980s and 90s. In an editorial in *Prophecy Today* I said:

I am deeply troubled by the amount of sexual promiscuity, adultery and marriage breakdown in the church today. I see and hear of these things, probably more than most Christians, because of my travelling ministry. Hardly a week goes by without my hearing of some leader who has been having an extramarital affair and has left his wife and gone off with another woman or a man... The Liberals have been led astray by their abandonment of the Bible as the authoritative word of God. At the same time, the Evangelicals have been diverted by pseudo-charismatics who have propounded exciting new teachings based upon experience rather than truth, while introducing lovey-huggy practices which have done much to overcome the inhibitions and restraints between the sexes.[5]

It was not only unbelief and sexual immorality in the churches in Britain that were holding back revival in the 1990s. There was a deeper underlying lack of trust in God and a failure to comprehend what was happening in society in the context of world events and a biblical understanding of the purposes of God.

Royal Family Breakdown

By far the most significant social phenomenon of the 1990s was the continuing rise in family breakdown. The domino effects of family and marriage breakdown ran through all other social institutions and affected every aspect of social life. The nation was shocked in the early 1990s by the exposures in the media of tensions and strife within the Royal family. 1992 was the *annus horribilis* of the Queen as she was forced to witness the breakup of her children's marriages. Fergie and Andrew had already separated, and in June 1992 Andrew Morton's book about Diana was published. This was highly embarrassing for the Queen, but worse was to come with the publication of the 'squidgy-gate tapes' revealing intimate conversations between Charles and Camilla. Diana had said that there were "always three" in her marriage and that Charles had always been in love with Camilla and he had never loved her. Morton's book and the tapes appeared to substantiate the truth of this.

The Queen's discomfort became even greater when Windsor Castle caught fire on 20th November 1992 and caused extensive damage which eventually cost £36 million to repair. Shortly after the fire, the Government said that the nation would pay for the damage, which caused an outcry against the already unpopular monarchy. Press comment widely reflected the mood of the nation and an opinion poll suggested that Britain no longer needed the Royal Family. It looked as though it was not only the marriages of the Princes that were following the national trend, but the existence of the whole Royal Family was under threat.

The Queen acted swiftly and four days after the Windsor Castle fire she broadcast to the nation confessing that this was her *annus horribilis,* as everything appeared to be going wrong in her life. She recognised that people were actually questioning the role of the monarchy and its place in the life of the nation, and she turned this and her own troubles to her advantage. She said "This sort of questioning can act as an engine for change," thus acknowledging that within the Royal family there needed to be changes. This led to greater transparency in Royal affairs and a new openness in public relations. She said that one of the changes she would make was to begin paying income tax, and Buckingham Palace would be opened to the public which would raise funds for the repairs to Windsor Castle.

Christianity on the World Scene

On the world scene the church was growing at a faster rate than ever before since the days of the Early Church. But this growth was not in the rich Western world, it was exclusively to be seen in the poorer nations among those who lacked material resources and in nations where there was persecution of believers.

The most spectacular growth of Christianity was to be seen in great spiritual awakenings that were taking place in Southeast Asia – China, Indonesia, Malaysia, the Philippines; and in Africa, south of the Sahara; and in many parts of South America. Hundreds of new churches were being formed every week and thousands of new believers were coming into the Kingdom. God was pouring out his Spirit with power as the gospel was received with joy and there were multitudes of signs and wonders that included spectacular healings, some of which Monica and I ourselves witnessed in many places on our worldwide travels, particularly in Indonesia where we had established links with Petrus Octavianus who was renowned as the 'Billy Graham' of Southeast Asia. We toured Indonesia with him on several occasions and taught at his Bible School in Batu up in the mountains of Java, where he was training Indonesians for the pastoral and evangelistic ministries.

Monica had written a book about our experiences[6] in which she contrasted the growth of the church in the poorest parts of the world with the decline in the rich nations. She concluded that the church in the West was in danger of being rejected by God for corruption, rebellion and promiscuity, whereas prosperity and growth were to be seen among the poorest communities. She cited incidents that revealed the limitations of the knowledge and experience expected of her with the title of Executive Director of the 'British Church Growth Association': in Indonesia she was asked for advice on church growth by a little group of elders who asked her, "When is the right time for us to appoint a pastor?" They said that their church, which was now three months old, had an attendance of 750. Should they wait until they were passed 1000 before making a pastoral appointment? Monica had never received questions like that in England! In the book she questioned who were the rich and who were the poor. She concluded that God was turning upside down the values of the world.[7]

A Role in Education
PWM and BCGA united to form the 'Centre for Contemporary Ministry' (CCM), to provide residential in-service training courses for clergy, which they held for a number of years in Bawtry Hall, near Doncaster. These covered a number of issues, from 'Pastoral Counselling' to 'Spiritual Gifts' – the most popular being 'Gaining a Wider Vision' and 'Turning Vision into Strategy'. They were especially geared to meet the needs of clergy, equipping them to understand the changes in the church and society. These five-day residential courses were seen as lifelines or last chances by many in despair who were thinking of leaving the church.

Social Issues
Far from being a 'Decade of Evangelism' in Britain, the 1990s, despite all the exciting things happening in the charismatic churches, proved to be a period of decline, not only in numerical church attendance, but in the influence of the church in society. Significant social changes were taking place in Britain that were largely being ignored by the churches. The most important changes that were affecting every aspect of life in the nation was the escalation of marriage breakdown and traditional family life. As Jack Straw, the Home Secretary, said in 1998, "The family is the building block of the nation." But the building block was crumbling, endangering the stability of the whole family institution which was central to the life and health of the nation. The churches, however were silent on the issue — probably the greatest social issue of the century.

Among the many factors responsible for endangering the health of family life, and especially of children, was the new social phenomenon of the video recorder which came onto the market in the early 1980s and by the end of the decade it was to be found in most households across the nation. In Chapter 7 of this book we described the Parliamentary campaign that resulted in the unanimous passing of The Video Recordings Act, July 1984, which imposed restrictions on all video films making them subject to classification for different age groups. But in many households children of all ages were still viewing films containing sex and violence. As mentioned in Chapter 13, in 1993 an incident took place that shook the whole nation, known as the 'Bulger case'. Two 10 year-old boys kidnapped a two-year old little boy, James Bulger, and took him to waste ground where they tortured and murdered him, leaving him beside a railway line. The boys had been viewing violent videos where a similar incident had taken place which they copied.

All-Party Parliamentary Group
The subject of violent videos had largely dropped out of public attention after 1985. But following the Bulger case a small group of Members of both Houses of Parliament who had been involved in the Parliamentary campaign for video control, continued to meet. They formed the 'All Party Family and Child Protection Group' under the chairmanship of Dame Jill Knight (later to become Baroness Knight). The group continued to monitor what was happening in family life and they had an ongoing concern of the link between media violence and crime. Although it was difficult to establish a direct link between watching violent films and committing violent crimes, the Bulger case appeared to support such a link. When the vice squad of Hampshire Constabulary reported to the Parliamentary Group that they had had five cases within the last year where a sexual offence was directly connected to pornography, the group decided to act. They contacted members of the Working Party who had produced the report on video violence and asked them to investigate.[8]

A new Working Party was formed that included three members of the Lords and three members of the Commons plus 20 professionals. I was asked to direct the Working Party. The new group included Gordon Heald the director of 'Opinion Research Business' who had organised a national survey in 1979 on the links between pornography and behaviour. It was decided to re-run this survey to give a comparative basis, but extend it with a number of additional questions. The results of this are covered in Chapter 13 on Family Matters. The Report was submitted to the Parliamentary All Party Family and Child Protection Group by a Working Party chaired by the Earl of Halsbury, which I edited and which was published by PWM from Bedford in June 1996.

Despite Tony Blair's personal acknowledgement of the importance of moral and spiritual values in society, the influence of secular humanist ideologies within the New Labour movement were strong. Notably, the rising influence of LGBT interests were seen in the Blair Government where powerful Cabinet posts were given to homosexual individuals such as Chris Smith who took control of Culture, Media and Sport. This was exactly the area where LGBT values could be subtly injected into the public life and was a notable triumph for the secular-humanist postmodern movement.

Ideological Battle

Women in the Blair Government such as Clare Short and Harriet Harman, with strong feminist orientation and secular-humanist values, also opened the way for the promotion of LGBT ideology. Disputes within the Cabinet reflected the ideological battle for the preservation/ destruction of the traditional family that was gathering momentum at this time. Jack Straw's endeavour to promote measures that would strengthen family life, as already noted above, were thwarted within the Cabinet and resulted in his failure to produce the promised White Paper to strengthen family life. This had major social consequences in the future of the nation.

What was not widely recognised at the time was the level to which LGBT values were based upon a fundamentally socio-anarchist objective. Although their 1972 manifesto had already stated their objective of destroying the traditional family, this was generally regarded as a foolish hyperbole that could be disregarded. Even today, their true objectives are not generally recognised.

The rising power of the LGBT lobby within the Civil Service, among politicians and in the media, presented a serious threat to the stability and health of the social structure of the nation which was not recognised in the 1990s. The warnings that were given in the 'Family Matters' report fell upon deaf ears. In hindsight it was probably Chris Smith's appointment that did the most serious damage to the nation at this time. As Minister responsible for Culture, Media and Sport he was influential in appointments to institutions such as the BBC that could profoundly affect the public presentation of LGBT ideology and values.

It was at this time that key appointments began to be made in other broadcasting and media outlets where homosexual men and lesbians were introduced. Their influence in the media cannot be exaggerated. They ensured that other key posts were also filled with pro-LGBT individuals. A report in October 2017 revealed that nearly 12% of BBC staff appointments were in the hands of LGBT individuals in comparison with a national average of 1.7%.[9]

This gross overrepresentation of LGBT people in the national broadcasting institution has had an influence on every type of programme put out by the BBC – introducing homosexual contestants in popular entertainment programmes such as *Pointless* and *Strictly Come Dancing* to the editing of news presentations in daily broadcasts. The presence of so many homosexuals or sympathisers on the BBC staff has undoubtedly had an influence upon the promotion of homosexuality as well as the advance of humanism and the broad secularisation in the nation. It is impossible to measure the extent to which the BBC as the state broadcaster, has been responsible for reshaping the nation away from its traditional Christian spiritual heritage into a secular-humanist model.

Notes
[1] *Prophecy Today*, September 1994, p. 13.
[2] See Chapter 9 of this book.
[3] 16th September 1989.
[4] Reported in *Prophecy Today* November 1989 under the title "Canterbury tales" p. 14.
[5] *Prophecy Today* July 1991, p. 5.
[6] Monica Hill, *Rich Christians, Poor Christians*, Marshall Pickering, London 1989.
[7] Monica Hill, *Ibid*.
[8] This is reported in Chapter 13, *Family Matters*.
[9] http://www.christian.org.uk/news/percentage-lgbt-staff-bbc-six-times-higher-population/

Chapter Sixteen

REBELLION AGAINST GOD

Undermining the Value System

The four social revolutionary movements of social change that hit Britain and the Western nations in the post-World War II period, coalescing between the 1960s and the 1980s, all had a number of common characteristics. All were driven by anti-creationism. Some had elements of anti-Semitism. All aimed at the destruction of the traditional family. All wanted to see the collapse of the Judaeo-Christian value system that was foundational in Western society.

The fact that these four movements should all hit the nation at the same time was a unique historical phenomenon. In sociological terms, the movements had both similar roots and objectives. Their roots are in the 18th century Enlightenment and the search for freedom, particularly freedom from divine law and restrictions. The philosophical objective of all four movements was reflected in the teaching of Matthew Fox, the New-Age teacher. He taught that through our communing with Nature and the Cosmic Christ we can achieve divinity. We no longer have need of the God of Creation. We can be masters of our own destiny.

All four movements were part of humanity's age-long rebellion against God that has existed since the beginning of Creation. **But God is never taken by surprise.** As he said to Jeremiah shortly before Judah fell to the Babylonians, *"I have been watching!"* (Jer 7.11).

God Prepares his Church

Of course, God is never taken by surprise. He knew what was going to happen in the second half of the 20th century. At the beginning of that century he began preparing his church for the forthcoming spiritual battle. The Pentecostal movement had its origins at this time, but although it grew quite rapidly in different parts of the world it did not penetrate the mainline churches in the Western nations. In fact, in 1911, just three years before Germany went to war with the rest of Europe, the German Lutheran Church declared the Pentecostal movement to be a heresy. It was to be some 70 years and two world wars later that the same church repented of that declaration and recognised Pentecostals as brothers in Christ.

Pentecostalism

Jesus said that the only sin that is unforgivable is the sin of denying the Holy Spirit — of saying that the Holy Spirit is demonic (Mark 3.29). This is what the German Lutheran Church did. Could it have been the rejection of the Holy Spirit that caused Germany to suffer the unspeakable disaster of two world wars? We will never know the answer to this question until we meet the Lord face-to-face in the life hereafter. The one thing we do know, from God's dealings with his covenant people Israel, is that the actions of the religious leaders of a nation are a determining factor in the history of that nation. We also know that the German Lutherans retained a great deal of the anti-Semitic views expressed by Luther towards the end of his life and that these views were reflected in Hitler's policy and the widespread support he received from the general population in his persecution of the Jews.

The Lutheran Church, however, was not alone in its rejection of Pentecostalism. In Britain, all the main denominations either ignored Pentecostals or simply regarded them as fringe sects and not worthy of recognition as part of the church scene. This was true even in 1980 when Monica and I were working for the Evangelical Alliance and we were responsible for organising the 'National Congress on Evangelism' at Prestatyn in North Wales. No Pentecostal church leaders were invited because the Pentecostal churches were not members of the Evangelical Alliance or recognised by them. That situation changed quite soon after that event.

We brought consideration of Pentecostals by the EA Council to the fore by including them in a great celebration of Pentecost in Trafalgar Square the following year. It was soon after this that AoG and Elim were admitted into the EA and within a few years a Pentecostal leader was elected (Eldin Corsie) chair of the EA Council. An important element in the acceptance of Pentecostalism was the Charismatic Movement that arose in the 1960s and penetrated the mainline denomination churches. God was merciful in allowing Britain a second chance in accepting the work of the Holy Spirit.

It was in the 1980s that the Charismatic Movement bloomed in many churches of all denominations and in its churchmanship in Britain, in America and throughout the Western world. This opened traditional churches to a new experience of the presence and power of God. Whole congregations were impacted in a new way which transformed their worship and their theology. The Third Person of the Trinity, the Holy Spirit, who had been neglected since the time the Western Church persecuted the Montanists,[1] was suddenly elevated to a position of great significance in both the personal experience of individuals and in the teaching of the church.

The openness of the 20th century Western church, in the second half of that century, to embrace the new experience of the Holy Spirit was quite remarkable. No doubt the traumatic experience of two world wars as well as the invention of rapid means of communication had some influence upon this. Reports of strange things happening among Christians at worship in churches, where they were more used to chanting "as it was in the beginning, is now and ever shall be", spread like wildfire across national boundaries as well as denominational and theological boundaries.

Charismatic Movement

In Britain, the Charismatic Movement was born at a time when a spirit of moral and social rebellion was triumphing in the battle with traditionalism in the secular world. In *Blessing the Church* we looked at the sociological background.

This was a time when the most socially destructive Acts of Parliament were put on the statute book. It was a time when it seemed as though the whole nation was intent upon overturning past tradition and rejecting the social values and moral precepts of their forefathers. This was the spirit of the age in which the Charismatic Movement emerged and there is good evidence for the contention that many of the social characteristics of that period were birthed into it.[2]

The new House Church Fellowships that were born at that time had something of the rebellious spirit of the age in their nature. This was a new day, God was doing a new thing and the old practices in the traditional churches were considered stumbling blocks to what God wanted to do among his people. Leaders of these new fellowships said that the Holy Spirit was sweeping away the dead wood in the institutional churches and there were many calls for people in the mainline denominations to come out of their churches, as God had finished with the denominations. This inevitably caused resentment among those church leaders who had not had a charismatic experience, and division and disunity increased. The 1970s saw the greatest fragmentation of the church in Britain for decades, but also reached a new height of social change and industrial strife in secular society.

The spirit of rebellion and discontent was running right through the nation with numerous strikes in industry, a vast increase in marriage breakdown, abortion, and sexual promiscuity, with an accompanying rise in youth crime and behavioural problems. The break with traditionalism in the Charismatic Movement reflected this discontent. But this does not imply that the Charismatic Movement was not part of God's purposes. God was indeed shaking the nations, and shaking the church was part of his purposes in order to free the church from the deadening chains of traditionalism and to create a new openness to the Holy Spirit for the battle for its very existence in the secular humanist environment that was reshaping the world.

One of the strengths of the Charismatic Movement was its emphasis upon individual experience and the personal relationship of each believer with God. This had its roots in Evangelicalism and the teaching of the Reformers on conversion and the individual nature of salvation. But a spirit of individualism was also growing in secular society in the 1970s, driven by marriage breakdown and the increasing weakness of the family.

Individualism penetrated the renewal movement, taking it away from its Hebraic roots in the teaching of Jesus whereby each individual made a personal commitment and then became part of a corporate community of believers — the Body of Christ.

Self Interest

By contrast to the teachings of Jesus, the Charismatic Movement became highly 'me-centred'. Each individual was encouraged to discover their personal spiritual gifting and the gifts were regarded as personal possessions rather than together making up the spiritual attributes of the community of believers. This individualisation of the spiritual gifts led to some erroneous teaching that God wanted his people to prosper, to be healthy and wealthy, which was fully in line with the desires and ambitions of Western acquisitive materialist society. The exercise of the spiritual gifts tended to reflect the personal needs within the fellowship rather than the equipping of the Body of Christ for fulfilling the Great Commission.

The servant nature of discipleship tended to be lost and charismatic worship reflected the 'me-centredness' with a large number of songs and choruses using the first person singular rather than the plural. These worship songs were found in denominational churches as well as in the new churches. So the character of the 'charisma' tended to move into a personal experience rather than a corporate movement empowered by the Holy Spirit to go out into the highways and byways and make disciples. There was a misunderstanding of the nature and purposes of God in giving the Holy Spirit to believers in Jesus. It reflected a lack of understanding of the teaching of Jesus at the Last Supper with his disciples when he said, *"You did not choose me, but I chose you and appointed you to go and bear fruit – fruit that will last. Then the Father will give you whatever you ask in my name"* (John 15.16).

The fruit of an apple tree is not just another apple (no matter how many), it is another apple tree.[3] This is what Jesus meant by adding the words *"fruit that will last"*. The edible apple will not last. It is easily consumed, but in order to bear fruit it has to fall into the ground and die.

Using the Gifts

The gifts were not given for personal use or self-aggrandisement. They were given to equip the church to fulfil the Great Commission: to make disciples of all nations, teaching them to obey everything that Jesus commanded (see Matthew 28.29).

A further weakness of the Charismatic Movement was the lack of basic teaching on moral values. Its anti-legalism left the door open to worldly standards of sexual freedom to become commonplace. Many charismatic churches suffered from adulterous relationships and marriage breakdown, not only in the new churches but in the mainline charismatic churches where some well-known ministers and clergy were involved in public scandals.

These sex-scandals were often due to a lack of clear biblical teaching of the whole Bible: dropping teaching on the Ten Commandments in favour of emphasising freedom from legalistic attitudes and a new freedom in Christ. Alongside this in some fellowships there was a lack of sound biblical teaching on the gifts of the Holy Spirit listed in 1 Corinthians.

An example was in the use of the gift of prophecy which was often mistakenly linked with the exercise of speaking in tongues: interpretations were given as 'words of prophecy' and would therefore be accepted by the congregation in times of worship without testing. This was in contravention of New Testament teaching where Paul clearly says that all prophecy must be tested (2 Thess 5.21). False prophecy thereby found a way into practices within the churches, which was often harmful. An example was when a Cardiff church in the late 1980s accepted an untested 'prophecy' that everyone should have a close intercessor/partner which led to many of the congregation, including the pastor, getting into adulterous relationships.

The Exercise of Power

Perhaps the greatest problems faced by the Charismatic Movement was in the exercise of power. The church was suffering from two decades of steep decline which leaders felt powerless to stem. Into this situation came John Wimber in the mid-1980s with a promise of power – divine power, Holy Spirit power – power available to all Spirit-filled believers who would allow themselves to be released from the shackles of ecclesiastical tradition and let the Holy Spirit flow freely through their lives. I have already described the impact of John Wimber's ministry in Britain in the 1980s but I am returning to this subject here because it is an important part of the turning away from biblical truth in the British churches.

Nothing could have been more seductive for church leaders in Britain who were weary of the uneven struggle to maintain decaying buildings with declining congregations and seeing little fruit from their labours. Wimber's message of power to triumph over the powers of darkness was exactly what was felt to be needed. The devil had had the church on the run for far too long and here at last was power to overcome the enemy. Wimber even taught that adversity, including sickness, could be due to demonic activity which could be overcome through the power of the Holy Spirit. Healing ministry leapt in popularity in many churches.

It was Wimber's teaching on power evangelism that really caught the imagination of church leaders. They flocked to his two visits to Britain in July and October 1990 without stopping to evaluate his teaching with its 'Latter Rain', 'great-end-time-harvest' to be reaped by an irresistible 'Joel's Army' of 'Overcomers'. The 1980s had already seen a number of highly publicised evangelistic outreaches fail to deliver the promised revival. The Pentecostal churches had organised the JIM campaign (Jesus In Me) and Reinhardt Bonnke had organised a much-publicised £6 million campaign with a postal drop of a booklet to every household in Britain. But nothing produced the much-prophesied revival that most Christians longed to see.

Repentance

Prophecy Today and the PWM team had been warning throughout the 1980s that there would be no revival in the Western nations until there was repentance in the church and the recognition of the responsibility that Christian leaders bore for the state of the nation. Church leaders did not recognise that the drift away from biblical truth in the church and the acceptance of the seductive teachings of secular humanism were linked with the forces of darkness that were driving socio-economic and political policy in society. Church leaders did not recognise the way in which the mission field, dominated by secular humanism, was dictating the mission of the church, because they did not understand the nature of the battle!

In the May 1990 edition of *Prophecy Today* we drew attention to these dangers, particularly in the context of the great expectations of revival that were being built up ahead of a visit to Holy Trinity Brompton scheduled for July 1990 which was widely advertised as the beginning of revival in Britain, with people expected to fall down in the streets slain in the Spirit and 'miraculous healings' occurring throughout the land and featured on TV. I said:

My response is 'Amen, Lord, let it happen!' But the Spirit within me declares this to be a false expectation and to warn against filling people with false hopes through crying 'Peace! Peace!' when the Lord is saying 'There is no peace!' **There will be no revival in Britain without repentance. Indeed, revival will come! But it will not come until the breaking of the nation and the church. The revival will come out of the brokenness, and not before.**

The true word of the Lord today is to prepare the people for days of darkness that are coming, that at least the remnant may be able to withstand the testing days and to take a firm stand against deception and compromise with the truth.[4]

The great revival prophesied by the Kansas City 'Prophets' under the ministry of John Wimber did not happen and caused great disappointment and disillusionment among a vast number of Christians and church leaders, not only in Britain and America, but throughout the Western nations.

This should have been the moment when church leaders stood back and took stock of the situation, recognising the extent to which biblical truth had been sacrificed on the altar of experientialism and fleshly excitement. Instead, just four years later, in 1994 when British charismatic and Pentecostal leaders were at an all-time low, they heard that something new was happening across the Atlantic.

Pragmatic Hope?

A new fountain of spiritual life was said to be flowing in Toronto! This was wonderful news that God was at last giving revival somewhere in the Western world! Even more exciting was that 'The Blessing' was transportable! Eleanor Mumford (wife of the leader of the South London Vineyard Fellowship) had been to Toronto and got it, and brought it back, and passed it on to others. If she could do it, surely others could do the same! Here was real hope for hard pressed pastors struggling to maintain their churches in times of disillusionment. They rushed to book flights to Toronto. Very few went to test the spirits in obedience to New Testament teaching. They were more interested in the simple pragmatic test – *does it work?* Can I get it and bring it back for my congregation?

There were mini-Torontos in some parts of Britain and there were several more outbreaks of enthusiasm in different parts of the world such as Pensacola and Lakeland in the USA, but the great revival sweeping through the Western nations and bringing millions into the Kingdom according to the false prophecies of the 1980s did not happen. This is not to say that that nothing that happened at any of these charismatic events was of God. That is certainly not what is being said here. Many people *did* get blessed, *but there were few actual conversions*. It was, perhaps, a time of spiritual refreshment among Christians rather than a time of outreach into the secular world.

The main thrust of enthusiasm generated by the Charismatic Movement in the second half of the 20th century was dissipated by the end of the century. But its lasting effects in challenging the dead weight of traditionalism and bringing new life into the churches, with a fresh recognition of the presence and power of the Risen Lord Jesus through the Holy Spirit, has undoubtedly been a permanent value. The spiritual value of the Charismatic Movement has not only been in the personal lives of many individual believers but it also has affected the institutions of the church, in its teaching and its worship.

It cannot be denied that a fresh move of God occurred during the second part of the 20th century. But this raises the question – what were God's purposes in raising a fresh awareness of the presence and power of the Holy Spirit? And were God's purposes realised?

If it were God's purpose to bring about a great spiritual revival

in accordance with many prophecies to that effect, then why did this not occur? We have to conclude that it was human failure rather than God's failure to achieve his purposes. God's promise is:

> *"As the rain and the snow come down from heaven and do not return to it without watering the earth and making it bud and flourish, so that it yields seed for the sower and bread for the eater, so is my word that goes out from my mouth: it will not return to me empty, but will accomplish what I desire and achieve the purpose for which I sent it"* (Is 55.10–11).

There were many warnings that both teaching and practice were drifting away from biblical truth and that therefore God's purposes could not be achieved. Back in 1995 I offered the following summary:

If the Charismatic Movement is to fulfil the purposes of God there has to be, first of all, a recognition that things have gone radically wrong (in the church as well as in the nation), and of the reasons why this has happened. There has to be, not merely a superficial repentance, but a radical turning away from the world and turning to God. The Bible has to be restored to its central place in the life of the church with a serious study of the word of God given great importance, not only among leaders and preachers of the Word, but in the lives of all believers. If this does not take place there will be serious consequences for the whole church in the Western nations.[5]

I also stated that the purposes of God cannot be thwarted, and the sovereignty of God ensures us that he can fulfil his purposes by different means. As John the Baptist declared to Israel, *"I tell you the truth that out of these stones God can raise up children for Abraham"* (Matt 3.9). In the same way, God could fulfil his purpose of bringing salvation to the world through other means. In the final pages of *Blessing the Church?* I said:

If there is no repentance among charismatics and no radical renewing of the Western church… it may well happen that God will allow the

Western church to disintegrate. As the church in the West dies so he will raise up the church in the East, and in the poorer nations, to be his servants and to bring the message of salvation to the world. This would be completely in line with the ways of God in Scripture.[6]

Is There a Second Chance?

The great question facing us today is whether or not there is another chance in the 21st century to do what we failed to achieve in the 20th century. In order to answer this question, we have to study, not only what God is doing in the world in the context of his biblically declared purposes, but also we have to understand what human beings are doing, and the nature of the battle against the powers of darkness that are presently threatening to overcome the Church in the West. Sometimes it is actually easier to discern what God is doing today by noting what the 'father of lies' is doing because he usually knows what is important to God, and that becomes the focus of his attack.

How is God working out his purposes for Britain? We know perfectly well that we are an unrighteous nation that has been squandering the biblical heritage of centuries since the 1960s when one ungodly statute after another has been passed into law by our Parliament. The summit of these laws, driven by the secular humanist movement that has so successfully infiltrated the political and social system of the nation, was reached in 2012 when Prime Minister David Cameron announced that he was espousing the 'same-sex marriage' ambitions of the powerful LGBT lobby group. This was not Cameron's brainchild. He had been present at an EU leaders' meeting in 2010 when it was decided to urge all EU nations to aim to introduce same-sex marriage by 2013. Cameron knew that pressures would soon be imposed, and as an ambitious politician he wanted to be ahead of the game. He did not, however, take into account that he would actually be putting himself against God and that this would begin the end of his political career.

Despite fierce opposition from a majority of his own backbench MPs, Cameron was able, with the help of Labour, LibDems and Scottish Nationalist MPs, to pass the Same-Sex Marriage Bill that redefined marriage which is part of God's act of creation – and thus put himself and the nation under severe judgment. Cameron was allowed a period of grace from the time the Act became operative in 2014 for a short time, just long enough to enable him to oversee a Referendum on Britain leaving the European Union. His political career ended in June 2016 with the vote that he and all the political pundits least expected.

Brexit

The Brexit decision that took Europe by surprise was all part of God's shaking of the nations. God both uses the socio-economic movements of change in society and also nudges them in the direction that achieves his purposes as part of the exercising of his sovereignty over the nations whereby, as the prophets of Israel recognised, nothing happens unless God either wills it or allows it. Brexit resulted from the social movement whereby the ordinary working people in the Western nations who had enjoyed a long period of relative prosperity since the end of World War II were now beginning to feel that prosperity draining away as economic power drifted from the monopoly exercised by the Western nations to the developing nations.

In Britain, America and most European nations, working people recognised that the austerity cuts that were making life increasingly difficult for them to make ends meet were the result of a small ruling elite of bankers, global investors and politicians making unjustifiable fortunes at their expense. As this realisation slowly dawned, people were looking for an opportunity of expressing their anger and disgust at the greed and corruption of the elite that had been revealed as part of the shaking of the nations, which had been growing in momentum since the 1980s.

But Brexit was not only the result of socio-economic disquiet; it also had a strong spiritual element resulting from a huge amount of prayer from Christians who discerned the significance of the shaking of the nations, and that God was exposing the demonic elements in the secular humanist forces of darkness that were driving the European Union towards self-destruction. Many evangelical Christians perceived the warning signs and in the months leading up to the June 2016 Referendum they organised specific, focused and believing prayer to get Britain out of the EU and no longer under the jurisdiction of the European courts of justice, which had an impact upon the result.

This corporate prayer movement came out of what has clearly been a move of God over several decades urging the faithful remnant to come together in small groups for prayer and study of the word of God. The movement has brought together Christians from all denominations and church traditions to meet in one another's homes with open Bibles, for prayer and fellowship, seeking to understand what God is saying to his people today. This is part of God's activity in mobilising his people for the great spiritual battle that is already raging over the Western nations.

Centrality of the Family

That battle is to be seen in the four great movements of social change that we noted in Chapter Six. We saw there that the central institution under attack from all four of these movements is the family. The family is of great significance because it is a foundational part of God's creation of humanity. We noted that all four movements of social change that coalesced in the 1960s not only had common roots, but there was also a similarity in objectives, particularly in the desire to destroy the Judaeo-Christian heritage of the Western nations. In order to achieve such an objective, the family was perceived to be the major barrier.

The importance of the family in Western society is undeniable. There is a huge mass of research showing that, despite all its imperfections, the traditional family, consisting of a husband and wife united in a covenant relationship of faithful marriage, provides the safest and most caring and supportive environment for the upbringing of children and ensuring their welfare, encouragement and education that fits them for personal fulfilment and stable adult life.

Research also shows that no other type of family is equally successful in providing an ideal outcome for children. Many single parents, of course, successfully raise their children and self-sacrificially provide the very best for their children; but this is not an ideal family environment. A massive amount of research shows that 'fatherlessness' is highly detrimental in the lives of children, especially boys who lack male role models and often seek a substitute in gang life that leads to various forms of anti-social behaviour, delinquency and crime. Research studies have shown that as many as 98% of young people involved in youth crime come from broken homes or fatherless families.[7]

Sociologist Prof Brigitte Berger argues that the nuclear family is not only good for raising children but it is fundamental to the structure of society. She says:

> It is of singular importance for us to remember that **only the family – and a very specific type of family – can spontaneously produce the social forms necessary for adequately linking autonomous individuals – regardless of ethnicity and social class – to the macro-structures of modern society.** This type of family, more than any other, is particularly suited for producing self-reliant, morally accountable, and entrepreneurial individuals who become the carriers of political responsibility and economic prosperity. In this the nuclear family in its 'bourgeois' form serves a mediating function between autonomous individuals and the mega structures of society. In this sense I think it is legitimate to argue that the fate of the bourgeois family and the fate of our type of society are inextricably intertwined.[8]

This is a statement of profound significance that was either not understood in the 1990s or was deliberately ignored in a society where the national culture was already being strongly driven by the LGBT lobby whose influence in the media was rapidly increasing. It was becoming increasingly fashionable in the Western media and among political lobby groups linked with the LGBT community to ridicule the nuclear family as part of their campaign to undermine and destroy the Judaeo-Christian values of society in order to advance their own agenda of social anarchy. No doubt this is the reason why there has been such a sustained attack upon the Church, with a particular focus upon the Church of England, due to its important position in society.

Homosexual Lifestyles

As we will see in Chapter 18, Archbishop Rowan Williams had to deal with a particularly difficult situation in preventing the appointment of a homosexual bishop soon after he became Archbishop of Canterbury.[9] The problems surrounding the issues of homosexuality in the clergy were to continue unresolved throughout Rowan's time at Canterbury and still be an issue passed on to his successor Archbishop Justin Welby.

The reason for this is not hard to see. For some who have adopted a homosexual lifestyle, their deepest desire is to have an assurance of the approval of God. They live in a society where historically homosexuality has been condemned and was actually illegal until the modern era of liberalisation. They carry with them that background and a sense of guilt from which they long to be free. But this presents a huge difficulty for Bible-believing Christians who cannot rewrite Scripture, or pretend that there is nothing in the Bible that condemns homosexual activity. Christians therefore aim to show love and acceptance in local Christian Fellowships, but this does not provide relief for those who are gay who carry a conviction that their lifestyle is not acceptable in the sight of God.

Among non-Christians there are many who simply want to get on with their lives quietly and with as little publicity as possible. But there are others who are aggressively vocal and have a political agenda that drives them. It would not be appropriate here to attempt to deal with the motives behind the activity of this group. It is, however, highly appropriate to note their *objectives*, because these not only affect the tiny minority of active homosexuals,[10] they affect the whole population. The declared objective of the LGBT community is to carry out a radical change in the structure of society by destroying the nuclear family which they see as the core social institution and what they regard as the root of their 'oppression'.

Political Influence

The LGBT movement is now highly organised on a worldwide basis which was considerably increased during the Obama period in the White House when America began linking aid grants with the promotion of family planning and LGBT values. Britain followed suit which is evidence of the considerable political power and influence the movement exercises in most Western nations, which is now spreading more widely.

The Marxist and Darwinian basis of their teaching puts it on a direct course of opposition to Judaeo-Christian biblically-based values, but politicians such as Prime Minister Theresa May don't appear to recognise the conflict with their professed faith. It was noticeable that one month after she revealed that she is a lesbian, Justine Greening was appointed by Theresa May as Secretary of State for Education, with responsibility for the education of the nation's children. Her influence was soon to be seen in the extension of sex education to five-year-old children in primary schools and in the increasing number of children being given treatment for what was euphemistically termed 'gender dysfunction' whereby children sought to change their birth gender. In July 2017 she announced that she was going to try to persuade the Conservative Government to pass legislation making it easier for people suffering from 'gender dysfunction' to change their gender. But opponents say that such people are really suffering from a form of mental illness and should not be helped to make physical changes that they will regret later in life. Greening lost her job in Education in a January 2018 reshuffle.

Church Influence

The Anglican Church in Scotland voted to recognise same-sex marriage in June 2017; and, in November 2017, Bible-believing Christians were outraged by Kelvin Holdsworth, the homosexual Provost of St Mary's Cathedral Glasgow, who called for Christians to pray for Prince George to be gay. He said that this would be the fastest way to force the Church of England to allow gay people to be married in Anglican churches.

In the July 2017 Synod of the Church of England held in York, John Sentamu, the Archbishop of York, urged the rejection of an amendment that would have committed the Church of England to evangelism among ethnic minorities in Britain. It was argued that for many years Britain has sent missionaries overseas to take the gospel to people of other faiths. Now they have come as immigrants to settle among us in Britain and yet we are doing nothing to evangelise them. The amendment was rejected but another amendment urging the writing of a ceremony to recognise the new identity of those who change gender was accepted with the approval of Sentamu and the nodding approval of Justin Welby the Archbishop of Canterbury.

Welby said that he looked forward to "radical new Christian inclusion" in the Church of England. He did not elaborate upon this, but it certainly sounds as though he expects the church to move away from its biblical foundations towards greater secularisation in conformity with the politically correct 'inclusiveness' in society. In November 2017

Archbishop Justin Welby sent a letter to all C of E primary schools encouraging them to facilitate cross-dressing among children. The reason for this was not stated but it looked to be in compliance with the LGBTQ+ objectives.

In January 2017, the Rev Dr Gavin Ashenden was forced to resign as Chaplain to the Queen because he protested against the reading of the Qur'an at St Mary's Cathedral Glasgow. The reading was on the Feast of Epiphany and it explicitly denied the divinity of Christ. Following his resignation, Dr Ashenden said,

> The hierarchy of the C of E have become so politicised that it matters more now that you are a feminist than a theologian or a baptised Christian... The C of E is much more comfortable with politics and power than it is with the Holy Spirit.... I'm not sure I see much point in a church that just wants to be accepted as a sort of not too irritating chaplain to a secular and hedonistic culture... The C of E has opted for a kind of spiritualised socialism and feminism in opposition to the gospel of our Lord Jesus Christ.[11]

Further comment seems unnecessary! I didn't think it was possible to get a worse Archbishop than Runcie – but maybe I was wrong.

Notes

[1] The Montanists were a group of Christians who held on to their belief in the presence and power of the Holy Spirit into the third century AD. Church history has dealt very harshly with them. When I was a young undergraduate anything to do with the Montanists was taught under the heading of 'heresies'. Church records of that time are so biased in favour of the church authorities that we cannot really know the truth about them. We certainly know that the hierarchy of Rome was mobilised to destroy them because they were seen to challenge the authority of the papacy and the priesthood, because they believed that the Holy Spirit was open to all believers. The fact that the great church leader Tertullian strongly supported them, should encourage a re-examination of history. He was not unaware of the value of persecution and martyrdom. His most famous saying was that 'the blood of the martyrs is the seed of the church.' But the church of Rome in his day was more interested in establishing the authority of its priests and hierarchy than in theologically examining the beliefs and practices of those who challenged the authority of Rome.

[2] Clifford Hill, Peter Fenwick, David Forbes, David Noakes, Eds, *Blessing the Church?*, Eagle, Guildford, 1995, p. 23.

[3] See also Chapter 12, p. 197.

[4] *Prophecy Today*, Volume 6 no 3 page 7

[5] *Blessing the Church?* p. 223.

[6] *Ibid.*, p. 226.

[7] Research published in June 2017 showed that self-harm among teenagers is linked to family breakdown. The same research showed that married couples enjoy better health than singles or any other form of couple relationship.

[8] Brigitte Berger, 'The Bourgeois Family and the Modern Family' in *The Family: Is It Just Another Lifestyle?*, IEA Health and Welfare Unit, Lancing, West Sussex, 1993, p. 24.

[9] See p. 264 in Chapter 18 for a fuller account of this incident.

[10] It is impossible to give an accurate number but most research suggests the number of active homosexual males in Britain to be between 1½% and 2%.

[11] An interview with VIRTUEONLINE: The Voice of Global Orthodox Anglicanism, published 29.01.2017.

Chapter Seventeen

SOCIAL ACTION

Centre for Contemporary Ministry

By the beginning of the 1990s the reshaping of the nation by the forces of secularisation was impacting every part of society. Family breakdown was having a particular effect upon all social institutions and was particularly affecting the health and welfare services. This had an impact upon the churches. Ministers and clergy of all denominations noticed the increased levels of stress in carrying out their pastoral work.

We were in touch with hundreds of pastors through our two ministries, PWM/PT and BCGA, and we recognised the need for pastoring the pastors. In response to this need we decided to provide in-service training courses for those in pastoral charge.

In the early 1990s Monica and I both believed that we were being led to leave London and establish a ministry base near Bedford. We eventually discovered Moggerhanger Park, a semi-derelict Georgian mansion in 1994 which we bought for £1.00 and set about restoring so that it could become a Christian ministry centre. We wanted to establish a community of believers who would be at the heart of the centre. They would share all things and be a serving community living by faith and sharing the gospel with members of the public and those who would come to our teaching courses.

This is not the place to tell the story of the amazing things that happened in our time there, but it is relevant to note that part of our objective was to bring both our ministries together, joining the Prophetic and Church Growth in a community project. In 1992 we had founded the 'Centre for Contemporary Ministry' (CCM) as an educational charity offering in-service training to those who were in pastoral charge and who wanted to increase their vision by gaining a greater understanding of what was happening in the contemporary world and how to be more effective in the pastoral ministry.

In 1992 we had begun offering three-to-five-day in-service residential courses at Bawtry Hall in Yorkshire, with a new course every two weeks, while we were searching for the right premises. The objective was to transfer this teaching ministry to the new base as soon as conference facilities and bedrooms were available. Soon after we had acquired Moggerhanger Park in 1995 it was upgraded to Grade 1 which meant that its restoration was going to be a much longer process than we had expected, and it was spread over the next 10 years costing in excess of £7 million. The house was designed by Sir John Soane, a leading 18th century architect, for the Thornton family who were first cousins of William Wilberforce.

We felt a strong affinity with Wilberforce because of his concern to apply the gospel to the great social issues of his day. Wilberforce not only campaigned against slavery but he also sought to improve the working conditions of those who laboured in the cotton mills of Lancashire, in the woollen mills of Yorkshire and down in the mines of South Wales. His especial concern was with the exploitation of children as young as seven years of age who often worked 12 hours a day in appalling conditions and were subjected to cruelty by their employers. Our experience of working in inner-city areas of London over a number of years had given us a great love and concern for the powerless, and those who were often victims of injustice. In particular our experience of working with Africans and immigrants from the Caribbean led us to identify what we believed to be a legacy of slavery among the Caribbeans. The mixed-race populations among whom we worked shared a variety of needs. Welding these together into a community was a particular challenge.

Transform-UK

Our vision throughout our years of working in Tottenham and in the East End of London was nothing less than the transformation of society to give hope to those who were depressed and hopeless, not simply with first-aid programmes, or 'soup kitchen' runs supplying food to the homeless, as some churches did. We did not despise this work, but our concern was changing lives as well as living and working conditions. We were deeply committed to a fully evangelical message as well as making structural changes in society which would give opportunity and hope to those who were not only hopeless but voiceless. Our community development programmes aimed to identify each individual's potential and to start where they were in meeting their needs.

We founded an organisation called *Transform-UK* which sought to follow Wilberforce and the Clapham group of evangelical social reformers with whom he worked. Their ethos was both social and evangelical, being concerned with both social change and personal salvation, which was very similar to the ethos that we had in our work in London. I discussed these concepts at some length with Archbishop Rowan on a number of occasions and with Members of Parliament of different parties who were Christians and who had a similar vision of being part of a modern day 'Clapham Sect'. Numerous meetings took place in and around Parliament and as part of this work we founded the 'Christian Workplace Forum' (CWF) that was linked with the Universities and Colleges Christian Fellowship (UCCF) now called 'Christian Unions'. Its objective was to provide a link between the universities and the workplace. This was in response to the many Christians who had enjoyed the fellowship and support of their Christian Union during their student days and then when they got into the workplace they found no similar support.

Christian Workplace Forum

By 2005 CWF was affiliated with 85 Christian associations in the professions, commerce and industry. Our objective was to get these associations recognised by their employers so they could contribute to the management, and where appropriate to wider activities among the employees. The outstanding example of success was with the Audit Commission where the Christian Association was invited to have a representative on the Management Board and were given permission to circulate by email a 'Thought for the Week' and to offer their services for counselling to any of the employees. This was a model that was widely circulated to other employers but we were disappointed that there were not many who followed the Audit Commission's example. This was not necessarily due to intransigence among employers, but also to the lack of vision among the Christian groups.

Christian Workplace Associations settled upon prayer meetings and engaging in evangelism. Many of them replicated 'church' at their meetings and there was no strong vision for seeking to change the nature of the institutions for which they worked. Several MPs were very good at hosting meetings in Parliament with representatives of Christian Workplace Associations but we were not very successful in transmitting the concepts of *Transform UK* into the workplace. We nevertheless followed the practice we had begun in the East End of London where we never had a 'failure' – we only had 'learning experiences'! We sought other ways of achieving the same ends.

In 2005 the *Transform UK* team undertook a national tour with meetings in different parts of the country seeking to generate grassroots activity using a similar strategy to that used by Wilberforce. The programme usually included a presentation of *The Walk,* which was a short play about the life and work of Wilberforce. It featured his struggle between wanting to be used in evangelism and his calling to be in Parliament, representing the County of York. It included an encounter with John Newton, the writer of *Amazing Grace,* who convinced William that he could best serve God by remaining in Parliament and fighting for the abolition of slavery.

Abolition of The Slave Trade

Monica and I were already members of a national committee set up to initiate plans for the commemoration of the 200th anniversary of the abolition of the slave trade in 2007. None of the plans were particularly ambitious, although they included a Thanksgiving Service in Westminster Abbey to be attended by the Queen and led by the Archbishop of Canterbury. In our prayers we believed there was something more that could be done which would dramatically communicate the horrors of the transatlantic slave trade and the legacy that we knew still existed among Caribbeans, not only in the Caribbean islands but also among migrants in Britain, especially in the under-achievement of boys in school, and health issues among adults.

Finding a Replica Ship
We decided to bring a replica slave ship into London and open it to the public. In August 2006 we discovered that the Square Rigger used in the film *Amazing Grace*, in which it was named the *Madagascar*, was moored in Charlestown, St Austell, Cornwall. The owners were willing to lease it for the period we required in March/April 2007. We went to see it in September and reached agreement on refitting it as a slave ship and re-naming it *The Zong*[1] after the most infamous of the 18th Century slavers. We also negotiated with the Port of London Authority for the use of Tower Pier and a mooring in the Thames adjacent to Sugar Pier.

The Royal Navy
We had earlier approached the Admiralty to explore the possibility of mooring alongside HMS Belfast. This was not possible due to the gigantic size of the Belfast against the tiny sailing ship. The Admiralty, nevertheless, expressed considerable interest in the project and offered to send a warship up the River Thames into the Pool of London to accompany the slave ship as part of the Navy's commemoration of their role in the abolition of the slave trade. The 1807 Act of Parliament banning the slave trade could not have been enforced without the active participation of the Royal Navy and they were proud of their role in keeping the Atlantic clear of slavers.

Funding
These negotiations enabled us to fix a provisional budget of £250,000. We had less than six months to raise this sum but support from a number of sources appeared to be encouraging and we had expectations of £100,000 from Walden Media, the makers of the film *Amazing Grace*, £50,000 from the Heritage Lottery Fund and £50,000 from the GLA.

By the end of November 2006 it became clear that none of these provisional promises were likely to materialise. We were faced with cancellation of all the arrangements and the abandonment of the project. Early in December the decision was taken to appeal to our ministry supporters. A letter went out in the second week of December 2006 at the height of the Christmas post. But by Christmas Eve we received promises of nearly £200,000 so contracts were confirmed. Donations continued to come from individual supporters in the New Year which enabled us to meet the final budget of £300,000 for which we truly gave thanks to God, as we saw this as an amazing answer to prayer.

Distressing Experience

The experience of going on board *The Zong* and down into the cargo hold where slaves had been chained and manacled was painful for many African-Caribbeans, knowing that this was how their forebears had been transported across the Atlantic. A coach party from Birmingham brought with them a large wreath which they placed in the slave-pen on the lower deck. This simple action added to the pathos for many visitors, some of whom were in tears when they climbed back onto the upper deck. The Birmingham group said they were particularly thinking of the 1.3 million Africans who lost their lives on the journey across the Atlantic as well as their own forebears who were enslaved on the sugar plantations in the Caribbean islands.

Some young people of African-Caribbean origins living in Peckham, South London came to visit *The Zong* because they saw it on the TV news and were impressed with the multiracial group of singers on board the ship as it sailed into London. They thought at first that this was a white man's attempts to whitewash the slave trade. But when they saw that the group of singers was black and white, young and old they decided to come and said they had learned a lot because they were 'never taught this stuff at school' and they wanted to know more about their roots.

The Hidden Period of History

The fact that this period of history had not been taught in school came out in conversation with hundreds of Caribbeans. The comments of older people showed that all the history they were taught in the West Indies was about English Kings and Queens. They were never taught about their own history beginning in Africa. Many of them said that slavery is a subject that is never even talked about privately in their family groups because it was a taboo subject back home in the West Indies. Slavery was in the distant past and older Caribbeans preferred to leave it there and not to discuss the subject. But among young people the 'Zong Project' revealed a real hunger to know their own history which they feel they have been denied for 200 years.

There was always an expert historian on hand and there were also trained counsellors available for those who found the experience on board *The Zong* to be distressing. All our staff and 120 volunteers were not only familiar with the subject but were also committed to the concept of reconciliation. This was emphasised in conversations with visitors, in the free literature that was given to each visitor, and other papers that were freely available.

Gospel Message

Reconciliation was also the focal point of an onboard prayer-time on Maundy Thursday evening, held on the deck of *The Zong* slave ship, where black and white people washed one another's feet in the way that Jesus had washed his disciples' feet at the Last Supper. It was a memorable time.

Research[2] of those visiting the ship showed that very few people knew much about the 300-year slave trade between the West Coast of Africa and the Americas including the Caribbean. Following the abolition of the slave trade in 1807 and the ending of slavery in the British Empire in 1833, the subject was not taught in most British schools until it was put on the curriculum in 2007, only to be dropped again a few years later. Any teaching on slavery was usually based upon the cotton fields of the American deep South rather than the Caribbean sugar industry and the cruelty of plantation life under British rule. The public exhibition we organised at 'All Hallows by the Tower' and on the replica slave ship attracted considerable public attention including TV news broadcasts.

The Zong was opened by Ken Livingstone, the Mayor of London, who called for the ship to be permanently based in London as "an iconic" historical feature. We did a lot of project planning and costing for mooring the ship permanently in the Royal London docks, but by the time we had carried out this work Ken Livingstone was involved in seeking to obtain a third term of office as London Mayor and he was no longer interested in the Slave-ship project.

Boris Johnson's Request

Boris Johnson, however, had heard of my links with black churches and community leaders and he asked to meet with me. I had no wish to become involved in party politics and political campaigning so I refused. Boris's team continued to pursue me and in February 2008 I decided to meet him to see if he might take over Ken Livingstone's interest in the Slave-ship project. We met in the disused former GLC headquarters on the South bank of the Thames. It was an eerie experience walking down those long empty corridors to find the room Boris had hired which had no furniture in it other than a table and two or three wooden chairs. We spent a couple of hours together discussing community issues and the plight of black young people in London. Boris promised full support of the Zong Project if he became Mayor and he asked if I would help him by using my influence to persuade black leaders to come to a breakfast meeting in the Emmanuel Centre Westminster.

I agreed to do this on the understanding that he would make youth and family issues in the Caribbean community a priority and that he would support the Zong Project. I was responsible for getting a good number of black church and community leaders to hear him speak which undoubtedly had a significant effect upon the election which surprised the pundits by the large number of votes for Boris, a Conservative candidate, from inner-city boroughs with large black populations. Sadly, once he became Mayor, despite numerous appeals to him, Boris was no longer interested in the slavery issue.

Financial Crash

In June 2008 I met with David Noakes and Michael Fenton Jones for a time of prayer, seeking the Lord together to understand what was happening in the nation. We were convinced that a financial crash was imminent and we decided to call a meeting of Ministry leaders. We booked the lower hall at the Emmanuel Centre Westminster for the first Saturday in October. Over a hundred were present and this proved to be the weekend when many of the great financial houses crashed due to the crisis caused by the sub-prime mortgage scandal in America. We had got our timing right. There was much animated discussion and prayer, seeking to understand what was happening in terms of the purposes of God.

Meeting in Parliament

There was a collective decision to approach our friends among MPs and Members of the Lords and to call a meeting in Parliament, which took place in December in the Upper House. The sponsors of this meeting were the Right Rev Peter Foster, Bishop of Chester, Alistair Burt MP, David Burrows MP, Jim Dobbin MP, Andrew Selous MP, Lord Hylton, Lord Anderson of Swansea, the Right Rev Nigel McCulloch, Bishop of Manchester. The meeting was called as a Private Consultation on *The Social and Spiritual Implications of the Current Financial Crisis*.

More than 80 attended the consultation, including lawyers, businessmen and church leaders. There were 12 listed speakers and then the meeting was opened up to anyone wishing to speak. A number of the businessmen had spoken of the greed and corruption in the financial services industry and this was picked up by other speakers who emphasised how the nation had moved away from its Judaeo-Christian heritage. Many of the speakers emphasised the need for spiritual renewal. Many Scriptures were quoted, including Deuteronomy 28 that lists the things that threatened judgment upon Israel. Several of the lawyers and MPs emphasised the opportunity that the financial crisis was giving for a re-examination of our values and a new emphasis upon biblical truth.

Declaration

A declaration was agreed as a press statement recognising that the financial crisis was not simply due to a monetary policy or faults in economic policy. It was due to greed and corruption creeping into the financial systems with the insatiable drive to increase profits and personal bonuses as well as to build up a vast mountain of debt which was dependent upon confidence and trust. Once that confidence was lost the whole edifice began to collapse like a house of cards. The resolution of the present crisis depended upon a re-examination of our values which lay at the heart of the present situation.

Day of Prayer

Alongside the declaration there was a call for a day of prayer and repentance. This took place on 28 February 2009 in the Emanuel Centre Westminster. The outcome was a clear message to the church in Britain to declare to the nation that God is at work in the things we are seeing in our daily newspapers and TV news. God was shaking the foundations of the nation to bring fundamental change into our social and personal values, politics, the economy, education, the media and the church.

God was reminding us that there is no other foundation upon which the church in the nation can live other than that which he has laid — Jesus Christ our Lord and Saviour. Through what we called the financial crisis, God was exposing the moral and spiritual corruption caused by our having turned our backs upon God, deliberately going our own way and doing things that are directly against the word of God. The word of God states:

> *"If at any time I announce that a nation or kingdom is to be uprooted, torn down and destroyed, and if that nation I warned repents of its evil, then I will relent and not inflict on it the disaster I had planned"* (Jer 18.7).

God was calling the church to be proactive in changing the nation and Christians to be much more active in:

- explaining to the nation what has gone wrong, and calling for repentance because we had turned away from the word of God
- describing God's purposes, his love and forgiveness
- declaring to the Nation the principles and values of the Kingdom of God
- bringing major changes into every part of the life of the nation
- ensuring that the values of the Kingdom are clearly seen in our own lives, words and deeds.

Heal Our Land

The year 2009 also saw the launch of a new musical Christian event *Heal Our Land*. It was based upon an original musical written and produced by Jimmy and Carol Owens in the USA. They were well known in Britain in the 1970s and 80s for their earlier musical events *Come Together* and *If My People*. Monica and I had gone with a party from our community in the East End of London in 1976 to the Albert Hall to enjoy the presentation of *If My People*.

Jimmy and Carol wrote a book entitled *Heal Our Land* to coincide with the production of the new musical. I wrote a few chapters in it and it was published by our own ministry.[3] The new musical was largely the work of Liz Doyle working with two Caribbean church leaders, Lloyd and Dennis Wade, who had updated the songs and written some new ones. The London premiere of 'Heal our Land' was at the Emmanuel Centre Westminster in the New Year 2010. It was then presented in Liverpool Cathedral by a local choir supported by a small professional choir led by Wade brothers. There were more than 1,000 people present and the musical was received with great enthusiasm. From Liverpool it went on tour to a number of places around Britain.

Notes

[1] The Zong, owned by two former Lord Mayors of Liverpool, sailed from the West Coast of Africa in 1781, being licensed to carry 292 Africans. The captain (Collingwood) took on board 442 men, women and children, for whom there were insufficient provisions for a journey to the Caribbean that lasted almost 3 months. When nearing Jamaica and knowing that his Africans were in such poor health they would fetch very little on the slave market, he decided to throw overboard 132 live men and women and claim insurance on them. The insurers opposed the claim which became a celebrity court case going right to the High Court in London where Lord Mansfield stated that under British law throwing slaves overboard was the same as throwing horses. They were chattels. However, Lord Mansfield held against the insurers, holding that the slavers were at fault.
[2] *The Zong Report*, CCM, Bedford, 2007 available from Issachar Ministries. The Movement for Justice and Reconciliation has been researching the legacy of slavery and has taken responsibility for the Zong project. Their plans for 2019 include sailing the ship around ports on the South and West coasts of England that were involved in the colonial slave trade.
[3] Jimmy and Carol Owens with Clifford Hill, *Heal Our Land, Strategies for Prayer and Action*, CCM, Bedford, 2010.

Chapter Eighteen

ARCHBISHOP ROWAN WILLIAMS

The Most Revd and Rt Hon Dr Rowan Williams
Archbishop of Canterbury December 2002 to December 2012
George Carey was succeeded by Archbishop Rowan Williams who
had a reputation of being a liberal and whose appointment was greeted
with dismay by many evangelicals. He had particularly attracted some
unfavourable press reports by attending a Welsh festival and participating
in a Druid ceremonial. English evangelicals saw this as participating in
a pagan ceremony, but that was not how Rowan saw it. He was invited
because of his poetry writings, in particular his poems in the Welsh
language. This ceremonial he simply saw as a celebration of Welsh
culture in which his contribution was recognised. But this view was
not shared by English evangelicals which increased their opposition to
his appointment when it was announced and this was reflected in some
unfavourable newspaper reports.

First Meeting
It was quite extraordinary how my friendship with Rowan began when
he was the Archbishop of Wales, based in Newport, South Wales. I had
been invited to speak at a meeting at Newport. It was an open public
meeting organised by the Revd Geoff Waggett on behalf of ARM (the
Renewal Group of Anglican clergy of the Church in Wales). Rowan as
Archbishop of Wales was listed as one of the speakers. I had woken
early on the morning of the meeting and in my prayer time the Lord had

spoken to me about the significance of this meeting and in particular of my meeting with the Archbishop which was to have far-reaching consequences. This seemed strange to me because I had never met the man and I knew nothing about him. I had not read any of his books so I was not familiar with his theology and I was a stranger to what was happening in the church in Wales.

I reached Paddington Station in good time for an early morning train from London to South Wales, but found that there were severe delays due to some problems down the line. It was some two hours later that the train left Paddington and I knew that the Archbishop was one of the morning speakers so I feared that I would not see him. I concluded that I must have been wrong in what I had thought God had said to me earlier in the day about the significance of my meeting with him.

I was met at Newport Station and driven to the school where the meeting was being held. As we drove into the car park my driver said, "Oh, there's the Archbishop just leaving." I walked quickly across the car park just as he settled into the passenger seat of his car. I tapped on the window which he opened and I said my name, adding that I had just come to greet him. He immediately smiled broadly and told his driver to switch off the engine and he got out to talk to me. We stood there talking for about twenty minutes or maybe even half an hour. We covered a number of things and then he asked me to pray for him. I followed my usual practice and simply laid my hand on his shoulder and quietly asked the Lord what I should pray for.

To my astonishment I heard the Lord say that this man was chosen to be the next Archbishop of Canterbury. Instead of praying with him I told him what I had heard. He laughed and said this was all the more reason why I should pray for him. As I began to pray I saw some of the things that lay ahead which would bring him great suffering. I saw the very testing times that he was going to have to face and I began describing them. This became so real at one point that I actually broke down and wept. This was incredibly unusual for me. I don't do tears. I was truly amazed and embarrassed that I was so overcome with grief. I actually wept while trying to pray with an astonished Rowan. In my confusion and apologies, I tried to describe what I was seeing, but words were so inadequate. I then prayed for strength and a double measure of the

Holy Spirit for him. He got back into his car, and I went into the school where the meeting was being held. After the lunch period, I spoke to the meeting, and spent the rest of the day there before returning to London; but I said nothing to Geoff Waggett or anyone at the Newport meeting of my strange encounter with Rowan.

Unlikely Friendship

I heard no more until there was a public announcement that he had been nominated as the next Archbishop of Canterbury. Shortly after that he contacted me and asked me if I would come to visit him in South Wales. He knew that the Lord had revealed things to me and he wanted to talk with me to know what God had said to me. I went several times while he was still in Wales, and spent time gently elaborating on the things that I had foreseen. I prayed with him on each of my visits and especially shortly before his move to London. Once he had moved into Lambeth Palace I began going regularly and Monica sometimes came with me to spend time with Jane. For a number of years we met at least once a month. By this time, I had learned a lot more about his theology and I wondered why God had brought me together with him.

I think that as an ordained minister, but a non-Anglican and therefore not under his ecclesiastical authority, I was useful to him. Our friendship deepened quite rapidly and he asked for my views on the draft of the address he intended to give at his installation in Canterbury Cathedral. I assumed that it was for this purpose that God had brought me into his life – to help him to fulfil a prophetic role in the nation, bringing the word of God into the public square at a crucial time in British history.

I made a number of suggestions, attempting to bring it more in line with the message of the biblical prophets as a declaration of the kind of ministry that I believed to be needed and I hoped he would exercise in the nation. I wanted to see something that recognised the changes that were reshaping the nation and a declaration of how the gospel could be on the front line leading social change in the nation. But Rowan resisted this and settled for a much safer and thoughtful piece. I was disappointed, but at the same time I recognised that this was his great occasion and he must fulfil his ministry as he felt called by God.

Problems Start

The revelation I had received of the problems Rowan would encounter in his ten years at Canterbury were by no means exaggerated. In fact, the problems began almost immediately after his consecration with the nomination of the Revd Dr Jeffrey John as the Suffragan Bishop of Reading in Berkshire. The vacancy came under the Diocesan Bishop of Oxford, Richard Harries, one of the liberal bishops appointed by Robert Runcie.

Jeffrey John was well known for his homosexual lifestyle. He was on the staff of Southwark Cathedral in south London and he had been on terms of friendship with Rowan Williams from the time when they were both at Oxford. In May 2003, there was an announcement that Jeffrey was to become the Bishop of Reading. This took Rowan completely by surprise as he had not been consulted on the appointment, as was his right.

There was an immediate outcry from a number of clergy in and around Reading and elsewhere in the diocese of Oxford. Evangelical clergy in particular, from a wide area, contacted Church House and Lambeth Palace to make their views known in no uncertain terms. Their views inevitably found their way into the press and other news media where anything controversial in the Church is eagerly seized upon. Rowan began to make enquiries as to why he had not been consulted and he was told that as he had only recently become Archbishop of Canterbury it was thought that he should not be burdened with the matter of a Suffragan Bishop in this early stage of his ministry.

Rowan then met with the Archbishops' Appointments Secretary in the Crown Appointments Commission. It was he who had sent the nomination directly to Richard Harries, bypassing Rowan. The letter had contained several names and stars had been put against the name of Jeffrey John. Richard thought that the paper had been approved by Rowan and he further thought that Rowan was responsible for putting the stars against the name of Jeffrey John. Richard Harries, well known for his liberal theology, welcomed the appointment but was dismayed when he heard that Rowan was querying it.

It certainly looked to me as though Rowan had been 'stitched-up' in the early days of his time at Canterbury, although this is just a personal opinion and I did not discuss this with him. Rowan, nevertheless, took some time to consider all the implications of appointing the first homosexual Anglican Bishop and he took note of the views of local clergy in the Oxford diocese as well as the strong representations from evangelical clergy and others in the Church of England that were sent to Lambeth Palace. His decision was made more difficult due to his own earlier writings that expressed sympathy with homosexual aspirations of equality and his concerns about the rejection some of them suffered, which he clearly considered to be unjust. His views on homosexuality were set out in publications such as *The Body's Grace* and *Open to Judgement*.[1] On his appointment, the Lesbian and Gay Christian Movement eulogised:

> This is extraordinarily good news and we are tremendously excited... For the first time lesbian and gay Anglicans can feel that they have a real friend in Lambeth. No longer will we need to feel shut out of the heart of the Church. Rowan counts many of us as his friends, his knowledge and understanding of the feelings of exclusion we have experienced can only lead to greater understanding of our lives.[2]

With this level of expectation upon him from the homosexual community, many of whom counted him as a friend, Rowan knew that he would be bitterly disappointing them if he did not appoint Jeffrey John. Nevertheless, Rowan was determined to explore all the different issues involved in his decision. He knew that going against those who counted him as a friend would be painful, but he had the wider implications to consider, not only in the Church of England, but in the worldwide Anglican Communion and its relationships with other parts of the Body of Christ. This was certainly not the kind of issue he wanted to face within weeks of arriving in London. He tried to find an amicable solution. In phone calls and correspondence with Jeffrey John and Richard Harries, Rowan tried to persuade Jeffrey to stand down, but he refused.

Rowan then invited them both to come to talk with him. The meeting was arranged for a Saturday and Rowan spent much of the day trying to persuade them both that for the sake of unity, not only within the Church of England but in the worldwide Anglican Communion, it would be much better if Jeffrey stood down. Both Jeffrey and Richard were strongly against this and in the end Rowan had to exercise his executive authority and refuse to allow the appointment.

It was an extremely difficult time for Rowan. His suffering that I had foreseen had begun. During the week prior to his meeting with Jeffrey I made three journeys to Lambeth Palace and spent many hours with him talking through the issues and praying with him. Rowan is by nature gentle and loving, with a pastoral heart, and he certainly had no wish to hurt Jeffrey or to disappoint Richard and many others who had welcomed his appointment as Archbishop, but it was becoming increasingly clear that he could not please everyone. In between each visit I made contact with many clergy and church leaders, sounding out their views, which I relayed to Rowan. We then spread them all before the Lord and got into prayer.

In the end, I don't think it was any individual view that weighed with him in making his decision, although, of course, I cannot speak on his behalf. I believe his central concern was to preserve unity within the church and that it was not right at that time to challenge traditional teaching on marriage which would inevitably have been a result of the appointment of a homosexual bishop.

It was widely reported that Rowan had blocked the appointment, and Richard Harries made no secret of his anger and disagreement, to which he referred publicly in his diocesan newsletter. I am not saying here any more than is already in the public domain. I am simply noting that for Rowan it was a costly decision to have to make within weeks of taking up his responsibilities and my role was simply to be alongside him and to pray with him.

International Problems

Issues of human sexuality were set to trouble Rowan for the whole of his time at Canterbury. The Jeffrey John incident was followed by the appointment of Gene Robinson as Bishop of New Hampshire in the Episcopal church of the USA. This man was not only an active homosexual living with his male partner, but he had been married to a woman and had children. He had done exactly what Paul denounced in Romans 1.27 – *In the same way the men also abandoned natural relations with women and were inflamed with lust for one another*. He had *abandoned natural relations* and broken his marriage covenant and the vows before God he had made to his wife. His wife was still alive so he was acting against the teaching of Jesus.[3] He had also left his children, thus abrogating his duties as a father. If he could not be faithful in keeping his vows to his wife and caring for his children, how was he fit to be a bishop in the church?

The additional difficulty for Rowan as head of the worldwide Anglican Communion was the strong objection coming from many of the African bishops who threatened secession if the Anglicans in America were not disciplined. Holding the whole Anglican Communion together as well as dealing with the problems of unity within the Church of England became a major feature of Rowan's time at Canterbury. It would probably be true to say that of all the multitude of problems he faced, especially in the administration of the unwieldy international institution of the Anglican Communion, the problems related to human sexuality and church unity were the most difficult.

Theological Problems

One of the complications for Rowan, however, lay in his own writings and the fact that he took no steps to deny or moderate the views that he had expressed earlier in his academic career. This was a problem that did not only relate to his views on human sexuality but the whole of his biblical theology which even mature theologians sometimes found difficult to comprehend. Dr Gary Williams published a short critique of Rowan's theology[4] at the time of his appointment to Canterbury. He expressed the fears of many evangelicals that the Archbishop would not exercise a biblical ministry and thereby fail to give the nation the lead that they believed was needed.

Our friendship, however, did not only involve discussing these problems and seeking guidance from God. We had many biblical discussions although we avoided the kind of theological issues he had grappled with in his published writings. Our relationship was not comparable with an academic seminar discussion. So, although I was aware of the issues raised by Gary Williams and the things that I had read in some of Rowan's earlier writings and I was now hearing quoted to me by my friends, I avoided these in the belief that God had brought me into this friendship in order to help Rowan fulfil a prophetic mission through his time in the leadership of the Anglican church and the influence that he could have in the nation.

I hoped (maybe mistakenly) that my own simple, direct and biblically-based faith might be helpful to him in fulfilling this calling, and what he needed to hear from me was more practical theology than lecture room theology. I did not feel that it was incumbent upon me to raise issues with him even in regard to sin and salvation which I knew his critics were querying, because nowhere in his published writings had he made a simple statement that Jesus bore our sins upon the Cross thus enabling us to enter a right relationship with God our Father. His teaching on the Cross was more in line with God offering comfort to sinners by having triumphed over the worst that human hatred could perpetrate.[5]

The help that I could offer included considering some of the important speeches he was required to make when he shared with me the draft of a forthcoming speech and invited me to comment. I think, for both of us, some of the happiest times we had were searching the Scriptures together. I was able to share with him my love of the biblical prophets and particularly the life and times of Jeremiah and Ezekiel, and the relevance of their messages for our own times. I appreciated Rowan's scholarship, and his knowledge of the Hebrew Scriptures.

Personal Cost

What Rowan did not know was the cost to me personally of our friendship. I lost many of my evangelical friends. Although I never discussed with them my visits to Lambeth Palace, they became aware that I had some kind of connection because of the Jeffrey John affair. I had been asking a lot of questions to gain as much information I could, particularly from Anglican clergy, and I was able to feed back some guarded information which showed that I had some connection with Rowan. Although the outcome was pleasing to most evangelicals there remained a deep suspicion of the new Archbishop and when I defended him disapproval was usually directed at me.

The most difficult time was when Rowan accepted an invitation from the trustees of Moggerhanger Park, our ministry base in Bedfordshire, to speak at a celebration marking the conclusion of a major restoration of the Grade 1 listed property. The backlash from many of our supporters created numerous difficulties in our ministry. But the most challenging was the reaction of the Editorial Board of the magazine *Prophecy Today* that I had founded and led for 20 years. I was in the process of handing over the senior editorship to a conservative evangelical. In handing the magazine over to him we made an agreement that I would remain as Consultant Editor and the magazine would always be open to me to publish my writings and it would support my ministry.

In December 2003 it became known that Rowan was to visit Moggerhanger in October 2004, and on the front cover of the January 2004 issue of *Prophecy Today* there was a photo of Rowan, and an editorial to the effect that the magazine would not support the Archbishop unless Rowan publicly declared that he upheld "the absolute authority of God's word for all matters of doctrine and morality". The editorial said, "I cannot permit the impression to be given that this magazine is associated with, or in any agreement with, his stance." I was removed from the Board and the magazine simply noted my name as Founder. But by the end of the year they dropped all mention of my name, and from different sources I heard that my position was being questioned by many evangelicals. It was a difficult time.

Defining 'The Church'
One of Rowan's problems, which became apparent quite early in his tenure at Canterbury, was in expressing himself simply, in terms easily understood by non-theologically educated people. At the July 2003 Synod of the Anglican Church he quite rightly stated his own understanding of the church. One section in the heart of his speech summarised his thinking on the Anglican Church.

What makes a church is the call of Jesus Christ, and our freedom and ability, helped by grace, to recognise that call in each other. The first reality is God's actions summoning us together as a people – in the words of Jesus, which make it clear that we can belong to God's people if we trust what Jesus says about God and does in God's name, and in the death and resurrection of Jesus, which actively remove the barriers we set up by our sin to communion with God.

To announce all this is to announce God's invitation. To accept the invitation, with all it carries of acknowledging what Jesus has done, is to be taken into Christ's living Body, finding there a company of unlikely people who have received and answered the same invitation.

The Church's life develops as we slowly and clumsily start working on the ways we recognise each other as called by the same God and Saviour... Our language, our doctrine, our worship all seek to be effective assurances that we are stepping to the same dance. At the centre of everything, the Scriptures provide the first test of that unity and coherence, to which all else is brought to be judged; then there are the basic identifying acts of the community which tell us that the life of the Risen Christ is promised if we once let go of the self-protection we cling to (baptism) and that it is to be celebrated and deepened as we literally respond to the invitation of the Risen Jesus at his table (communion).[6]

These thoughts about the Church would be understood by theologians, but it is doubtful if many members of the public reading the speech, or indeed, members of the General Synod, understood its language. I recognised quite early in our friendship the difficulty Rowan had in communication. His definition of the church above is actually quite an orthodox statement but it does not contain a simple basic statement of the gospel that Jesus died for our sins and that we are part of a community of the redeemed. It does not communicate with the prophetic fervour of a Martin Luther King describing his mountaintop experience and how he had to go down into the valley where the people were. I longed to see Rowan transform his insights and understanding of the church and its mission in the modern world into terms that ordinary people could understand in the way that Donald Coggan had done in his 'Call to the Nation'. It was very largely because of his use of language and inability to express things clearly in simple English that he ran into problems with the media.

This was shown in the problems he had when speaking about Islam. He told a reporter that he intended to refer to Islam in his Christmas Day sermon in Canterbury Cathedral 2003 where he wanted to say something about promoting peace and tolerance. Unfortunately, it provoked a storm of protest including a fierce rebuke from Home Secretary David Blunkett, gleefully reported in the *Daily Mail*[7] under the headline "Blunkett Blasts Back in Archbishop Terror Row". Rowan wisely deleted it from his Christmas sermon and stuck to a more conventional presentation of the Nativity message. But I was concerned that this incident appeared to show that Rowan had little understanding of the explosive social issues surrounding Islam in the nation.

Islam

On one occasion Rowan had received an invitation to address the senior Islamic scholars in Egypt at their most prestigious Mosque. I saw this as a God-given opportunity for presenting the gospel, and I suggested he should make a comparison between the teaching of Jesus and that of Mohammed.

I also wanted him to tackle some of the issues of segregation among immigrants which were creating ghettos in some of our cities. I was particularly concerned that terrorists were justifying their atrocities by using references in the Qur'an which urged Muslims not to make friends with non-Muslims, and other references urging Muslims to kill Jews and Christians. These were being used by Al Qaeda and the Islamic State fighters and others whom the West labelled terrorists or 'extremists'.

But Rowan chose a much less controversial but more intellectually demanding subject of explaining the Christian concept of the Trinity. This, of course, was no easy task although it was certainly very relevant, as Islam teaches that Christians are not monotheists – that they worship three gods. Rowan felt that tackling this basic theological misunderstanding of Christian doctrine would be a way of opening dialogue that could lead to a consideration of other doctrinal issues between Islam and Christianity. In the event, the Muslim scholars listened to him attentively, but there was no indication that they were willing to enter into a continuing dialogue. I was disappointed in this and felt that it was a missed opportunity.

On other occasions when he made statements about Islam in Britain, particularly referring to the relevance of Sharia law for the migrant communities of Muslims, he was severely rebuked in the media. But once again, I found myself comforting him and Jane. I think that he was trying to see these issues from the standpoint of the Muslims in Britain and the needs of their communities. But his words were seen as undermining British Common Law. I personally did not think that Rowan ever really understood the spiritual as well as the political issues at the heart of Islam. He was treating Islam on the same basis as any other philosophical concept instead of seeing it in the context of Islam's own history of forceful conversion and Mohammed's strong antagonism towards Jews and Christians who did not accept his new religion. I don't think that Islam can be understood without recognising the influence upon Muslims of the commands in the Qur'an to kill Jews and Christians as part of their service to Allah.

Although we often took different views, there were many issues on which we were in full agreement and I grew to respect not only Rowan's scholarship, but despite the differences between us, also his love for Jesus. I was continually urging a much more prophetic and biblically-based forthright approach to issues using simple language, but he was not gifted with that kind of leadership although he was usually patient when I was often a thorn in his flesh.

Pastoral

Despite the wide range of demands upon his time, Rowan never forsook the pastoral responsibilities of his calling. On one occasion I drew his attention to one of my friends, Peter Lawrence, who was the Vicar of Canford Magna in Dorset, and author of several books on the Charismatic Movement.[8] I had known Peter for many years as we had a lot in common – both ministering to inner-city congregations. Peter was in Birmingham when I was in the East End of London. Peter had recently been diagnosed with terminal cancer and Rowan immediately wrote to him a lovely pastoral letter and he continued in correspondence with him until Peter passed away.

The Clapham Sect

Rowan and I both had a great respect for Wilberforce. I had spent several years researching for a book on Wilberforce and the Clapham Group and their work to abolish the slave trade, the 200th anniversary of which was commemorated in 2007.[9] Rowan was kind enough to read the manuscript for me (despite his many commitments) and make a number of helpful suggestions and amendments to the text. He also wrote the Foreword to the book for which I was most grateful.

We often spoke about the need for a similar group to the so-called 'Clapham Sect' which Wilberforce led and which had a transforming effect upon British social history. They not only succeeded in the abolition of the slave trade in 1807 despite huge opposition, and slavery throughout the British Empire in 1833, but they applied their evangelical faith to a range of issues in the nation, such as the exploitation of children in industry. I spoke about my own visits to the Caribbean on behalf of the British Council of Churches in the 1960s and my extensive work among the immigrants in London and the time I used to broadcast a regular weekly 'Letter from London' to the Caribbean on the BBC Overseas Service.

The book *The Wilberforce Connection* was launched at a special event at Moggerhanger Park[10] where Monica and I were Ministry Directors, following a £7 million refurbishment and restoration of the buildings. Rowan very kindly came to the event and spoke to the large gathering at this special celebration. During the visit he also prayed a prayer of dedication in the chapel which was newly established for worship. The house had connections with Wilberforce through its owners, the Thornton family, who were first cousins; and in his address Rowan referred to the need for an application of the gospel to the social and political affairs of the nation in the same way as Wilberforce had done. I was greatly encouraged by this and I took it as a sign that his time at Canterbury may have the prophetic outcome for the nation that I longed to see.

Hebraic Roots and Israel

We often spent time talking about theological issues and I expressed my own love of exploring the Hebraic roots of the Christian Gospels and the harm done by the widespread existence of 'Replacement Theology' in churches of all denominations, especially in the Church of England. I spoke about my own conviction of the importance of studying God's dealings with ancient Israel and his Covenant with the Jewish people that is still valid today. This enables us to understand the purposes of God in the context of what is happening in the contemporary world. I spoke of my many visits to the modern State of Israel and my many friends among the growing number of Israeli Jews who are believers in Jesus as their Messiah. I described what had happened at the international gathering of men and women with prophetic ministries at Mount Carmel and the international conference in Jerusalem in which I had been involved.[11]

I also referred to my friendship with many Jewish Messianic leaders such as Lance Lambert and the Berger brothers who led the Hebrew church at Christ Church in the Old City of Jerusalem which is the oldest Anglican church in Israel. Rowan confessed that he had never met a Messianic Jew and he eagerly agreed with my suggestion of organising a one-day seminar with Jewish Hebraic scholars. Rowan would host this in one of the meeting rooms in Lambeth Palace.

I immediately set about making contact with a number of Messianic Jewish leaders in Israel, Britain and America, whom I knew to be outstanding biblical scholars. It was agreed that we should limit the number to ten and invite each to submit a paper on some aspect of Romans 9 to 11. They were each also asked to submit a few paragraphs about themselves and their ministry. The meeting took about six months to organise and finally took place in November 2004. Rowan chaired the seminar and he also invited his personal chaplain, David Marshall, and Christopher Herbert the Bishop of St Albans who was the Chairman of the Council of Christians and Jews and the senior Anglican responsible for Jewish relationships.

The Land and the Remnant
All those present had seen the Archbishop's paper that had been read to the 'Sabeel' Conference in Jerusalem in April 2004, organised by Palestinian Christians, in which he had stated his firm conviction that the land of Israel belongs to God, and that he has entrusted it to the stewardship of his Covenant people Israel. This was referred to appreciatively a number of times by the Hebrew scholars when the subject of the land was discussed.

There was much discussion of the identity of the 'remnant' in Romans 11.5 and the conclusion that Paul was referring to the Jewish believers in Jesus in his own day. There was agreement that a small remnant of Jewish believers in Jesus have survived the centuries and are now blossoming in Israel and other nations which has an eschatological significance. This was linked with Galatians 6.16, with its reference to 'The Israel of God'. There was discussion on the identity of the 'Israel of God' and God's end-time purposes for believing Jews in the context of world evangelisation and their place in the 'one new man' in Christ. It was recognised that the people of Israel are the true vine into which believing Gentiles are grafted in accordance with Romans 11.24 where Paul looks forward to the day when all Israel will be saved and be grafted back *into their **own** olive tree'*.

Rowan greatly enjoys theological discussion, especially investigating biblical textual meanings. So he appreciated the contributions of these Hebrew scholars. It was recognised that the three outstanding events of the 20th century were the *Shoar* (Holocaust), the rebirth of the State of Israel on May 14, 1948, and the emergence of a sovereign movement of Jewish believers in Yeshua. It was stated that many Christians and theological scholars believed that the existence of JBY (Jewish Believers in Yeshua) would only be a short-lived phenomenon, but both in Israel and in the diaspora, numbers are growing. In Israel today, there are more than one hundred Messianic congregations and growth is so considerable that they represent a significant minority in the population that can no longer be ignored.

Replacement Theology
The great stumbling block is that the Gentile churches have so far not recognised either the existence or the significance of JBY. This is due to the theological concept of 'supersession' or 'Replacement Theology' (the replacement of Israel by the church in the purposes of God) a theology which is still alive and growing within churches of all denominations and is especially associated with left-wing politics. Numerous churches still claim to be the legitimate heir of the 'congregation of Israel'. While JBY share a common faith in the Bible together with Gentile believers, at the same time they also view themselves as the natural successors of the first century Jewish disciples of Yeshua. Historically all the first disciples were Jews who took the gospel to the Gentiles. Therefore, they also highlight the fact that they do not abandon their Jewishness and actively identify with their Jewish brethren – even if, as a result, the

universal church treats them with suspicion and displeasure.

One of the papers presented was on the history of Messianic Jews, from a Messianic pastor who has a doctorate from the Hebrew University in Jerusalem on this subject. In his paper he said that the number of believing Jews in Israel has been increasing throughout the past 40 years and the present rate of growth is making it impossible for the Israeli Government to ignore them. This led to discussion of the difficult relationships between St George's Cathedral in Jerusalem with its Arab Bishop, Abu El-Assal, and Christ Church with its Anglican and Hebrew congregations.

The JBY scholars greatly appreciated the invitation from the Archbishop to meet with him and they were hoping that the outcome might be the denouncing of 'Replacement Theology' in the Anglican church and the recognition of JBY as brothers in Christ. Sadly, this did not happen. I don't think that Rowan perceived the spiritual significance of recognising the growth of the Messianic congregations in Israel as a genuine move of God. Thus, the opportunity was missed of bringing great blessing upon the Church of England, and also upon the nation, through aligning with what God is doing and enjoying the blessing that would follow according to the promise of God to his Covenant people in Genesis 12.3 *"I will bless you, and whoever curses you I will curse; and all peoples on earth will be blessed through you."*

The day concluded with the Archbishop thanking the Jewish scholars and saying how much he had learned from them. He warmly responded to an invitation to speak to a gathering of Messianic leaders when he next visited Israel. However, there was no noticeable shift in the Church of England moving away from Replacement Theology. Rowan stated clearly that he himself did not believe in Replacement Theology but he made no public pronouncement along these lines, which was a considerable disappointment to the Messianic leaders as elements of the Church of England are regarded by many Israelis as anti-Semitic.

Once again, I was greatly disappointed as here was an opportunity for the Church of England to lead the way with a huge theological leap that would reconnect with the Early Church and the days when it was largely composed of Jewish believers in Jesus. I personally have gained so much in understanding the Jewish roots of the Christian faith from my

Jewish brothers in Christ and I wanted to share this with Rowan. But he did not appear to recognise the significance of Israel in the purposes of God which I believe is the key to understanding what God is doing today.

Search for Truth

Our relationship changed after Rowan's interview with John Humphreys which was broadcast by the BBC. This was part of a series in which Humphreys talked with various religious leaders about their faith in a search for truth. Rowan chose to use an intellectual argument whereas I thought that he would have been much more effective by giving a simple testimony of his own faith in Jesus and I was forthright in what I said to him, which was not well received. I was quickly penitent because I had not meant to upset him. I wanted to make the point that a simple testimony of faith is often much more powerful and effective than a complex intellectual argument. I believe that the point I made was particularly painful because he was always hard on himself after any event and he knew that he had difficulty in expressing things simply. Later, we were able quietly to discuss our difference. But we both knew that this could affect our relationship for some time.

I went home and immediately wrote a long letter and posted it that afternoon. As soon as I had departed, Rowan must have sat down and written me a long letter and also posted it that afternoon. Our letters crossed in the post, but we had already agreed to take a break in our meetings, so we left it for two months before we met again. If we had been engaged in a theological or philosophical discussion things would have been more straightforward because Rowan would have been fully confident and simply countered my statements. But in querying the way he publicly professed his faith I went to the heart of his own problem.

Our friendship, of course, continued, but this incident undoubtedly made a difference. I was always much more careful in how I expressed my views after this incident, but it also meant that I was not as forthright in looking at issues with him, which I thought was the purpose of God bringing us together. I had to realise that Rowan brought his own personal gifts to the office of Archbishop and he could not go beyond that. I wanted him to exercise a prophetic leadership in the life of the nation and to express his thoughts in simple direct language, but this was beyond his gifting. I suppose I still had the model of Donald Coggan in my mind. I hoped that what William Temple had prophetically foreseen, and Donald had attempted to fulfil but been unable to achieve, Rowan might actually accomplish. I believed that it was for this purpose that God had brought me into contact with Rowan and I was prepared to accept the personal cost, but I don't think he ever fully understood the kind of ministry that I was advocating.

I wanted to see him declaring biblical truth into the nation. We often touched on these things but not in the depth that I wanted. Nevertheless, towards the end of his time at Canterbury we discussed the possibility of him speaking on a joint platform with Vincent Nichols, the Archbishop of Westminster, who often spoke forthrightly about moral and spiritual issues in the nation. I also wanted the Chief Rabbi, Jonathan Sacks, to be included as he also often spoke prophetically on national issues. The intention was to give them the opportunity of speaking about these issues. Rowan seemed quite keen on this and there was a lot of correspondence about it and meetings with representatives of 'Churches Together in England'. The original objective had been to try to organise such a meeting to take place before the General Election of May 2010, but for various reasons this was not found possible and then eventually the whole event was abandoned. The bureaucratic forces in the institutional churches had once again triumphed. This was probably another milestone in the reshaping of the nation in accordance with the secular humanist agenda.

In both sociological and spiritual terms, I was very aware of the destructive forces at work in society and although we often spoke of the things that were happening in Britain as well as on the international scene, I don't think Rowan was ever able to think in the same dimension. He has a brilliant brain for philosophical and theological concepts, but he is not gifted with the kind of prophetic thunder of Jeremiah or Amos or any of the biblical prophets. He is kind and gentle and a great scholar, but he is not a prophetic leader.

Looking Back

Looking back on our friendship in that period, I know that it was the John Humphreys incident that made me realise that I was no longer being a blessing to Rowan, as I think I was in the early days of his time at Canterbury. I had to realise that I was trying to push him to fulfil *my vision* of the kind of leadership that should be exercised by an Archbishop, instead of simply recognising his gifts and supporting him in the fulfilment of *his vision*. I know there were times when he hated the job, so maybe I should have been more supportive. But that was not the purpose for which I believed God had called me into this relationship. We talked about him resigning but he is so conscientious that having set his hand to the plough he would not cease his endeavours until he had completed his term.

It was not until the summer of 2011 that Rowan made the decision to leave at the end of the following year. My mind flashed back thirty years to when, in the same place, I had discussed the same thing with Donald Coggan. I had had a huge sense of disappointment then, but now I was simply glad for Rowan that he would be released from the burdens he had been carrying and would now be able really to be himself once again. I think he was greatly relieved when he could leave Lambeth Palace and go back into the academic world where he really belongs and is fulfilled.

Notes

[1] *The Body's Grace*, Lesbian and Gay Christian Movement and the Institute for the Study of Christianity and Sexuality, London, 1989, second edition 2002.
Open to Judgement, Longman and Todd, London, 1994 and 1996, 2001, 2002.
[2] Press statement issued by the LGCM on the announcement of the appointment of Rowan as Archbishop of Canterbury.
[3] Luke 16.18.
[4] Gary J Williams, *The Theology of Rowan Williams: An outline, critique, and consideration of its consequences*, Latimer Studies 35, London, 2002.
[5] *Open to Judgement*, page 57.
[6] Dr Rowan Williams, Presidential Address, General Synod, York, Monday 14th July 2003.
[7] *Daily Mail*, Monday 22 December 2003.
[8] Peter H. Lawrence, *Signs and Blunders: Learning to Risk Mistakes for Jesus*, Monarch. Crowborough, 1994.
[9] Clifford Hill, *The Wilberforce Connection*, Monarch Books, Oxford, 2004.
[10] See Chapter 17.
[11] See Chapter 8.

Chapter Nineteen

REVIEWING THE NOUGHTIES

The Meaning of the Millennium

The beginning of the year 2000 was no ordinary New Year. It was not just the start of a new century, but the beginning of a millennium. So how was it celebrated? More importantly, how was its significance recognised? Of course, there were plenty of celebration events, feasting and dancing, but also there was fear. What did the new millennium hold? There were lots of scare stories as the year 2000 drew near and promises of chaos and confusion with computers crashing, being unable to adjust to the new century. There was even foreboding in some circles about the possibilities of an end of the world scenario, but for the majority of the population it was just another New Year, part of the Christmas holiday package that usually came around at this season.

The Daily Telegraph, helpfully, engaged Gallup to carry out a national poll to find out what people knew about the new millennium and its significance. On New Year's Eve at the very end of the 20th century, the *Daily Telegraph*[1] printed a full-page cover story entitled 'The depths of people's ignorance on the Christian faith is almost unfathomable'. It then featured a Gallup poll of a question put to a representative sample of the population across Britain. The question was "What event does the millennium celebrate?" Only 24%, less than one quarter of the population, knew that the millennium was to celebrate the 2000th anniversary of the birth of Jesus Christ. The result, 29%, was only slightly better for those who claimed to be Christians. The majority of the population, including Christians, gave some other answer, while 11% admitted that they did not know.

Among those who claimed to be Christians, 56% could name all four Gospels. But 15% expressed doubts in God, 33% had doubts about the resurrection of Christ, 33% about his virgin birth and 62% had doubts about his second coming. *The Telegraph* report said, "Once upon a time, believing Christians were motivated by both the hope of eternal salvation and the fear of eternal damnation. The hope apparently lives on, but Gallup's findings make it clear that the fear of judgment has largely vanished"[2] – 67% believe in heaven but only 40% believe in hell.

Among those claiming to be Christians, only 35% claimed to pray frequently, 35% said that they go to church, 'more-or-less every Sunday' or 'quite often' and 71% said that they believed that Christianity and the church will still exist in 1,000 years' time. At least The Telegraph report ended on this note of optimism!

Clearly, the home mission field at the beginning of the 21st century was vastly different from the beginning of the 20th century, at the close of the Victorian era, when most of the population went to church regularly. Even halfway through the century, in 1949, a poll showed that in the whole population 61% were able to name all four Gospels, as compared with 48% in 1999. These results showed that there was still a remnant of faith remaining from the Victorian biblical heritage in Britain. If these figures had been broken down into age groups it would no doubt have been found that those over the age of 40 had a far greater knowledge of Christianity than young people whose education had not included any biblical teaching. Many church leaders were concerned that their congregations consisted of mainly elderly people but few had any idea how to reach young people with the gospel in 21st century Britain.

Christian Outreach

One Christian leader who was concerned about Christian outreach was Gos Home, the proprietor of the Christian Resources Exhibition (CRE) an annual event attracting thousands of Christians held at Sandown Park racecourse. In 2005 he came to consult Monica in her capacity as Director of the British Church Growth Association. She had been one of those whom he had consulted before starting the Exhibition twenty years previously. The CRE had flourished under Gos's leadership but he was concerned that it had become largely a commercial event and he wanted to see it serving the churches and promoting the gospel more effectively. Monica had noted a distinct trend in new evangelistic outreaches coming onto the church scene since the start of the new millennium that were not yet established or strong enough to hire stands.

I was drawn into the conversation and together we suggested having a section in the Exhibition that was purely about new outreaches in mission that had begun in the 21st century and could benefit the churches. Gos agreed to provide free stands for any new group, and this became known as *The Sharing Show – Good News and How to Give It Away*. It gave many new enterprises an introduction to the wider church scene. This is where 'Food Banks' organised by the Trussell Trust and many other activities first came to public attention and some have become part of the national scene.

The Sharing Show presented imaginative new outreaches to the Christian public. These included groups working with motorbike enthusiasts, canal barge travellers, and many others including groups reaching different ethnic minorities. These attracted considerable attention and interest at the CRE and were useful in stimulating others to see what can be done to communicate the gospel in different parts of society.

There were also larger organisations who took the opportunity of having a free stall at the CRE where they could show what they were doing and recruit additional volunteers. Organisations such as 'Christians Against Poverty' and 'Street Pastors' demonstrated the range of Christian outreach activities that have been generated in churches up and down the land since the beginning of this century. These larger organisations caught the imagination of many Christians in different denominations to see the opportunity of expressing their faith in practical ways.

To take 'Street Pastors' as an example: this was founded by the Rev Les Isaac of The Ascension Trust who founded this work while pastoring a church in Brixton South London, where he was deeply concerned about the number of young people on the streets late into the evenings and nights who were often involved in excessive drinking and were getting into trouble with the law. He began by recruiting some local Christian men to go on the streets at weekends to talk to these young people and to help them.

'Street Pastors' rapidly spread in city areas where churches saw the opportunity of making a positive contribution to a social problem that was involving an increasing number of young people. 'Street Pastors' are clearly identified by their dress and are recognised by the police for their assistance which has saved countless arrests and unnecessary police time. 'Street Pastors' often calm difficult situations that might otherwise get out of control. In addition, they have many conversations with young people in which they are able not only to express practical care but also to speak about the love of God and to offer the gospel to those who have never heard the word of the Lord.

Evangelism

The Sharing Show also gave birth to a number of 'Love Events' in different areas around the country. These evangelism outreaches were the result of several groups involved in the CRE who so enjoyed working together in the Exhibition that they wanted to do something practical together. Invitations came from a group of churches in Cornwall to do a month of outreach in September 2006.

This was ideal timing and many of the churches in the county actively participated in 'Love Cornwall' in 15 different locations, with the support of 45 home-based prayer groups scattered around Cornwall. Street evangelism, which included drama and a Christian rapper, handing out free burgers and praying for people in the streets, resulted in more than 100 giving their lives to Christ. The month concluded with a well-attended tent meeting on the Wadebridge County Show ground where many more decisions were made and a spectacular healing of a man who had been pushed into the meeting in a wheelchair ending by him dancing on the stage! 'Love Cornwall' was followed by a number of similar events such as 'Love Leicester', 'Love Ashford', 'Love Croydon' and many others, each having a unique outreach content.

Slave Trade Abolition

The CRE May 2007 gave an opportunity to display the 200th anniversary of the abolition of the Slave Trade and to highlight the horrors of the

Transatlantic Slave Trade through which the British nation had gained their wealth at the time of the Industrial Revolution. We were members of a national committee stimulating and coordinating events across the country to mark this event which included a service in Westminster Abbey attended by the Queen.[3] As mentioned, our personal contribution was in bringing the Zong, a replica 18th century square rigger ship refitted as a slaver into London and opening it for visitors in March/April 2007.[4]

Prayer Movement

Probably the most significant development among churches of all denominations in the past two or three decades has been the increase in the commitment to prayer among Christians. It is often said that all revivals begin with a movement towards prayer. This is certainly true of the Wesleyan revival in the 18th century that is said to have stemmed from the prayers of the Moravians who were influential in John Wesley's life.

Since the beginning of the House Church Movement in the early 1970s, increasing numbers of groups of Christians have been coming together in one another's homes to pray and to study the Scriptures. Many of these groups have been linked to wider Christian prayer networks such as 'Intercessors for Britain', 'Together for the Nation', the 'Ladies Prayer and Bible Week', the 'International Lydia Fellowship', 'Christian Friends of Israel' (CFI) and numerous others.

This commitment to prayer and Bible study is generally recognised as a response to the unsettled times in which we are living. Christians who know the Bible can see many things happening today which are similar to events prophesied in the Bible, which gives them a hunger for more in-depth Bible study in which they enjoy sharing with other like-minded Christians. Inevitably such Bible study draws them to greater prayer commitment, seeking to hear from God as well as to speak to him. They also recognise the powerful forces of secularisation that are driving the nation which leads many to a greater commitment to intercede on behalf of the nation and its leaders.

Politics

The year 2000 began with the scrapping of the tax allowance for married couples.[5] This was a massive political blunder with huge social consequences. It sent a signal to the nation that marriage was no longer important. It showed an incredible ignorance among politicians of the social significance of marriage and it revealed the magnitude of the forces arrayed against the family. It showed that the family was at the centre of the battle for the soul of the nation.

Members of the Lords and Commons Family and Child Protection Group (LCFCPG) chaired by Gerald Howarth MP recognised that weakening the family would have severe consequences not only for social stability but also for the economy. As we have noted, the group decided to commission a programme of research to show the cost to the nation of the breakdown of family life. The report[6] contained severe economic warnings as well as evidence of the social consequences of family breakdown. But even these warnings did not change political policy – the relentless secularisation of the nation, reshaping its moral and spiritual character, continued in defiance of all the empirical evidence.

Legislation

As noted in Chapter 13, Jack Straw MP, when responding to the Report *Family Matters* on 15th July 1998 had promised a White Paper outlining measures to strengthen the family. That White Paper was never produced, but instead a Green Paper was published by the Home Office for public discussion. This was a reflection of the battle Jack Straw was facing within the Cabinet with those who wished to promote the LGBT agenda, a battle that was carried over into the new century. The Green Paper *Supporting Families* had correctly stated that marriage was the most reliable framework for raising children, but this caused dissension in the Cabinet.

The rallying cry of the secular humanists driving Government policy was "The family is not deteriorating, it is only changing." They said that the flexibility of the modern family can accommodate all kinds of family and all are of equal value. This was the beginning of Government policy focusing upon 'equality'. Hence the value of the married couple family could not be taught in school because a child from a one-parent family might feel inferior if we say that two parents are best. So, in defiance of all the evidence, children were taught what was becoming known as 'alternative facts' which laid the ground work for 'fake news'. This was another milestone in the reshaping of the nation in accordance with the secular humanist objectives.

In the LCFCPG it was recognised that family breakdown is at the centre of most of our social ills. Poverty, health, drugs, mental health, child and youth behaviour, crime – all stem from marriage failure and family breakdown. The evidence is conclusive and incontrovertible but 'Political Correctness' prevents us dealing with the real issues. The Foreword to the Report *The Cost of Family Breakdown* stated the problem clearly:

> Different sexual and child rearing lifestyles are decisively not equal in the sense of equality that is applied in all other areas of legislation, that is, equal in their average results for good or harm on the present population and on generations to come. Aristotle defined injustice as treating unequal-things equally... The reconstructed families of today must all enjoy the privilege of the lifelong monogamous family, without having to bear the monogamous family's burdens of continence, fidelity and permanence. Whatever the future may hold, for 40 years the choice has increasingly been made in favour of the new pseudo-family options.

Reshaping Marriage

The conclusion reached in the Parliamentary Group was that the importance of marriage for family stability, the health and well-being of adults and children had been irrefutably established by mountains of research. Society had to decide whether it wanted to recover the ideal of fatherhood and the covenant of marriage, and if so there needed to be a major reappraisal of social values and individual priorities. If we were to set about the task of rebuilding a family-friendly culture based upon faithful marriage and personal commitment, society had to identify and acknowledge the issues involved and then develop sound strategies for addressing them. Although the Report was warmly received by MPs on both sides of the House and in the Upper House, there was no change in Government policy. It was as though a veil was drawn over the eyes of politicians of all parties shielding them from the truth.

It was clearly stated at that time, July 2000, that if current trends in society were to be reversed many agencies would have to be involved. The churches needed to give a clear, unambiguous lead. We said that Government must acknowledge its duty to guide, lead and set the tone. Rather than sit on the fence, Government must be prepared to discriminate positively in favour of marriage, and take more vigorous action to uphold marriage as an ideal. The situation would not be changed or family life strengthened unless there was a change in corporate and individual values in society. What was needed above all was a cultural change at grassroots level which acknowledges that the traditional family is the central foundation stone of a stable, prosperous and caring society.

The Family and Child Protection Group produced two more reports early in the decade. *Sex under Sixteen* was a report on teenage pregnancy sponsored by the Family Education Trust published in the year 2000, shortly after the publication of *The Cost of Family Breakdown*. That was followed in the following year by the publication of *Does Your Mother Know?*, which was a study of underage sexual behaviour and parental responsibility. That was published in July 2001.

Despite the widespread acknowledgement of the cost of family breakdown, in Parliament and in the national press, the secular humanist agenda continued to be pursued by politicians of all parties. The transfer of premiership from Tony Blair to Gordon Brown resulted in no significant change of policy and the Labour Government lasted until 2010 when a General Election produced a hung parliament with the Government presided over by David Cameron and Nick Clegg. Their combined secular humanist agenda paved the way for the legalising of same-sex marriage in 2013.

Postmodernist Reshaping

Step-by-step throughout the first decade of the millennium the nation was reshaped by what we now know as the Postmodernist agenda of secular humanism. Parliament approved legislation which inevitably undermined the stability of society by destroying the basis of family life which was rooted in the Judaeo-Christian concept of the covenant of marriage. The first such regulation in the new millennium was the Human Reproductive Cloning Act 2001 which was repealed and replaced by the Human Fertilisation and Embryology Act 2008. This Act permitted embryo research for developing treatments for serious diseases. Effectively, the Act allowed cloning human embryos and experimenting with creating human life.

This was followed in 2004 by The Civil Partnership Act which was introduced by the Labour government but supported by both the Conservatives and Lib Dems. The Act granted in the United Kingdom similar rights to that of heterosexual civil marriage. The same year also saw the passing of the Gender Recognition Act which granted trans-sexual people legal recognition as members of the sex opposite to their birth gender, either male or female.

The Equality Act 2006 created the 'Equality and Human Rights Commission' (EHRC) and a similar Act in 2010 drew together all the other Acts that had relevance to 'equality and human rights', bringing British law fully in line with the European Equal Treatment Directives.

The reshaping of Britain to conform to the Darwinian secular humanist concept of society continued relentlessly in total disregard of the damage being done to family and marriage and the foundational structures of society. A list of Ungodly Laws (with explanatory notes) passed by the British Parliament since 1950 is included as an Appendix to this book (see pp. 341ff).[7]

Notes
[1] *Daily Telegraph*, Friday, December 31, 1999.
[2] See reference to Jeffrey Hadden's research in the 1960s, Chapter 5 on p. 79.
[3] See Chapter 17.
[4] See Chapter 17.
[5] Referred to in Chapter 13, p. 205.
[6] *The Cost of Family Breakdown*, FMI, 2000.
[7] A printed copy of the Ungodly Laws is available from Issachar Ministries 5 Shannon Court, Sandy Beds SG19 1AG or by e-mail: info@issacharministries.co.uk

Chapter Twenty

SOCIAL CHANGE IN CHURCH AND STATE

This final chapter aims to offer a brief overview of church and state in the period of rapid social change we have been reviewing, and to look ahead to where current trends are pointing.

In Chapter Six of this book we outlined four movements of social change that hit Britain in the 1960s. They were Cultural, Spiritual, Political and Sexual. We will look briefly at the way they have developed since the 1960s.

Cultural Change

Cultural Change, in the modern era since the end of the Second World War, has seen the move from the early days of rock and skiffle bands and discos to a multi-million dollar, culture-setting industry that exercises a controlling influence over the minds of young people. Its rap songs and lyrics that are unintelligible to older people dominate the minds of the young and form a powerful sub-culture.

Other major cultural changes that have come in since the 1960s are linked with the invention and development of the Internet, the smart phone and the iPad which have led to the massive industry of social media that also has a powerful influence over the lives of millions of young people, introducing them to pornography, violence, hate-speech and bullying.

Of course, the internet also has its good side in opening up a world of knowledge to young people of which former generations could not contemplate. But in terms of personal health and well-being for so many, social media represents oppression and darkness rather than freedom of expression and enlightenment.

Other major social changes have occurred through immigration and the development of a multi-religious society and the influence of secular humanist philosophy that has resulted in half the population becoming agnostic or declaring that they have no religion. The loss of social standing of the church and the decline in church attendance have been contributing factors in the secularisation of society.

But the major cultural change since the 1960s has surely been in the realm of social values. Revolutionary changes in attitudes have taken place that cannot be adequately summarised in a few sentences. They cover everything from the value of life to the redefinition of family and marriage. The former has resulted in legislation abolishing capital punishment (1965), the legalisation of abortion (1967) and the ongoing campaign to recognise euthanasia as legalised mercy-killing. The latter has resulted in the Same-Sex Marriage Act of 2013 and the introduction of sex education in schools to children as young as five.

But in sociological terms the significance of the cultural revolution since the 1960s lies in its effect upon the value system of society. Social systems, like physical organisms, are constantly changing. No social system remains unaltered indefinitely, nor when disturbed does it return unaltered to its original state. Thus, the stable model of society is virtually unknown in the modern era. Each of the major institutions in society when disturbed affects the other institutions. This is because of the complex interrelatedness of institutions within the social system.

When a significant change takes place in one of the major social institutions all the others are affected.[1] What we have witnessed since the 1960s is a unique sociological phenomenon unknown until the post-World War II era: all our major social institutions have been experiencing fundamental changes at the same time. This has created an incredibly volatile social situation in which the forces of change generated within each institution have been dynamically affecting each other. These changes have been working their way through the entire system and have reached the underlying value system that forms the foundations of our civilisation. In Britain and most Western societies this is rooted in our

Judaeo-Christian biblical heritage. It is this heritage that is now under attack and will undoubtedly crumble unless there are radical changes in social policy to recognise the essential nature of Judaeo-Christian values for the health and well-being of society.

Spiritual Change

Spiritual change has seen New-Age concepts become part of everyday life and acceptance into the general culture of the nation. But it has also taken on a more aggressive stance in terms of the practice of Satanism that has become mainstream in youth culture through its introduction into the world of music and art, where its devotees rejoice in various forms of darkness. Both the Paris and the Manchester terrorist attacks in 2017 occurred when the performers at a concert were indulging in music linked to Satanism.

The influence of Satanism has led to the suicide of many young people. Its influences are also to be seen in the attack upon the value of life, both in its beginnings and end. Abortion is accepted as a means of birth control (including the 'morning-after-pill' now freely available to schoolchildren without parental knowledge) and has been made socially acceptable by secular humanist campaigns regarding women's rights over their own bodies (regardless of the rights of the unborn child). Euthanasia is increasingly becoming a political arena for humanists who use the suffering of individuals to call for the right to end life. These campaigns raise ethical issues regarding the sanctity of life in an age where medical science has the ability to prolong life indefinitely despite a person being brain dead.

The major decline of Christianity in Britain, however, has to be located in the rise of unbelief and the loss of biblical conviction among professional church leaders of all denominations of the Christian church. Biblical criticism is at the heart of this unbelief although it should be recognised that the scholarly study of the origins of the various books in the Bible should not lead to unbelief but to a greater understanding of the nature and purposes of God.

Scholarly study of the Bible has been taught by many academic institutions, not in the context of faith, but in the pursuit of false and destructive philosophical concepts that undermine faith and lead to unbelief. Unbelief in the pulpit inevitably leads to unbelief in the pew and in simple terms this is exactly what has happened in the church since the 1960s. The secular humanist values of the world have massively penetrated the church, undermining the faith of many clergy and leaders of all denominational churches. In many cases this has led to ungodly behaviour, sexual offences, marital breakdown and public dishonour which has further reduced the social honour in which the church in Britain has been held for centuries.

The doubts and uncertainties among professional church leaders have been aided and abetted by false teaching and a wide range of unbiblical beliefs and practices that have entered the church from many sources. These have caused confusion and controversy resulting in division and an immense amount of unhappiness and suffering among Christians, some of whom have left the denominational churches and either found their way into new groupings of Christians or have become disillusioned with all organised forms of the Christian religion.

Political Change
Political change has seen an emphasis upon opposite ends of the political spectrum. This is not just being seen in Britain but in most Western nations in different forms. Both far right and far left political parties have benefited from the rise of 'populism' which, in Britain, is seen as a modern form of 'peasants revolt', a rejection of established forms of authority. Its results have been seen in the USA with the election of Donald Trump; in France with the election of Macron; in Austria with the election of a Green Party President and a right of centre Government; in Italy with the election of the 'Five-Star Movement' to political power. In Britain the populist movement is widely believed to have influenced the EU Referendum with its decision to quit the European Union.

Secular humanism has been the major concept driving political change since the 1960s and has resulted in the development of a philosophy of 'political correctness' that has limited freedom of speech in an age where the traditional concepts of politeness, good manners and deference to age and gender have largely been swept away in a tsunami of cultural change. Legal controls on violent behaviour have increased in a society where individuals fail to exercise personal self-control and many children no longer have these values taught in family life.

Truth has become the major casualty of all four major movements of social change since the 1960s, although none so marked as in the political arena where 'fake news' and 'alternative facts' have become accepted as the norm of political life. An American journalist speaking on CNN in a New Year 2018 debate on Donald Trump's first year in office justified the President's boasting about his personal achievements by saying, "Well, we all massage the truth to fit our own narrative" – a remark that reflects the cavalier attitude to truth in much of the present-day media. As Jeremiah said just before judgement fell upon Jerusalem: *Truth has perished; it has vanished from their lips* (Jer 7.28).

Sexual Change

Sexual change progressed rapidly after the passing of both the Abortion Act and the Sexual Offences Act in 1967. The legalisation of abortion has led to the killing of more than 8 million unborn babies with about 450 abortions taking place daily in British hospitals, mostly at the expense of British taxpayers – a vivid illustration of the nation's lack of value for the sanctity of life which inevitably affects all our social values and even contributes to the steep rise in knife crime and acid throwing among young people who lack the stability of a caring family.

The legalisation of homosexual practices which the Bible describes as being 'detestable to God' (Lev 18.22) was the first major step in undermining traditional attitudes regarding sexual practices and social values in terms of family and marriage. The original Act in 1967 decriminalised homosexual acts in private between consenting men over the age of 21. The age of consent was reduced to 18 in 1994 and then in the year 2000 it was made equal to the heterosexual age of consent at 16.

There was strong opposition to this measure in the public arena and in the House of Lords. But the Government of Tony Blair was determined to abolish 'Clause 28'[2] which protected children by prohibiting the promotion of homosexuality in schools, and it was this determination that caused them to use the 'Parliament Act' to drive the Sexual Offences (Amendment) Act through Parliament in 2003, although the Parliament Act was traditionally only used for measures of extreme constitutional importance. This demonstrated the extent to which MPs were driven by a destructive spirit determined to undermine traditional family life and to introduce children to homosexual practices that could actually reduce their life expectancy by as much as 30 or 40 years.

This was despite the fact that the Family Research Institute of Colorado Springs USA, had recently published research showing that only 2% of homosexual men died of old age, 65 or older.[3] The average age of homosexual males who died of AIDs was 39; and of those who died from other causes, the median age of death was 44.[4]

In sex education in schools today, children are taught that all forms of sexual intercourse are allowable according to each individual's wishes, but they are not taught the health risks involved in male homosexual practices that could reduce their life expectancy.

Understanding the Times

There is plenty of evidence of a powerful spirit of destruction driving the nations today. This is not only to be seen in the Western nations but also in Islamic nations in the Middle East. In the West the ultimate objective is the destruction of the Judaeo-Christian values underlying Western civilisation. In the Middle East the objective is to overthrow the dynasties of power that rule Islamic nations and oppress the people, as well as to destroy Israel and the Judeo-Christian religion.

We may then ask the question, "What is the origin of the spirit that is driving the nations? Is it the same spirit in the West and in the East?" If the spirit driving the Western nations (postmodernism, but also Islamic terrorism) is aiming to destroy Judaeo-Christian values, is the spirit in the Middle East aiming to destroy the values of Islam? Those who have studied the teaching of Islam in the Qur'an and elsewhere know that followers of Allah are instructed to kill Christians and Jews and to subdue the nations of the world. So, can the same spirit be at work in both East and West – seeking to destroy the Judaeo-Christian heritage in the West and to destroy the *enemies* of Judeo Christianity in the East?

That simply doesn't make sense; because we are asking the wrong questions and we are coming at the subject from the wrong starting point. When we find the right starting point the answer is simple.

What we are looking at in both the West and the East is the activity of human beings. As always, they are either led by a Spirit of Grace and Truth, or they are driven by an evil and destructive spirit. The Bible teaches us that we are either led by the Spirit of God or we are driven by an evil spirit.

Paul expresses the theology of this conundrum in Romans chapter 7 where he describes his own personal wrestling with the problems of good and evil. He finds the good he wants to follow he is powerless to do,[5] and the evil he hates has immense power over him. In despair he cries out: *What a wretched man I am! Who will rescue me from this body of death?* He finds the answer in Christ and gives thanks to God that: *through Christ Jesus the law of the Spirit of life set me free from the law of sin and death* (see Rom 7.24 – 8.2).

What is God doing?

Bearing this teaching in mind we are then in a position to return to our study of what is happening in the world today. We then begin with the right question: which is, 'What is God doing?' 'What has God said to us, both through the teaching of the prophets and through Messiah, Jesus our Lord and Saviour?' As the writer to the Hebrews says:

In the past God spoke to our forefathers through the prophets at many times and in various ways, but in these last days he has spoken to us by his Son, whom he appointed heir of all things, and through whom he made the universe (Heb 1.1–2, NIV).

The prophets of Israel, the Lord Jesus and his apostles, all speak of a forthcoming time of great turbulence and destruction among the nations. Jesus links this with a number of things such as the coming of deceivers, false prophets, and false messiahs; and the falling away from the faith of many, at the same time as the gospel reaches multitudes when *it is preached in the whole world.*[6]

Among the prophets of Israel are many prophecies of God shaking the nations such as Isaiah foresees as a time when: *the Lord Almighty has a day in store for all the proud and lofty, for all that is exalted, and they will be humbled.* He says that this will happen when God *rises to shake the earth* (see Is 2.12 and 19).

But it is the prophecy of Haggai 2: 6-7, repeated in Hebrews 12, which is of the greatest significance as Hebrews was one of the last books in the Bible to be written, towards the end of the first century A.D., and the fulfilment of this prophecy was still in the future. It speaks of the great shaking of the world of nature as well as the nations. Hebrews interprets Haggai's prophecy as being linked to the establishment of the Kingdom of God on earth. The prophecy says that everything that is founded upon human values will be shaken: *that is, created things — so that what cannot be shaken may remain* (Heb 12.27).

If we are right in applying this prophecy of God shaking the nations to what we are seeing today then we can say with some confidence that whatever is happening, including the destructive things, God will in some way use to work out his purposes. Of course, it does not mean that God either initiates or approves the terrible atrocities that are perpetrated by human beings. But in order to understand this we have to bring our theology in line with that of the prophets of Israel. Their fundamental conviction was that everything that happens is either in line with the will of God or because God has allowed it in order to work out his purposes.

The Testimony of Jesus

In John 5.19 Jesus said that he could do nothing on his own. He could only do what he saw his Father doing. He repeated this statement a number of times. *"I do nothing on my own but speak that which the Father has taught me"* (John 8.28). And in John 12.49 he said *"For I did not speak on my own accord, but the Father who sent me commanded me what to say and how to say it"*. These statements are of great importance for us in seeking to know how God is working out his purposes today and what he is saying to us his people.

We can see how the shaking of the nations throughout the Western world is exposing corruption, exploitation, injustice and unrighteousness, in business and commerce, in politics and in the world of media and entertainment. We have seen this in the collapse of great financial houses in 2008, in the humiliation of politicians at Westminster in 2009 in the exposure of their Parliamentary expenses and allowances; and in the sexual scandals involving well-known personalities in the media and entertainment, and even in bishops and other church leaders.

But these exposures of corruption and unrighteousness, which are shaking those who hold power in the nations, are only a preliminary to the working out of God's purposes. We know that his ultimate purpose is the establishment of the Kingdom of God on earth, but what we do not know is whether that will come suddenly through the Second Coming of the Lord Jesus or whether there will be a period of preaching the gospel of truth throughout the world in preparation for the Kingdom before the return of Christ. It is not easy to discern where we are in God's timetable, although clearly we are entering days foreseen in biblical prophecy. But we have to remember the warning that Jesus gave to his disciples: *"It is not for you to know the times or dates the Father has set by his own authority"* (Acts 1.7).

It may be that we have yet to see other things happen that Jesus referred to in Matthew 24 such as, *"nation will rise against nation and kingdom against kingdom"*. With a world armed with the most incredible weapons of mass destruction and the rising tensions on the international scene, it is hard to believe that human beings will not take the world farther down the road to utter destruction of the kind foreseen in Isaiah 24.3, *The earth will be completely laid waste and totally plundered.* The great unknown is whether or not God will intervene before that happens.

The one thing we can say with certainty is that God is exposing evil and corruption to prepare the way of the Kingdom. That may mean that God is preparing the way for a great time of proclamation of the truth to which human beings may respond. In the West that would be seen as a time of great revival. In the Far East it would be an extension of the spiritual awakening that has been gaining momentum in China, Indonesia, Singapore, the Philippines and other parts of that region for the past 20 or 30 years. In the Middle East it would be breaking the power of Islam which God has already begun doing by exposing the hatred and violence that was demonstrated to the world through the 'Islamic State' and the spirit of darkness and oppression that is at the heart of Islam.

At the same time as God is shaking the nations, in Britain, he is also drawing together small groups of believers to study the word of God and to pray. Collectively they form a 'community of believers' whom God will use in the fulfilment of his purposes to communicate truth to the people of the world.

It is important for believers to understand what we are seeing and hearing in the world around us, and that we are rightly discerning what God is doing, so that we can be his faithful witnesses in the 21st century. Those who obey Jesus' command to *"watch and pray"* are being drawn together in small house fellowships, in increasing numbers throughout the country. This is a major move of the Holy Spirit that is drawing together the faithful remnant of believers, giving them a hunger to understand what is happening in our times. This hunger is bringing a strong desire to study the Bible, to discuss its meaning and to pray with other believers. The movement is drawing together some believers from all denominations and traditions. It is giving a new unity that goes beyond the denominational churches and breaking down barriers.

Church Leaders
In the decades of rapid social change in the second half of the 20th century the nation was needing Godly leadership provided by the Church. There was a great opportunity for exercising a prophetic role and steadying the nation. It was an opportunity for stressing the unchanging nature of the fundamental values that were part of the social and moral fabric of the nation stemming from our Judeo-Christian heritage. Sadly, throughout that period of rapid and radical social change the leadership of all the mainline churches was weak and uninspired. A succession of ineffective Archbishops of Canterbury set the tone of church leadership in the nation. In the same period there was a lack of outstanding leaders in the Nonconformist churches, so there was no national voice from the Church to give guidance and direction throughout the second half of the Twentieth Century – the period of the greatest social change in the history of the nation.

Looking back over the 60 years of rapid and radical social change, the silence of the church has been deafening. In a time of confusion when there was a desperate need for the proclamation of unchanging truth to steady the nation and to point the way ahead, the churches were unresponsive, thus missing the greatest opportunities for creative leadership in the history of the nation. The short reviews of the Archbishops of Canterbury in the period covered by this book that we have presented shows that none of them have followed the lead of William Temple of offering creative leadership in both the social and the spiritual affairs of the nation.

As already noted,[7] William Temple set up a Commission in 1943 to produce a plan for the post-World War II re-evangelisation of Britain. He said, "If we have to choose between making men Christian and making the social order more Christian, we must choose the former. But there is no such antithesis!" In the Foreword to the report published in 1945 it was stated of William Temple that he was known as a 'great Christian social reformer'. It continued:

But the people of England are not sufficiently aware that his love for his fellow man was constrained by a deep love of Christ, that emerged naturally from the heart and mind of a great evangelist who knew the message, had personal experience of its truth, and was himself a mission preacher.[8]

The history of the Church of England since the end of World War II shows that none of its leaders had the ability and the spiritual dynamic to carry out the imaginative and far-reaching reforms of the church that were essential for the fulfilment of the plan of action conceived by the Commission set up by William Temple. The nearest anyone got to fulfilling the vision of William Temple was Donald Coggan and the Lambeth Group who embraced the same vision that Monica and I were following in the East End of London of being both fully involved in social action and evangelism. But Donald was virtually 'crucified' by the liberal bishops of the Church of England.

It is revealing to look at the record of Michael Ramsay who was Archbishop of Canterbury immediately prior to Donald Coggan. Ramsay was Archbishop from 1961 to 1974 which was probably the most critical 13-year-period of social change in the second half of the 20th century, when the most far-reaching measures of social change were debated in Parliament and put onto the Statute Book. The following is a short list of the most significant Acts of Parliament in this period. But Ramsay cared for none of these things.

- 1962 Commonwealth Immigrants Act
- 1964 The Obscene Publications Act Amendment

- 1965 The Race Relations Act
- 1965 The Murder (abolition of the death penalty) Act
- 1967 The Abortion Act (legalising abortion)
- The Sexual Offences Act (legalising homosexual practices)
- 1968 Commonwealth Immigrants Act
- 1968 The Theatre Act (abolishing censorship in the theatre and publications)
- 1969 The Divorce Reform Act (making divorce easy)
- 1972 The European Communities Act (taking Britain into the Common Market and eventually into the European Union)

Throughout the whole of this momentous period of social change in the nation, Ramsay took little or no interest in what was happening in Parliament other than to support the law to legalise homosexual practices, although he did oppose apartheid and support immigration from the Commonwealth. His main interest was in promoting ecumenical relationships. He actively pursued closer relationships with Rome, with Eastern Orthodox Churches and with the Methodist Church — none of which produced any positive results. He became President of the World Council of Churches which showed that his prime interest was in developing the institutional structures of the church. But he showed no interest in leading the Church of England to transform the nation at the most decisive period of political activity in the reshaping of the nation.

Nonconformist Leaders

In the first half of the 20th century what was known as the 'Nonconformist Conscience' was a powerful force in the nation. This came from formidable preachers in the latter part of the Victorian era whose dynamic ministries exerted considerable influence in both church and state. They spoke on social and political issues, bringing moral and spiritual values into national debates. They were prophets to the nation, declaring the word of the Lord on national issues. In the middle of the 20th century there were still a few outstanding preachers in the Nonconformist churches in Britain, mainly in the London area, such as Leslie Weatherhead at the City Temple Holborn, Sylvester Horne at Whitfield's Chapel Tottenham Court Road, Donald Soper at Kingsway

Hall, Edwin Sangster at Westminster Central Hall, Martyn Lloyd Jones at Westminster Chapel, and Elsie Chamberlain who was the first woman preacher to become Head of Religious Broadcasting at the BBC.[9]

These Nonconformist leaders all attracted large crowds and were much more influential than any of the Anglican clergy, where for many performing correct liturgy was more important than declaring the word of God – with few exceptions such as John Stott at All Souls Langham Place and Dick Lucas at St Helen's in the City of London. Soper was the only one who openly engaged in political issues. His Christian faith led him to be an enthusiastic Christian Socialist whose outspoken views delighted the crowds at Tower Hill and Speaker's Corner, Hyde Park. These outstanding preachers were well known in the 1950s and 60s, but with the advent of the Charismatic Movement in the 1970s and 80s great preaching gave way to experiential phenomena, especially in the 1990s. From this point the Nonconformist conscience died in Britain, which opened the way for secular humanism to spread across the nation unopposed by spiritual giants in the mould of previous generations. There were none who exercised the sort of leadership that excited public attention and inspired the nation. The voice of the church became muted.

Liberal theology had been taught in theological colleges and universities since the 1920s, but its content changed in the 1960s with the advent of ultra-liberal 'God is Dead' teaching, which was destructive of personal faith. Liberal clergy tended to be more concerned with social activities and meeting personal needs than in dealing with fundamental issues in society. The Bible-believing sector of the church was either preoccupied with the wide range of charismatic phenomena sweeping churches of all denominations in this period, or arguing among themselves regarding what was deception and what was a genuine work of God.

At the same time, many of the traditional churches of all denominations plodded along in the same way as they had for many decades, struggling to maintain decaying buildings with diminishing congregations and declining income. They were mostly without vision and without hope, adrift in a stormy sea of social change without a compass or rudder. They didn't understand the social issues and lacked the dynamic power of the gospel to stem the advance of secular humanism in society or unbelief in the church. So, from the mid-1960s to 2015, which was probably the most challenging 50-year period of radical social change in the history of the Western nations, the opportunities for creative leadership were squandered by Christians. There were two basic reasons for this:

First, many church leaders were simply unbelievers, lacking confidence in the Bible as the revealed word of God and the ultimate standard of truth.

Secondly, they did not understand the social processes that were driving the nation.

Church leaders thus were unable to join the battle against the secular humanist forces that were reshaping the nation because they did not understand the nature of the battle and they were not equipped with the right weapons. They were like King Saul's army facing the Philistines – *On the day of battle not a soldier with Saul and Jonathan had a sword or spear in his hand; only Saul and his son Jonathan had them* (1 Sam 13.22). If church leaders are not armed for the battle they will not be able to teach their people to understand the complex mission field that faces us today, nor equip them fearlessly to declare truth to a dying nation. Sadly, by the 1970s when the Charismatic Movement dawned, the institutional church had already been overwhelmed by a spirit of unbelief from libertarianism. **The world had reshaped the church. The prophetic voice was silenced.**

This is the great tragedy of the 20th century, carried over into the 21st century, that the world has reshaped the church – clearly demonstrated in the weak and ineffective leadership of churches of all denominations. As Donald Soper used to say, "The trouble with the clergy is that we've only got the laity to recruit from!" With fewer Bible believing preachers in the pulpits there will inevitably be fewer Bible believing laypeople in the pews. The church and its leadership reflect the secular humanist world in which we all live.

This has always been the problem facing the people of God. It was there throughout the history of Israel recorded in the Bible. The first reference is in the early days of the settlement in Canaan when the people came to the prophet Samuel and said *"We want a king so that we can be like all the other nations"* (1 Sam 8.19). But this was the very thing they were not supposed to be! For God to use them to reveal his nature and purposes and his salvation to the world, they had to be different!

Even after the tragic destruction of Jerusalem when its leading citizens were taken into slavery in Babylon, the people still did not learn this lesson. Their elders came to Ezekiel, the prophet of the Exile, saying *"We want to be like the nations, like the peoples of the world, who serve wood and stone"* (Ezek 20.32). But the very purpose of the exile was to cleanse the nation of idolatry and to enable them to learn to put their total trust in God the Creator who had revealed himself to their fathers Abraham, Isaac and Jacob. God's purpose for the exiles was made clear by Isaiah: *"I will also make you a light for the Gentiles, that you may bring my salvation to the ends of the earth"* (Is 49.6).

This is the tragedy of the church today. The church wants to be like the world so that the world likes the church. Archbishop Justin Welby, leader of the established church, has said that he wants the church "to be more inclusive" – which is politically correct code for saying that he wants the church to fall in line with the values of the secular humanist LGBT-friendly society. In other words this is the same spirit as the people who said to Ezekiel, *"We want to be like the people of the world who serve wood and stone"*. So we now have an idolatrous institutional church, an apostate church, a church purporting to be Christian, but with a Christianity without Christ and without a gospel of redemption.

Political Activity

Opportunities for impacting society had never been greater than in the post-1960s, but neither also had been the challenge to the gospel and to the very survival of the biblically-based foundations of Western civilisation. The level of social change ran far deeper than most people realised at that time, because the changes were drip-fed by one measure of change after another. This was rather like the parable of the frog in the bowl of water that was slowly raised to boiling point. He could have jumped out at any point but he did not recognise the danger slowly developing. Something similar happened in the Western nations through the impact of the four major movements of social change, all of which had a similar secular humanist and demonic spiritual driving force but they were slowly developed in society one measure at a time.

In political terms the only major social change fought by the churches was in defence of Sunday Observance. The 'Keep Sunday Special' campaign was successful in generating widespread public support, and The Sunday Trading Act was the only Government Bill lost by Margaret Thatcher. She later redrafted and successfully reintroduced it. But many significant changes in law that had a profound effect upon reshaping society slipped through with hardly a ripple of dissent in the nation. It may seem quite extraordinary that the churches paid so little attention to what was going on in society despite the fact that we have a free press, we all have access to our local Member of Parliament, and there are plenty of media outlets to make our concerns known to the public.

Throughout that half-century of rapid and radical change, Christians had the opportunity to express their views, but it was only minority groups, usually those involved in parachurch organisations,[10] who focused upon any of these issues or made any attempt to draw public attention to the dangers of the far-reaching and revolutionary changes that were taking place. Preachers in the mainline churches remained aloof from what was happening in the nation.

This was the fruit of the early 20th century when evangelical Christians would have nothing to do with politics and the social sciences were despised by Christians. Politics was considered to be a dirty game and political careers were shunned by evangelicals who warned their children against such ungodly and worldly pursuits. The result was that Christians stayed out of politics at all levels — local government and national. Christians especially avoided becoming involved in the Trades Unions, which increased the gap between the church and the working classes.

When we moved into the East End of London in 1970, less than 1% of the local population were regular in church attendance. This was not a new phenomenon: as far back as the 19th century, studies showed that church attendance was largely a middle-class activity and few working-class people were regular churchgoers. This was noted by E.R. Wickham in a study of Sheffield back in the 1960s.[11] But middle-class Christians generally thought of politics as a dirty game, one to be avoided by respectable people. Thus, throughout the 20th century, few committed Christians became Members of Parliament and so the word of God was rarely heard in the Palace of Westminster as it had been in Victorian times when the Bible was regularly quoted in debates. This separation of Christianity from the affairs of the nation hit a new high point when Tim Farron resigned as leader of the Lib Dems in June 2017, saying that he had found it to be incompatible to be a Christian and a leader of a political party in Britain.

A further reason for the church's silence on social affairs was the middle-class character of churches of all denominations and in all environments. Too often the most able ministers went to middle-class suburban areas or high status provincial areas. Inner cities were places where clergy only went if they could not get a church in a 'good' area. In strange contrast to the ministry of Jesus, most ministers of the mainline churches avoided working among the poor. In 2007 I was speaking to the annual conference of 'The Black Clergy and Ministers Association' when one Anglican vicar complained that the only churches they were offered were in inner-city areas of Britain. Others also spoke saying that they were never offered middle-class parishes.

Whose Responsibility?
A sound biblical principle running right through Scripture is that God holds the spiritual leaders responsible for the nation. In Jeremiah's day God said to him,

> *"Among the prophets of Jerusalem I have seen something horrible: they commit adultery and live a lie. They strengthen the hands of evildoers, so that no one turns from his wickedness"* (Jer 23.14).

When church leaders fail to give an exemplary example to the nation, it strengthens the hands of unbelievers. Ezekiel received a similar hard word about the leaders in his day who were caring for themselves rather than for the flock,

> *This is what the Sovereign Lord says: "I am against the shepherds and will hold them accountable for my flock"* (Ezek 34.10).

The central theological conviction that was at the heart of the message of the prophets was the sovereignty of God. That conviction has largely been missing in the life of the church for the past fifty years which has blunted both the message and the mission of the church at the most critical period of social change in modern history.

The most outstanding need today is for the message of the biblical prophets to thunder through the naves of our cathedrals and from the pulpits of our churches, declaring the unchanging word of God amidst the uncertainties of the times in which we live. But, of course, the preachers have first to believe the word of God so that, like Paul, they cannot keep quiet, the truth of the word of God just flows from them: as Paul says, *Woe to me if I do not preach the gospel!* (1 Cor 9.15).

The problems we are facing go very deep — right down into the value system of Western civilisation, which is causing the foundations to crack. The impact of globalism and elitism in the economic and political sphere, and libertarianism and the LGBTQ+ movement in the social and moral spheres, have been at the heart of the shaking of the nations in the Western world since the 1960s. But now there are signs that God is preparing to destroy the very movements that he has used to shake the nations in the same way as he overthrew Babylon after 70 years. It had achieved the purpose of God in the exile of his people and the time had now come for the wickedness and cruelty of Babylon to be exposed and discarded. This is how the sovereignty of God works.

We can see that God is turning on the light, exposing the greed and corruption in society, in the major social institutions, in politics and government and in the business and commercial world as well as the world of media and entertainment. But will this also include the Church? Is the writing on the wall for the many denominations of the Western Church? If they are no longer serving the purposes of God they will be discarded.

The Western nations desperately need to hear the message of the prophets and to be reintroduced to the Creator God who holds the nations in his hands. *He stretches out the heavens like a canopy... He brings princes to naught and reduces the rulers of this world to nothing"* (see Is 40.22-23). Paul goes to the heart of the dilemma of the nations that have known biblical truth for centuries and rejected it. He says: *The wrath of God is being revealed from heaven against all the godlessness and wickedness of men who suppress the truth by their wickedness, since what may be known about God is plain to them* (Rom 1.18). Paul sees three stages[12] in the corruption and degradation of society beginning with the rejection of God the Creator. Once the fundamental truth of the Creator is rejected, people do not worship nothing – they worship *anything*, and they descend quickly into successive stages of depravity. This is what has been happening in the reshaping of Britain since the 1960s.

Understanding the Battle

Church leaders throughout the past fifty years of radical and rapid social change did not understand the significance of the processes of social change and therefore they did not discern the spiritual nature of those processes. Unbelief was spreading across the churches from the theological institutions training church leaders, sapping the spiritual powers of discernment as it gradually undermined the confidence of preachers in the record of what God had done in the past, thus diminishing fundamentally their knowledge of the nature and purposes of God and their confidence in his power to transform the nation.

Breakdown of Family and Marriage

The central issue facing the Western nations today is the breakdown of traditional family life through the highly successful lies and deception that have sugar-coated the secular humanist onslaught led by the LGBTQ+ lobby, using the false and seductive concept of 'equality' in their campaign for same-sex marriage. Their objective, as stated in their 1972 Manifesto[13] has always been to destroy traditional family life which is the cornerstone of our Judaeo-Christian heritage and a central part of God's creation. **If Western civilisation is to stand any chance of survival, Christians must recognise the spiritual nature of this battle. The Postmodernist battle we are witnessing is a satanic attack upon the purposes of God. It is no less than an attack by the powers of darkness to destroy God's good purposes for humanity.**

Part of the fruit of the successful attack upon the family can already be seen in Britain and many other Western nations. In Britain, in most of our cities, gang life among young people is becoming increasingly virulent and aggressive with an increase in knife crime, acid-throwing, street warfare, drugs and violence. The gangs are substitute families giving identity, security, and belongingness that is absent in fatherless and inadequate families. Thousands of children are excluded from our schools for behavioural purposes, lacking discipline that is not taught in the home where so often family life is chaotic.[14] Our prisons are overflowing, placing an unbearable strain upon prison officers and, as violent crime increases, law and order in society is under threat, placing unacceptable pressures upon the police forces. So far, society has had no answer to inner-city problems which are already spreading to other areas around Britain.

In April 2018 there was an outcry that there had been more than 50 murders of young people on the streets of London in the first three months of the year. There were many calls for strong measures including the reintroduction of 'stop and search' by police, but none of the politicians and social commentators appeared to notice the root cause of these social problems that lie in family breakdown and the weakening of family life which is the cornerstone of society.

The breakdown of marriage and family life is very largely responsible for the mental health problems that are expanding to epidemic proportions throughout the UK. This is largely due to the stresses and strains of modern life which are exacerbated by strife within marriage and family breakdown, and spread by social media. Teaching schoolchildren that they can change gender at any time in their lives if they so wish increases the emotional problems of childhood and increases their insecurity and uncertainty about their personal identity.

The harm being done to children by sex education in schools and the lack of teaching about marriage and stable family life is doing untold harm to a whole generation of children and increasing the level of mental breakdown. Children already have to deal with the enormous emotional stress of social media and the multitude of data that pours into their mobile phones and other devices, often leading to bullying, insecurity and self-harm, problems that are often carried over into adult life. In 2016, some 300,000 employees left work due to mental health problems, placing an additional strain upon the NHS and the whole of our health and caring services, which increasingly produces crises in wintertime. These are just a few of the outcomes of the breakdown of family life which has been deliberately created by LGBT policy.

Church Leaders' Responsibility

Church leaders of all denominations (although primarily the Church of England as the established church) must bear responsibility for the present state of the nation. I recognise that I personally bear some responsibility for failing to speak out against the proposed law on abortion which slipped through the Commons with hardly any public notice. I regularly preached to a large congregation but I didn't even notice when the Bill went through Parliament so I made no mention of it. I have often come before the Lord in repentance since then, but laws are more easily made than changed. We are all part of a sinful nation and reformation begins with repentance. Perhaps every preacher should regularly be reading Daniel 9, a model prayer of repentance.

Collectively, over the period covered in this book, church leaders failed to discern the nature of the battle that was assailing the nation in a time of maximum social change – particularly failing to discern its spiritual roots. In the words of Paul: *Our struggle is not against flesh and blood, but against the rulers, against the authorities, against the powers of this dark world and against the spiritual forces of evil in the heavenly realms* (Eph 6.10 – 12).

This lack of discernment among church leaders has had a devastating effect upon the battle to save the nation from the disintegration of family life. As already noted, the nadir of the lifelong monogamous family was reached in July 2000 and it needs repeating here. The Government's paper *Supporting Families* had correctly stated that marriage was 'the most reliable framework for raising children'. A peer attempted to include that statement in the Education Bill going through Parliament so that all children would be taught the value of marriage and family life.[15] Writing about this political incident, sociologist Norman Dennis, said,

> The ecclesiastical historian of the future might well take the view that 18th July 2000 was a landmark in the development of the Church of England's attitude to 'holy matrimony'. Nine bishops voted against the amendment. If they had voted the other way the amendment would have been carried.[16]

This was another milestone in the reshaping of the nation. It was but a short step from this, 17 years later, for the Archbishop of Canterbury to encourage primary school children to experiment with cross-dressing. Gender and family, central to God's act of creation, were no longer upheld by the state church and defended at all costs. Former Archbishops chose to go to the stake and be burnt alive for less than this.[17]

Future Outlook

If these trends continue they will lead not only to widespread social breakdown but also to economic disaster, hastening the day when the nation will not be able to afford to support the welfare services. With fewer working people supporting a rising number of elderly retired people, with the unemployed, unemployable, dependent people, plus a huge pensions bill and the mountainous national debt, the strain on the economy will become insupportable. If the economy can no longer support the welfare services, the level of public protest and the breakdown of law and order on the streets may become uncontainable.

This is not an exaggeration, it is a realistic forecast of what will happen in the foreseeable future with the rising level of crime in society, unless there is a radical change in social policy that recognises the destructive nature of LGBTQ+ activity which is destroying family life. It is the deliberate destruction of the family that lies at the root of most of our social problems today. It is like pulling away the central pillars of a great building as Samson did in the temple of Dagon. For such a change to take place there has to be a radical change in attitudes towards 'political correctness', especially the stifling of debate on sensitive issues.

The present social-media-fuelled policy among students and young people of refusing to listen to any ideas or concepts that they don't like, has to be broken. This is a new phenomenon that has arisen in the 21st century. Prior to that, universities and colleges of higher education were bastions of debate, where new ideologies could be safely aired and rationally discussed. Today, young people want to tear down statues and remove plaques that relate to historical events that do not have the approval of today's ethical forum. But blotting out unacceptable parts of our history means that we will learn nothing from past mistakes. 'Political Correctness' promotes today's ignorance and tomorrow's folly.

At present the outlook is grim. The battle against truth is so great that the very future of humanity is under threat. Is there any hope?

Opportunities

Today, the rate of social change shows no sign of abating and the rate of technological change is actually accelerating as we approach the robot era. If we accept the biblical revelation of the sovereignty of God, we also have to accept the responsibility of Christians for failing to recognise the way in which God is working out his purposes today. The great question facing Britain, and all the Western nations, is whether or not the church is able to rise to the task of declaring truth to the nations, prophetically proclaiming the whole counsel of God for these days. The power of God through his Holy Spirit is available to Christians. What is lacking is *trust*, as well as *discernment* and *knowledge of the truth*.

Sadly, there are still some churches promoting the dangerous false teaching of the 'Latter Rain' heresies that were so divisive and did such harm in the 1990s. These teachings that distort Scripture are presented as exciting revelations and they appeal strongly to young people (especially through music and worship songs) who have little understanding of biblical truth and do not know how to weigh and test what they are hearing, so they are easily misled. They are subtly transmitted to young people through music where worship songs have become infected by false teaching.

A New Day Dawning

The opportunity for the re-evangelisation of the nation, as we have already said, was missed in the period of 1965 to 2015 which was a time of great social change. But a new day is dawning. The intensity of the great shaking of the nations is increasing rapidly. We may all soon be engulfed in a modern 'Babylon' of unbelievable intensity. But God is offering to Christians the most incredible opportunity, because only those who have their trust in him will be able to stand and be 'overcomers'. Living in 'Babylon' has never been easy. The 6th century BC Jews discovered this in the Exile, but their faith survived and thrived.[18] The Christians in the Early Church faced the cruel persecution of the Roman Empire, and through the presence of the Risen Jesus among them they not only survived, but they thrived, and the blood of the martyrs became the seed of the church as their numbers vastly increased to bring the message of salvation to the world.

This can happen again!
God always uses these periods of shaking the human institutions of the nations as an opportunity for spiritual intervention and for communicating his truth. If Christians had understood the nature of the battle and had rightly used the power of the Holy Spirit that was available to the church in the second half of the 20th century, history could have been very different. The question now is "What is the future?"

Spiritual revival could have swept through Britain in the 1970s and 80s because of the uncertainties created by socio-economic change which opened a large part of the population to the recognition of the moral and spiritual bankruptcy of society. God was at work uncovering the corruption in the finance and political institutions of society, but the church did not recognise what God was doing. Widespread public disquiet triggered the populist/anti-establishment movement that lasted well into the 21st century, influencing such things as the Brexit vote in the UK and the election of Donald Trump in the USA, Emmanuel Macron in France, Sebastian Kurz in Austria, Luigi Di Maio and the Five-Star Movement in Italy, Viktor Orban in Hungary, and other political upheavals in the Western and Arab nations, including the Arab Spring.

Today, as we go farther into the 21st century, we are heading into an even greater period of uncertainty and instability, as the shaking of the nations intensifies. It is a different kind of battle from the 1970s. The 21st century battle requires careful discernment. Bible-believing Christians will know that every battle requires a different strategy. Joshua had to learn this. The strategy God gave him for demolishing the walls of Jericho would not have worked at the next city of Ai. But Joshua did not stop to ask God for divine directions, which led to disaster (see Joshua 7). In a similar way, we have to seek the Lord to understand what is happening at each stage of social change in the nations today.

The Battle is the Lord's

We have to discern *God's* strategy for *his* people to achieve *his* purposes of bringing *his* truth, justice and righteousness to the nations. We have to discover fresh ways to communicate the knowledge of God's love, his salvation and his good purposes, to the nations. But we need constantly to be reminded that the battle is the Lord's. It is one that we cannot win alone: the spiritual forces of darkness in this battle are too great.

The word of the Lord to his church today is to mobilise the faithful remnant of believers scattered across the churches and fellowships of all traditions. They need to be alert to the great opportunity for evangelism that God is already giving to his people today in the midst of the shaking. But is the faithful remnant strong enough and courageous enough for the task of turning the tide of secular humanism? Can there be the equivalent of a populist movement in the church? The denominational leaders have failed to give effective leadership and the institutional churches are crumbling – will God raise a grassroots movement among Christians to accomplish his will? The task is immensely more difficult today than it was in the 1970s. But God does not depend upon numbers, as Gideon learnt. His tiny army of 300 was sufficient for achieving God's purposes (see Judges 7).

Prayer was a major force leading the British people to vote for Brexit against all the expectations and threats of those who held political and economic power. But for Brexit to be a success there has to be trust in God and obedience to his word otherwise the enemy will prevail. Without trust, God's good purposes will not succeed. The power of prayer needs to be focused upon discerning the will of God today. We will then be able to understand how God is using the shaking of the nations in the 21st century to bring his truth to the people. God does not require a democratic majority before he answers prayer; he responds eagerly to the faithful intercessions of his people.

The Final Great Decision

The major sociological factor that needs to be understood is that the reshaping of the nation that has taken place over the past fifty years has not been a simple process of Darwinian social evolution. Neither has it simply been the outcome of following a secular humanist agenda. A far more sinister force has been at work that has not been understood by politicians of any political persuasion. It has not been discerned by many Christian theologians. **It has been the product of an anarchist agenda, the driving force of which has demonic spiritual elements in that it is driving humanity to self-destruction: it is a spirit of death — its ultimate objective is the destruction of humanity.** This spirit of death has been in evidence many times in recent years in public events such as the scenes of jubilation in Dublin at the announcement of the result of the referendum on abortion in May 2018. The scenes of overwhelming joy and victory were a demonstration of how far Western civilisation has departed from the fundamental biblical values of absolutes – justice, truth, love – upon which it was founded. How many of these people realised the significance of what they were celebrating – the wilful murder of children: the destruction of human life, the condemnation of thousands of unborn babies to be torn from their mother's womb and thrown into the incinerator? This is the spirit of the age. It is the ancient spirit of the 'Moabites' (roundly condemned in the Bible)[19] and pagan tribes in ancient history who believed that by burning babies in the fire this would improve the fortunes of the people, their reproductive powers and the productivity of nature.

This even happened as late as the sixth century BC during the exile in Babylon where Ezekiel lambasted the elders who came to him seeking a word from the Lord:

"Therefore say to the house of Israel: 'This is what the Sovereign LORD says: Will you defile yourselves the way your fathers did and lust after their vile images? When you offer your gifts – the sacrifice of your sons in the fire – you continue to defile yourselves with all your idols to this day. Am I to let you enquire of me, O house of Israel? As surely as I live, declares the Sovereign LORD, I will not let you enquire of me'" (Ezek 20.30 – 31, NIV).

In biblical terms it is the equivalent of the Antichrist whose objective is to defeat God and his good purposes for his creation and especially for humanity, the summit of his creation. Its objective was set out in 1972 in the Gay Pride Manifesto that declared its intention of destroying the family which it saw as the source of oppression. But we cannot over-emphasise that the family is the lynchpin of society, and once the family disintegrates the whole social structure begins to crumble and the foundations of civilised society begin to fracture and shatter with devastating consequences.

This is what we are seeing today as the Postmodernist forces of darkness drive the Western nations. In Britain the process is so far advanced in destroying even gender differences that it may be impossible to redeem society. The only hope of saving Western civilisation from total implosion lies in the rapid recognition of the direction of social change that is now raging through the Western nations like a forest fire driven by raging storm-force winds, and repentance before God.

Will the eyes that are blind among the leaders of the Western nations recognise the danger and be prepared to change course? [20] Will the eyes of humanity be open to the truth and call upon God for help and allow him to reshape the nations?

Future Prosperity

In Jeremiah 29.11–14 God gave a promise to the exiles in Babylon and I believe he is saying something similar to us in Britain today. His promise then was:

"For I know the plans I have for you," declares the Lord, "plans to prosper you and not to harm you, plans to give you hope and a future. Then you will call upon me and come and pray to me, and I will listen to you. You will seek me and find me when you seek me with all your heart. I will be found by you," declares the Lord. (NIV)

In Britain the hope for the future lies not in the institutional churches which have been largely infiltrated by the values of the world. The hope lies in what God is doing in reshaping his church – the true ecclesia of the Lord – by drawing together Bible believing Christians in small groups and re-energising their prayer life as they study the word of God together.

Throughout the Bible we see evidence of God doing a new thing in the worst of times. In the time of King Jehoshaphat when a united army of hostile neighbours were mounting an attack upon Jerusalem which, humanly speaking, could not be resisted by the tiny army of Judah, the King recognised the plight of the nation and called the people to prayer. God answered his prayer of faith.

'Do not be afraid or discouraged because of this vast army. For the battle is not yours, but God's...' (see 2 Chron 20.15, NIV).

Similar things have happened in my lifetime. I have seen with my own eyes the amazing growth of the church in China and the most amazing miracles under severe persecution from the Communist Government. I have seen the same happening in Indonesia under severe persecution from Islam. In both nations God is at work answering the prayers of faith in ways that would be incredible in the sceptical nations of the West.

It may be that here in Britain, God is waiting for the faithful remnant to recognise their utter dependency upon the Lord and to cry out to the Father for help. Undoubtedly, when that happens he will open the windows of heaven and pour out such a mighty blessing that will sweep multitudes into the Kingdom.

Notes

[1] The five major social institutions recognised by sociologists are the Family, Economy, Education, Law (Government and law enforcement) Religion. There are many other institutions such as the media, the arts, health and welfare; but only the five major institutions have structural significance.

[2] 'Clause 28' was an amendment to the Local Authority Act 1988 which protected children from the promotion of homosexual teaching in school sex-education classes. It banned the promotion of "the acceptability of homosexuality as a pretended family relationship."

[3] *Medical Consequences*, Family Research Report Newsletter, Number 25, Family Research Institute, Colorado Springs USA, 1998.

[4] Medical science has advanced considerably since the late 1990s when this research was completed. Nevertheless, male homosexual practices still involve considerable risks to health although, as far as I am aware no recent research has been carried out in Britain on life expectancy among homosexuals.

[5] See Rom 3.17.

[6] See Matthew 24.1-14.

[7] See Chapter 1 p. 15.

[8] *Towards the Conversion of England*, Church Assembly, London, 1945.

[9] In strong contrast to today, where the Head of Religious Broadcasting in the BBC, appointed in 2017, is reputed to be an atheist.

[10] CARE, Family Education Trust, Intercessors for Britain (IFB), Barnabas Trust, London Institute of Contemporary Christianity (LICC), Lawyers Christian Fellowship (LCF), Christian Medical Fellowship (CMF), as well my own ministries, were all active in the 1980s and 90s. More recently they have been joined by Christian Concern, Voice for Justice, The Christian Institute and numerous others.

[11] E.R. Wickham, *Church and People in an Industrial City,* Lutterworth, London, 1969.

[12] The three stages are in Romans 1.24-32.

[13] Gay Pride Manifesto, London 1972.

[14] Government Report on BBC News, 11.06.18.

[15] This is dealt with in Chapter Thirteen, *Family Matters*.

[16] Norman Dennis, (Visiting Fellow at the University of Newcastle upon Tyne and Director of Community Studies at the Institute for the Study of Civil Society) writing the Foreword to *The Cost of Family Breakdown*, a report by Family Matters Institute for the Lord's and Commons Family and Child Protection Group, Bedford, 2000.

[17] As did Archbishop Crammer in 1556.

[18] See: Clifford and Monica Hill, *Living in Babylon*, Handsel Press, Edinburgh, 2016. See also the accompanying workbook *Living* Victoriously *in Babylon*, published by Issachar Ministries in 2017, which includes sections on how the Jews preserved their faith in six century BC Babylon, how the Christians in the early church survived under the persecution of the Roman Empire, and the situation facing Christians in the contemporary world dominated by secular humanism.

[19] Jer 7.30–8.3; Psalm 106.35 – 39; 2 Kings 16.3 and 17.17; Ezekiel 20.31. These are all references to times when the people of Israel indulged in the pagan practices of idolatry and sacrificed their sons and daughters in the fire, to the abhorrence of the prophets who spoke fiercely against these evil practices.

[20] See Isaiah 24:1, *See the Lord is going to lay waste the earth and devastate it*, and Isaiah 3:2 *The Lord is angry with all nations… He will give them over to slaughter.*

EPILOGUE

Since the middle of the 20th century we have seen, in Britain, a social revolution in the nation and the slow suicide of the church. The social revolution has been of such depth that it has reached right down into the value system that forms the foundations of the nation. The driving force behind this revolution has been a combination of Darwinian philosophy, Marxist economics and the hedonist idealism of the Enlightenment.

During the same period of *social* revolution, a *spiritual* revolution of similar depth has taken place in the institutional church, reaching down into the foundations of belief. The driving force has not been so much an *external* attack from secular world forces as an abandonment of biblical values by many who have been entrusted with the guardianship of the gospel of Jesus Christ (clergy and ministers) and who have embraced another spirit and produced another gospel of their own invention, one that is acceptable in a secular humanist environment. Instead of a radical church challenging the values of the world we have a compliant church seeking to be 'inclusive' and not to offend anyone.

We have occupied many pages in this book recounting the changes that have taken place in Britain since the 1960s, during which time there has been no significant public prophetic voice in the church or nation. The nation has been driven by a succession of postmodernist reformers in political parties of all persuasions; and many mainstream churches have been subjected to false teaching and fed with false hopes and aspirations that have little or no basis in biblical truth. We have now reached a critical stage in the history of Britain with the long-running Brexit battle on the political front and an Archbishop who wants the church to be more 'inclusive' in its beliefs and practices.

In this Epilogue we will seek to understand from both a sociological and spiritual standpoint what has happened in the past 50 years in this country to reach this point, and we will also seek to trace a way forward that could lead to the health and prosperity of the nation.

The Social Revolution

In purely sociological terms the major tragedy that has overtaken the nation during the period of revolutionary social change since the Second World War has undoubtedly been the disintegration of the family leading to the widespread destruction of family life. The family is the most important of all the major social institutions in any society, both agrarian and industrial. It is the lynchpin that holds together all the other social institutions such as the economy, education, the health and welfare services, government and law and order.

In most societies the family occupies a position that is undergirded and empowered by tradition and religion. In Britain the family has been based upon 1000 years of Judaeo Christianity, regulated by biblical teaching and sanctified by being part of God's act of creation in which he created human beings, both male and female, in his own image; and he instituted marriage between a man and a woman in a covenant relationship of love and faithfulness for the sustaining of the human race.

The pivotal significance of the family in the life and prosperity of a nation may well be illustrated by the recent history of China. For centuries the family and religion, centred upon ancestor worship, was the controlling factor in the social and economic structure of the nation. Traditionally the whole family was involved in the same economic pursuit, which can even be seen today in Chinese restaurants in Britain. The Communist era under Mao Zedong pursued the deliberate destruction of the family and its traditions. But since the end of that era in 1979 and the loosening of social and economic controls, the entrepreneurial family has regained its central significance and has materially contributed to the economic success of China today as a world leading economic power.[1]

In chapter 16 we quoted sociologist Brigitte Berger[2] as saying that "Only the family — and a very specific type of family at that — can produce the social forms necessary for adequately linking autonomous individuals, regardless of ethnicity and social class, to the macro structures of modern society". She also referred to the role of the family in other types of society and then made this significant statement,

It would be the ultimate irony of history if at the very moment when one country after another around the globe begins to discover this salutary role of the bourgeois type of family not only in the formation of their political economy but also in the organisation of their social life, the West is losing faith in the legitimacy of the manner of life that has made for its ancestry.

According to respected sociologist Talcott Parsons:

The basic and irreducible functions of the family are two: the primary socialisation of children so that they can truly become members of the society into which they have been born: second, the stabilisation of the adult personalities of the population of the society.

Parsons saw these two irreducible functions as essential for the stability and health of society – only within the family could children be socialised and young men and young women attain sexual and civic maturity.[3] But the family was seen by many in the 1960s as the location of patriarchy, a place where men, and only men, hold power and control the patterns of socialisation which determine male-female positions in society, condemning female roles to be subservient to males. Homosexuals also saw the family as the source of their oppression through its reinforcing of gender stereotypes. It was at this point that feminists and homosexuals joined forces to attack the family, which began the movement that over the next 50 years produced the LGBTQ+ movement of today.

The Secular Society
Britain today is rapidly becoming a fully secular society. It has taken only 50 years to destroy almost completely the Judaeo-Christian heritage of 1000 years. The process of normalising the abnormal[4] has been extended right down to the primary school and nursery. It uses a process known as CHIPS – 'Challenging Homophobia In Primary Schools' using "heart-

warming stories about lovable, cute and cuddly animals (e.g. the rabbits in *Rabbityness,* penguins in *And Tango makes three* and cats and kittens in *The Whisperer*) to plant and entrench ideas about 'difference' and 'homosexuality'."[5] It uses certain words frequently to implant them into the minds of small children. This is part of a process of "emotional conditioning" to indoctrinate the children to accept homosexuality and gender transition as normal conditions of human existence. Brian Hadley states, "CHIPS starts to deconstruct the true meaning of 'male' and 'female' as being a person's biological sex, by planting the idea in young children's minds that they can create for themselves any gender and sexuality they wish."[6]

Militant Secularisation

The fact that two major social processes have occurred during the past 50 years that have coincided with the rise of militant secularisation is highly ominous for the future health and well-being of the nation. The two major social processes are:

1. the collapse of the family and
2. the reduction in influence of the church.

This means that with small children being indoctrinated in state schools with the secular humanist values promoted by the LGBTQ+ movement with state funded resources and specially trained advisers to direct the activities of the teachers, there is little chance of children adopting values other than those of a secular humanist society. The breakdown of both church and family means that very few children will be taught in Christian households and receive a different set of values in the home, where children have traditionally been socialised.

Berger quotes a number of other sociologists such as Norman Dennis in *Families Without Fatherhood*[7] as all agreeing that the destruction of the family in contemporary Western society will lead to the demise of Western civilisation and culture.

Collapse of Law and Order?

The fruit of the destruction of the family can already be seen in drug addiction; the epidemic of sexually transmitted diseases among young people; the formation of gangs in inner-city areas which provide young people with a substitute family, with identity and self-worth; the rising crime rate whereby 60 young people died on the streets of London in the first four months of 2018; the rise in hate rage, self-harm, mental breakdown and suicide. All these are symptoms of a sick society at the centre of which is family breakdown.

What we are seeing today is the beginning of what could become the collapse of law and order as the structures of society begin to crumble. Historically, it had been the strength of family life that had ensured stability and even the survival of the nation in times of crisis. This has been demonstrated many times such as whole families in every community volunteering their men for service during the First World War. In the inter-war years of economic recession, unemployment and poverty, families closed ranks and supported one another in the most difficult and testing times. There were no riots, no breakdown of law and order, no revolutionary challenge to government. In poverty, families shared what little they had and the nation came through to face the challenge to its very existence in the Second World War where the little boats at Dunkirk and the men of 'Dad's Army' and the women of 'The Land Army' symbolised the strength of family life and the unshakeable faith of a praying nation in the face of invasion and annihilation.

If we are to face any similar crises, political or economic, in the future without the strength of the family and the Christian religion, the consequences, in purely sociological terms, will be dire. Without the restraining influences of biblical values taught in the home and in church and Sunday school, the breakdown of law and order in times of high unemployment and economic severity are inevitable. If the state is no longer able to pay welfare support and unemployment benefit it will be extremely difficult for the police and law enforcement services to restrain the violence that we may see on our city streets.

But how did we get to this point? How can any nation undergo such radical change in a single lifetime such as I have seen in mine? It is here that we may look for a biblical comparison.

Biblical Comparison

The period under review in this book has some similarities to that which Jeremiah found in late 7th and early 6th century BC Jerusalem after the demise of the godly King Josiah who was succeeded by his ungodly son Jehoiakim. It was a time of growing threat on the international front from the rising power of the Babylonian Empire, but the leadership of the nation were unconcerned with any of these things. Jeremiah was told by God:

> "Go up and down the streets of Jerusalem,
>   look around and consider,
>   search through her squares.
>   If you can find but one person
>   who deals honestly and seeks the truth,
>   I will forgive this city ."

(Jer 5.1, NIV)

Jeremiah realised that these were only the ordinary working people with little education or theological knowledge, so he resolved to go to the leaders and speak to them, saying,

> "... surely they know the way of the LORD,
>   the requirements of their God."
>   But with one accord they
>   too had broken off the yoke
>   and torn off the bonds.

(Jer 5.5b, NIV)

This was a devastating revelation for the prophet. The political and religious leaders of the nation had thrown off their links with the God of Israel who had brought them out of Egypt into the Promised Land and who had given them incredible blessings, protection and prosperity over the centuries. Jeremiah spent 40 years of his life warning the leaders and the people of the indescribable suffering they would bring upon themselves unless they put their trust in God. But from the King to the humblest workman, they would not listen to his words and they had ignored all the warning signs that God had sent to them. The word of the Lord came to Jeremiah,

"From the least to the greatest, all are greedy for gain; prophets and priests alike, all practice deceit. They dress the wound of my people as though it were not serious." (Jer 6.13-14, NIV)

The spiritual principle that we learn from this incident in the history of Israel is that God holds the leaders – both political and religious – responsible for the state of the nation. Ezekiel, who was a contemporary of Jeremiah, confirms this. He says:

This is what the Sovereign Lord says: I am against the shepherds and will hold them accountable for my flock. I will remove them from tending the flock so that the shepherds can no longer feed themselves.
(Ezek 34.10a, NIV)[8]

Both Jeremiah and Ezekiel could see the impending catastrophe facing the nation, of which the leaders of both state and religion appeared to be unaware. Both prophets emphasised that God held the leaders responsible for the moral and spiritual state of the nation as well as for the safety and prosperity of the land. But the prime responsibility lay with the religious leaders who had not taught the politicians and the people the word of God.

Post-War Britain
Bearing in mind this biblical principle of responsibility, we turn to the period covered in this book. But it is worth noting that as far back as 1943, when William Temple issued an urgent call to evangelism, he recognised what he described as the "sickness of our society and the sickness of individual souls". He said:

- In its approach to social change the church should fasten on what is closely akin to its own message. God created men and women for fellowship with himself and therein with one another. Our task is to mould society into such a fellowship and train citizens as members of it.
- Our aim is defined as the development of persons in community.

- To this end we shall urge the necessity of adequate housing; of wholesome food, light and air; of education to full maturity (to age 18).[9]
- The church will work with all who share its immediate aims; but will never conceal its own ultimate aim – **the fashioning of men and women and young people as children of God** in community not only with one another but with God the Father made known to us in Christ.[10]

This was the legacy William Temple bequeathed to the church. It was similar to the 'community-based evangelism' that Monica and I were practising in the 1970s – fully evangelical but also committed to social action. Sadly, it was despised by his successor, Geoffrey Fisher, a high-ranking Freemason, which began a spiral of ineffective leadership provided by the church.

In Chapter One we noted that at the Lambeth Conference in July 1978, just days after the bishops had blocked the plans for Monica and me to join him, Donald Coggan had said,

We have stopped listening to God and our spiritual life has died on us, though we keep up the appearances and go through the motions.[11]

Church Leaders' Unbelief

Donald Coggan clearly recognised that the church was committing spiritual suicide through unbelief. The spiritual life of the Church of England was dying. That did not mean that every local parish church was in a similar state, but that the *institution* of the Anglican Church was in a similar state to that of the Temple authorities in Jerusalem at the time of Jeremiah's Ministry – *with one accord they had broken off the yoke* (Jer 5.5) that connected them with the God of Israel. Their spiritual life was no longer directed by God, which put the church in a similar position to any other social institution in the nation – to being driven by the secular humanist forces of social change. **The institutional church had put itself outside the protective cover of God.**

Donald Coggan was the only Archbishop of Canterbury since the end of World War II to have understood the social and spiritual condition of Britain although, like all the other archbishops since William Temple, he lacked the dynamic of leadership abilities which would have given him the strength to challenge the institutional structures of the church and to follow through his 'Call to the Nation'. He raised expectations but was unable to deliver the fruit. All the other archbishops failed to understand the nature of the complex issues facing the nation. I am not saying that they were not good and sincere men. Even Robert Runcie, with whose theology I profoundly disagreed, was a good man doing his best according to his beliefs and was honest with his doubts. But none of them had the remotest idea how to exercise effective spiritual leadership in the nation. This was tragic for the church in Britain at a time of radical social change when a strong biblically-based spiritual leadership was desperately needed. **If we are to offer an honest assessment we would have to say that for 50 years the leadership of the institutional churches of Britain have failed the nation and are to a large extent responsible for the moral and spiritual state of the nation today.**

The Institutional Church

The greatest handicap of the Church of England lies in its institutional structures that are based upon the models of a secular nation and principles of democracy. There is no such thing as democracy in the Bible! What the Bible upholds is a *theocracy* in which the Lordship of God is Sovereign. The structures of the Church of England as the state church are modelled on that of the democratic state. Even when its leaders meet in solemn assembly it is in the form of a Parliament considering resolutions and taking votes rather than a community of believers under the Lordship of Jesus.

The churches in the Western nations are moulded upon the principles of democracy rather than theocracy. Their weakness lies primarily in their departure from the model of the New Testament *ecclesia* and its biblical basis rooted in Judaeo-Christian concepts. Leadership (clergy and Nonconformist ministers) has been moulded in conformity to democratised Western standards, setting them apart from the rest of humanity while conditioning the laity to accept the men (and women) of the cloth as possessing divinely empowered authority. But too often that authority is vested in the *institution of the church* rather than in the Lordship of Jesus.

By contrast, the New Testament church is a 'community of believers' not an institution. Its leadership is in teams with different roles and shared responsibilities,[12] not the 'one-man-band' who does a little bit of everything and carries all authority. It is the institutionalisation of the *koinonia* (fellowship) of the New Testament communities of believers that is the heart of the problem of the modern Western church. It changed the whole nature of the faith from a purposeful community of believers with a mission to transform individuals and society into an organisational structure taking its place alongside other institutions in society.

Church Unity

The most subtle form of error that has entered the church in a huge measure during the period of this study has been the desire for unity. Each of the Archbishops of Canterbury that I have known, even Donald Coggan, has desired some form of union with the Church of Rome and actively sought closer relationships with the Pope. This desire for unity has some basis in biblical truth.

The psalmist extols the virtue of unity:

> How good and pleasant it is
> when brothers live together in unity!
> It is like precious oil poured on the head,
> running down on the beard,
> running down on Aaron's beard,
> down upon the collar of his robes.
> It is as if the dew of Herman
> were falling on Mount Zion.
> For there the LORD bestows his blessing,
> even life for evermore.
>
> (Ps 133, NIV).

Clearly, God loves to see unity among his people and he bestows his blessing upon such unity. But this does not mean that we depart from truth in order to attain some form of unity. In fact, this demonstrates our lack of understanding of godly unity which is a *spiritual* rather than an *institutional* quality. In fact, there is no biblical support for merging our institutions to give a semblance of physical unity. Amos makes it clear that unity is a spiritual quality. He says: *Do two walk together unless they have agreed to do so?* (Amos 3.3). And Paul emphasises the spiritual nature of unity when he calls for believers to *Make every effort to keep the unity of the Spirit through the bond of peace* (Eph 4.3). True unity is where believers are of one heart and mind.

When truth is sacrificed on the altar of unity it becomes error. It is this error that has driven the Church of England for decades, leading the institution of the state church farther and farther from the truth. This was stated clearly by Dr Gavin Ashenden when he resigned as chaplain to the Queen, saying, "The Church of England is much more comfortable with politics and power than it is with the Holy Spirit."[13] The obsession with unity at all costs has proved to be an alien spirit driving the Church of England into error.

Theological Error

This obsession with unity reveals a fundamental theological problem in the Church of England that goes right back in its history to the time of James I and the translation of the Authorised Version of the Bible. James I (formerly James VI of Scotland) wanted the Bible to be available to all people. Until Bibles in printed English appeared in the 16th century, the only Bibles available in England were hand transcribed in the monasteries or in the Latin Vulgate version, which many even among the clergy could not read. James wanted a version in the English language, so he appointed a group of scholars capable of translating from the original Greek and Hebrew. Half were Anglicans and the other half were scholars from the Puritan tradition (nonconformists).

Their work progressed well, but in translating the New Testament there was one word on which they could not agree, so they consulted the King. It was the word 'ecclesia' (ἐκκλησια). The Church of England scholars wanted to maintain the word 'church' in line with the Latin translation, thus keeping the state church as close as possible to the Roman Catholic Church: but the Puritan scholars maintained that ἐκκλησια should be translated 'congregation' as a true representation of its New Testament context. The King, who disliked the Scottish Presbyterian system that gave too much power to the people, ruled in favour of the word 'church'.

Thus, the only place in the New Testament where the word ἐκκλησια is correctly translated in most English Bibles is in the description of the riot at Ephesus in Acts 19, where the whole population of the town came together in an assembly (ἐκκλησια) to demonstrate against the teaching of Paul.

Inevitably the Church of England is seen as an 'institution' instead of a fellowship of locally based 'assemblies', 'congregations' or 'communities of believers'. Sadly, all the Nonconformist denominations followed suit, and they too, in different degrees, have taken the form of institutions with centralised administration and a hierarchy of authority in their structures, essentially losing the New Testament concept of the Lordship of Jesus in the gathered company of believers in holy assembly. The institutional concept of the church follows the pattern of secular organisations and opens the door for the values of the world to play an influential part in its life. In Britain, the devil is no longer fighting the church – he has joined it!

In fact, the church has been taken over by the world and this is the reason why we have seen so little evidence of the genuine power of the Holy Spirit emanating from the church in the past 50 years. But what is happening today is of immense significance. We are seeing the crumbling of the institutional church in Britain. Instead of bemoaning this and crying out to God to strengthen the church, we should be rejoicing that God is at work refining the institutional churches that purport to be the bearers of his word.

All across Britain mature Bible-believing Christians are coming together in small groups not simply to share their grief at leaving fellowships they have loved and served, but to search the Scriptures together to find understanding of what God is doing today and to pray together with a new sense of unity and freedom in the Holy Spirit.

A New Creation
God is doing a new thing today in preparation for a mighty work of salvation in Britain and other Western nations. The word of the Lord to Christians today is:

Forget the former things; do not dwell on the past. See, I'm doing a new thing! Now it springs up; do you not perceive it? I am making a way in the desert and streams in the wasteland… For I will pour water on the thirsty land, and streams on the dry ground; I will pour out my Spirit on your offspring, and my blessing on your descendants. (Isaiah 43.18-20 and 44.3 NIV).

In order to understand what God is doing we have to put it in the context of the revelation of his nature and purposes throughout the Bible. He is not only the God of Creation but the God of re-creation and at the heart of his creation there is the principle that the seed has to fall into the ground and die in order to give new life. God is the God of new life and resurrection. He even allowed his only begotten Son to die in order to bring new life and salvation to sinful human beings.

The ways of the Lord are clearly demonstrated in his dealings with his covenant people Israel. Time after time God had to deal with their waywardness when they fell into idolatry and corruption and he raised up prophets to declare his word, to warn of danger and to point to the way of salvation. There were even times when he had to allow disaster to come upon his people in the Northern Kingdom of Israel: *"I am planning disaster against this people, from which you cannot save yourselves"* (Mic 2.3 NIV). A similar word was given to Jeremiah of what God intended to do with Judah and Jerusalem. *"The Lord said to me, from the North disaster will be poured out on all who live in the land"* (Jer 1.14 NIV).

The basic spiritual principle we see throughout the Bible is that we have to get to the point where we recognise that we are totally unable to save ourselves through our human strength and cleverness. When we get to that point of recognising our helplessness and we cry out to the Lord in repentance and absolute trust – then he is able to do his work of salvation, transforming the situation.

This is beautifully illustrated in 2 Chronicles 20 where Jehoshaphat recognises the absolute inability of the tiny army of Judah to resist the mighty army that was coming against them. He called the whole nation to come together and pray. His prayer is a model of intercession which climaxed in a call for help: *"For we have no power to face this vast army that is attacking us. We do not know what to do, but our eyes are upon you."* Immediately the Lord responded: *"Do not be afraid or discouraged because of this vast army, for the battle is not yours but God's"*. The rest of the narrative shows how God turned the whole situation around without Judah's army firing a shot.

Understanding the Battle

It is of vital importance for Christians to understand the nature of the battle today in order that we may pray in line with what God is saying and what he is doing. In the ministry team of which I have been a part since the early 1980s, we have had many words from God warning of a time of great trouble in the years to come. As far back as 1979 when I was writing the book *Towards The Dawn* I was told that there would be no revival in Britain until a time of disaster struck the nation which would cause people to be open to the word of the Lord for the first time in many years.

Then in 1986 at the gathering on Mount Carmel we all heard God saying that he was going to shake all nations. The words of Haggai 2 repeated in Hebrews 12 show that all 'created things' will be shaken. Part of the word received by Lance Lambert speaks specifically of how the great shaking will also envelop the church:

In the midst of all the turmoil and shaking and at the heart of everything is my church. In the heavenlies she is joined to me in one Spirit and I have destined her for the throne. You who are my beloved whom I have redeemed and anointed – you are mine. I will equip and empower you and you will rise up and do great things in my name, even in the midst of darkness and evil. For I will reveal my power and my grace and my glory through you. Do not hold back nor question my ways with you for in all my dealings with you I have always in mind that you should be part of my bride and reign with me. Do not forget that this requires special discipline and training. So, yield to me that I might do a work in you in the time which is left for I plan even during all this shaking that the bride will make herself ready.

Everything will be Shaken

From that point we began teaching that everything that is not of God will be shaken including the institutions that we call churches. It was a message that was not well received. I remember speaking in a church with a large congregation in a wealthy part of Surrey when I warned that the church would come under judgment for the corruption and false teaching that was being given in many churches. I was vigorously opposed by the minister who declared that the church could never come under judgment because it is the body of Christ. But this simply showed the extent of the misunderstanding of the nature of the church and the failure to distinguish between the true ecclesia and the man-made institutions that we call churches.

We began teaching that our prayers of intercession must reflect our understanding of what God is doing because if we pray for him to preserve or protect something that he is shaking we can put ourselves against God. At that stage, I don't think we realised the extent to which the shaking would affect all our lives although I remember David Noakes receiving a prophecy during one of our team prayer times calling upon us to teach people how to walk upon water. The prophecy began:

In the days that are to come, that part of the church which will survive and prevail as 'Overcomers' will be that part which has learned to walk upon the waters, trusting only in me. The ways of traditional church organisation will not be adequate for the needs, because they will be too rigid and inflexible to withstand the wind and the waves, and those who have put their trust in them for their security will be like those who find themselves in a boat which is overwhelmed and doomed to sink.[14]

No Revival without Repentance

The message we declared in the early 1980s and right through the 1990s was that there would be no revival in the nation until there was repentance in the church. It was not a popular message and we lost many friends who were caught up in the waves of enthusiasm coming through the charismatic movement and the words of false prophets and teachers.

It is not easy carrying a message that is contrary to popular sentiment.

I often identified with Jeremiah whose warnings of impending disaster were hated by his fellow priests as well as the general population. He was even banned from the temple and had to speak on the steps outside the gate. But he could not keep quiet. He had heard the word of the Lord and he knew what was coming upon Jerusalem and the people he loved. I understood his despair when he cried out, *"Alas, my mother, that you gave me birth, a man with whom the whole land strives and contends"* (Jer 15.10 NIV). Many times, I begged the Lord to give me a different message but always the answer was the same, *"My grace is sufficient for you."*

A Dramatic Incident

I had some relief when Monica and I were speaking to a conference in Adelboden high up in the Swiss Alps. It was January and the men's downhill ski race was taking place on the mountain slope outside the village. We were not speaking that afternoon so we joined the huge crowds at the foot of the mountain watching the young men risking life and limb to shave milliseconds off their time on each run. I had a strong sense that God had a message for me so I carefully watched each competitor, but there was nothing that spoke to me.

Then as we were walking back along the narrow winding mountain path the air was suddenly rent with the cries of a child. A little girl about three or four years old had evidently slipped underneath the guardrail and was sliding down a steep snow-covered slope towards the edge of a precipice with a drop onto rocks below. It was a sight I will never forget — the terror in the child's eyes and her piercing screams echoing across the valley from the mountains the other side. Suddenly another dramatic event took place as a man whom I later learned to be the child's father leapt over the guardrail and began running down that steep slope. He ran so fast that he overtook the child and managed to stop himself and was lost in a flurry of snow as he stopped a few yards short of the precipice sweeping up the child into his arms. Then he began the slow climb back up testing each foothold before he put his full weight and the weight of the child on it.

There were hundreds on the path who all stopped to watch the drama of this rescue and many arms were reached out over the guardrail to lift the child back to her mother and to help her father back onto the path and safety. As he climbed back uphill I heard the Lord say to me "This is what I brought you here to see. Did you see how that father did not hesitate to risk his own life for the sake of his child, that is how much I love my people."

Tell My People I Love Them

I found myself saying "Lord your love is wonderful", but immediately I felt a sense of rebuke and the Lord saying that his love is at least as great as human love and a million times more. And then I distinctly heard the words, "Tell my people I love them". I saw a new depth in the gospel message that God so loved those whom he had created in his own image that in Jesus he not only went to the edge of the precipice but he actually died on the cross to save us.

Many times since then I have thought about this incident. There were scores of men in the crowd close enough to rescue the child and I was one of them. But only one man moved in response to the child's cries for help — her father. I was one of those men who simply stood and stared, and I have often asked myself, if that were my child, would I have gone to help her? I don't know the answer to that, although I like to think that I would have done so even though I might not have been so successful in my lightweight trainers as he was in his snow boots. But I am not proud that I did nothing. Only the child's father responded to her need and this is the message that is desperately needed in this age of family breakdown and fatherlessness. Millions of children in Britain suffer the breakdown of family life and lack the warmth and security of a father's love, which makes it very difficult to teach about the Fatherhood of God: but it is the message millions need to hear.

The New Message

I was drawn back to this message as I was finishing writing this book. The new message which I had longed to receive for 30 years came to me in the summer of 2018 when I was crying out to the Lord about the state of the nation and the message I was to give on my bi-monthly CD that goes out to our ministry supporters. Suddenly, for the first time in 30 years, I began hearing the Lord speaking about revival in Britain!

For several years we had been growing increasingly concerned about the number of people who were out of church: mature Bible-believing Christians who felt impelled to leave their denominational church because of false teaching and departing from the word of God. They were either alone struggling to understand what was going on in the world around them, or linking with a few other equally dismayed believers. A year ago, we had heard the Lord saying to our Ministry team, "Find my sheep: search for those who feel lost and lonely: feed my sheep."

We had been carrying out a small piece of research helping us to understand the needs of the 'out of church' so that we could provide for their needs. Many were bewildered by the speed of change in the secularisation of the nation that was even limiting freedom of speech so that Christians were losing their jobs for taking a stand on biblical principles; street preachers were being arrested for preaching the gospel and in the midst of all this churches were either silent or in some cases were even preaching another gospel.

At the same time the TV news and the papers were full of strife and forecasts of doom. The Brexit battle was in full swing among politicians presenting a picture of chaos and confusion while at the same time on the social scene more than a hundred young people had died on the streets of London since the beginning of the year: gang life, drugs, knives and violence were rife; prisons were reported to be overcrowded and similarly filled with drugs and violence: there was no end to the picture of gloom; shops were closing on the high street, well known brands were disappearing, plunging people into local unemployment with threats to the future of the economy. Family breakdown continued at an unstoppable pace, while revelations of historic sexual abuse in the church filled the newspapers. The church had never been at such a low level of public esteem in my lifetime.

A Clear Picture

Suddenly, I felt that all the little pieces of a jigsaw were coming together and I could see the hand of God in all the confusing scenes that were being played out on our TV news and what we were seeing around us. This was what I had foreseen 50 years ago! Way back in the 1960s when the cracks first began to appear on the social and political scene, and we felt impelled to move from the race riots of Tottenham in North London into the social cauldron of the East End of London where we saw the need for a creative movement of social and spiritual renewal – I had seen then the rising tide of destructive forces sweeping across the nation.

At the same time, I had seen at first hand the spiritual atrophy of the church and when, during the 1970s, I was drawn into the highest circles of church leadership of the C of E and the denominations, and when I blew a trumpet of warning I had met the same stiff-necked unbelief that had assailed Jeremiah. He warned that God would not protect a corrupt generation even of those who were in a covenant relationship with him. He heard God saying *"Therefore say to them, this is the nation that has not obeyed the Lord its God or responded to correction. Truth has vanished; it has vanished from their lips"* (Jer 7.28). Truth was indeed fast vanishing from the public square in Britain.

Those destructive forces of social change that I had seen in the 1960s as one ungodly law after another was passed in our Parliament, with hardly a single voice raised in protest from any church leaders, caused me to know that the die was cast for the reshaping of the nation. In this book I have tried to trace the long line of social change in the nation that has been accompanied in the churches of most denominations by a mixture of complacency, blindness or deception. Now we have a nation where more than half the population has no faith in God and our political leaders have no idea how to deal with the social scene, the economic scene, or the political scene with its complex negotiations with the European Union and the desire for trade deals with the rest of the world.

The Conditions for Revival

But this is exactly the situation that is needed for revival in the nation! All that is needed is the recognition of the hopelessness of the situation in social, economic and political terms! The scene is set for the fulfilment of the prophecy received at Mount Carmel in April 1986 of the great shaking of the nations. But the message to the church was:

For in the midst of these judgments multitudes upon multitudes will be saved from the nations. You will hardly know how to bring the harvest in, but my Spirit will equip you for the task. And to Israel will I also turn in that day, and I will melt the hardening which has befallen her. I will turn her blindness into clear sight, and tear away the veil on her heart. Then shall she be redeemed with heart bursting joy, and will become a fountain of new and resurrection life to the whole company of the redeemed.

Do not fear for these days, for I have purposed that you should stand with me and serve me in them. Fear not, for I love you and I will protect you and equip you. I, the Lord, will anoint you with a new anointing and you will work my works and fulfil my counsel.[15]

But this was a message to the true ecclesia of the Lord, not to the denominational structures known as 'the church'. God is separating out the true believers who have not bowed the knee to the Baals of this world, or succumbed to the seductive teachings of the false teachers and prophets who have muddied the waters of evangelism and injected the honeyed messages of deception into the spiritual arteries of those who do not have a sound grasp of biblical truth.

The message of God to his Bible-believing faithful remnant today is that the days are coming when he will respond to their prayers. Just as judgment begins at the house of the Lord where we are seeing the crumbling of the denominational structures of the church, so repentance must begin there. God is not waiting for the whole nation to repent. He is not a God who looks for democratic majorities. He is waiting to see a spirit of repentance among the faithful remnant of believers who know his word and who plead on behalf of the nation, *"We do not know what to do, but our eyes are upon you."* These are the prayers of faith that God is longing to see among his people – the recognition that we can do nothing in our own strength to deal with the corruption in the nation. His promise is:

Blessed is the man who trusts in the Lord, whose confidence is in him. He will be like a tree planted by the water that sends out roots by the stream. It does not fear when heat comes; its leaves are always green. It has no worries in the year of drought and never fails to bear fruit (Jer 17.7-8).

The Hand of God

It is in the midst of judgment that we will see the hand of God moving in revival – not to revive the corrupt old structures but to touch the hearts of men and women and young people who recognise the mess that the nation is in and who long to see something new and different from the old pattern of society that has been followed by our leaders in both church and state for the past 50 years.

This new openness to truth and search for a way of life that is truly satisfying presents the greatest opportunity for Christians for more than a hundred years: the opportunity to declare to their friends and neighbours and to all those whom the Spirit of God will be touching – this is what God our loving Heavenly Father is saying to his children. I love you with an unending and unbreakable love:

"Turn to me and be saved, all you ends of the earth; for I am God, and there is no other. By myself I have sworn, my mouth has uttered in all integrity a word that will not be revoked: before me every knee will bow; by me every tongue will swear. They will say of me, in the Lord alone are righteousness and strength" (Isaiah 45.22-24).

Notes

[1] See Gordon Redding, *The Spirit of Chinese Capitalism*, De Gruyter, New York, 1990.

[2] See Chapter 16 p. 244.

[3] Talcott Parsons, *Family Socialisation and Interaction Process*, New York, 1956, p. 16.

[4] Lisa Nolland et al., *The New Normal: the Transgender Agenda,* Wilberforce Publications, London, 2018

[5] Brian Hadley, 'Education or Indoctrination? An assessment of CHIPS', in Lynda Rose, ed., *What are they teaching the children?* Wilberforce Publications, London, 2016, p. 140.

[6] Ibid., p. 149.

[7] Norman Dennis, *Families Without Fatherhood*, IEA Health and Welfare Unit, London, 1992.

[8] Ezekiel uses the word 'Shepherd' in reference to both political and religious leaders.

[9] This was a revolutionary statement at a time when the school leaving age was 14.

[10] William Temple, *Social Witness and Evangelism*, the Epworth Press, London, 1943, p. 17.

[11] See p. 32 of this book.

[12] The fivefold ministries of the church are set out by St Paul in Ephesians 4 – they are Apostles, Prophets, Evangelists, Pastors and Teachers.

[13] See p. 247 of this book.

[14] The full text of this November 1994 prophecy is published in: *Hearing from God: Prophecies to Church and Nation*, published in the magazine Prophecy Today since 1985. Available from Issachar Ministries, Sandy, Beds.

[15] This is part of the prophecy given by Lance Lambert, referred to in chapter 8 of this book.

LAWS THAT RESHAPED BRITAIN SINCE 1950
(with selected bible references showing how these laws contravene God's creation order and plan for mankind)

1951: The Fraudulent Mediums Act abolished **The Witchcraft Act (Deut. 18:10-13).** This legalised witchcraft in Britain (which had been banned for centuries) and made occult activities legal.

1959: The Obscene Publications Act (Mark 7:21-23) required proof that a publication had "a tendency to corrupt and deprave", making prosecutions for obscenity harder. Later amendments and **The Broadcasting Act 1990** extended the law to cinema and television.

1967: The Abortion Act (Gen. 4:10-11 and **Psalm 139:13).** The Act made abortion legal up to 28 weeks gestation in the UK with the exception of Northern Ireland. In 2017 it was reported that more than 8 million unborn children had been killed in the 50 years since abortions became legal.

1967: The Sexual Offences Act (Lev. 18:22 and **Rom. 1:22-27).** This Act legalised homosexual acts between consenting men over the age of 21.

1994: The Criminal Justice and Public Order Act reduced to 18 the homosexual age of consent.

2000: The Sexual Offences (Amendment) Act equalised the age of consent for homosexual and heterosexual sex at 16.

1968: The Theatres Act (1 Thess. 4:7) virtually abolished censorship of the theatre. Although 'obscene' performances are prohibited, in practice explicit sexual acts are permitted.

1969: The Divorce Reform Act (Mark 10:2-12) introduced the principle of the irretrievable breakdown of marriage as the sole ground for divorce, to be proved by adultery, unreasonable behaviour, or desertion; or by two years separation with consent to a divorce, or five years separation without consent to a divorce. It opened the way for easier divorce.

1972: The European Communities Act, the EC (Amendment Acts) of 1986 and of 1993) (Deut. 32.8). The 1972 Act took Britain into the European Economic Community (later into the European Union) and made European law supreme and, with later Acts, seriously diminished our sovereignty.

1989: The Children Act (Deut. 4:9 and Deut. 6:6-7). The Act aimed to increase the protection of children, but it removed the traditional concept that parents are the best judges of their children's welfare.

1990 Amendment to the Abortion Act (Jer. 7:31 and Psalm 106:37-38). This reduced the age at which an unborn baby could be aborted to twenty weeks and legalised the abortion of seriously handicapped babies up to the time of birth.

1990: The Human Fertilisation and Embryology Act (Eccles. 11:5). This Act legalised the creation of embryos, for experimentation or storage in laboratories. (As mentioned above, this Act also amended the Abortion Act 1967, resulting in abortion on demand for 'seriously handicapped' babies up to the time of birth.)

1993: The Sunday Trading Act (Ex. 20:8-11). This Act allowed widespread trading on Sundays which was against God's command to observe a Sabbath day as a day of rest each week.

1994: The National Lottery Act (1 Tim. 6:9-10) instituted a State national lottery, encouraging people to gamble and increasing the level of personal debt.

1996: The Family Law Act (Mal. 2:16 and Matt. 19:8) replaced the five grounds for divorce in the Divorce Reform Act 1969 with a so-called 'no-fault' divorce system. The Lord Chancellor announced in 2001 that this part of the Family Law Act would not be brought into effect and would be repealed in due course.

1997: The Amsterdam Treaty (Deut. 27:17). This reinforced the identity of the European Union as a legal entity and further eroded national sovereignty.

1999: The Finance Act (Mal. 2:13-15) removed the Married Person's Allowance, further degrading the value of marriage.

2001: Regulations to the Human Fertilisation and Embryology Act 1990 (Ex. 23:7) permitted embryo research for developing treatments for serious diseases, allowing the cloning of human embryos and experimentation with the creation of human life.

2004: The Civil Partnership Act (Matt. 19:5 and Eph 5:3) granted civil partnerships to same-sex couples with rights and responsibilities very similar to those of civil marriage.

2004: The Gender Recognition Act (Gen. 2:23 and Isaiah 5:20) granted transsexual people legal recognition as members of the sex opposite to their birth gender, either male or female.

2006 to 2010: Equality Acts (1 Cor. 6:9-10) The 2006 Act created the Equality and Human Rights Commission (EHRC) and the 2010 Act drew together the Acts and statutory instruments enacting European law relating to equality and human rights. These introduced the "protected" status of homosexual orientation and gender reassignment, restricting the freedom of Christians.

2013: The Marriage (Same-Sex Couples) Act (Rom. 1:24-27 and 1 Cor. 7) redefined marriage which had always been between a man and a woman. It allowed two persons of the same gender to enter into legally recognised marriage.

35000151R00195

Printed in Poland
by Amazon Fulfillment
Poland Sp. z o.o., Wrocław